Q & A SERIES
CONFLICT OF LAWS

SECOND EDITION

Cavendish
Publishing
Limited

London • Sydney

TITLES IN THE Q&A SERIES

BUSINESS LAW
CIVIL LIBERTIES
COMMERCIAL LAW
COMPANY LAW
CONFLICT OF LAWS
CONSTITUTIONAL & ADMINISTRATIVE LAW
CONTRACT LAW
CRIMINAL LAW
EMPLOYMENT LAW
ENGLISH LEGAL SYSTEM
EQUITY & TRUSTS
EUROPEAN UNION LAW
EVIDENCE
FAMILY LAW
INTELLECTUAL PROPERTY LAW
INTERNATIONAL TRADE LAW
JURISPRUDENCE
LAND LAW
PUBLIC INTERNATIONAL LAW
REVENUE LAW
SUCCESSION, WILLS & PROBATE
TORTS LAW
'A' LEVEL LAW

Q & A SERIES
CONFLICT OF LAWS

SECOND EDITION

Jason Chuah, LLB, LLM (Cantab), M Ilex
Senior Lecturer in Law
Kingston University
and
Alina Kaczorowska, PhD, DEA, BCL, Barrister (Paris)
Principal Lecturer of the Law Faculty
Southampton Institute

Cavendish Publishing Limited

London • Sydney

Second edition first published in Great Britain 2000 by Cavendish Publishing Limited, The Glass House, Wharton Street, London WC1X 9PX, United Kingdom

Telephone: +44 (0) 20 7278 8000 Facsimile: +44 (0) 20 7278 8080

e-mail: info@cavendishpublishing.com

Visit our Home Page on http://www.cavendishpublishing.com

First edition 1996

Second edition 2000

British Library Cataloguing in Publication Data

Chuah, Jason

Conflict of Laws – 2nd ed – (Cavendish questions and answers series)

1 Conflict of laws – Examinations, questions, etc

I Title II Kaczorowska, Alina

340.9

ISBN 185941 413 3

Printed and bound in Great Britain

Preface

This book is designed for use in a private international law course as taught in many undergraduate law schools. The materials attempt to cover a wide array of 'popular' issues in these courses. The questions are tailored to the syllabuses of most undergraduate programmes.

Whilst the book has been arranged into delineated chapters on jurisdiction, choice of law in specific matters, recognition and enforcement of judgments and awards, it should be emphasised that these are but an artificial vehicle to assist the student in his or her revision. It should not be perceived as presenting the substance of private international law as discrete packages. The law is, of course, the result of a combination of those issues.

We believe that the introductory notes in every chapter help the student identify the relevant issues for examination purposes. The book does not seek to replace the textbook but to complement it. Student numbers have grown considerably over the years and, where there was the personal tutorial, now there is mass education. Innovative distance learning modes have also necessitated the use of a book of this size and nature. A book like this, if used carefully and as a supplement, should assist the student in studying intelligently and discovering the acceptable approach and structure of a legal essay. Some of the legal skills that are considered in this book to be important include: fact analysis; issue identification; statutory interpretation; legal application; clarity of argument; and critical legal analysis.

The academic substance of private international law is not, however, compromised. There are endnotes inviting the student to do further reading. There is a comprehensive index and the table of cases should assist the student in locating the primary sources. The questions have been designed to accommodate recent and potential legal problems in private international law and the theories of private international law. Students are reminded of the theoretical underpinnings of the 'practical' outworking of the law. In the 'answers', students are exhorted to note that there is very often no 'one right answer'. The essential criterion is well structured legal analysis.

Alina Kaczorowska has been primarily responsible for the following topics: domicile, jurisdiction, family law and tort; and her introduction and questions and answers have been marked with an asterisk. Jason Chuah has been responsible for the residual areas.

We should like to thank Jo Reddy at Cavendish Publishing for her support and encouragement in seeing this project to completion. Alina wishes to thank Chris Ireland at Ireland's Commercial Lawyers of North Hampshire. Jason Chuah thanks Mark Herrett and Isabelle Brodie for providing the vital distraction – *dulce est desipire in loco* (Horace, Od, IV.xii.28) – 'it is pleasant to play the fool on occasion'.

We have attempted to state the law as it stood on 1 January 2000.

Jason Chuah
Alina Kaczorowska
March 2000

Contents

INTRODUCTION*

Private international law, or conflict of laws, is a body of rules designed to determine whether English or foreign law is to be applied when an English court is faced with a claim that contains a foreign element. The peculiarity of private international law is that it has no material content, in the sense that it does not provide any immediate solution to a particular dispute, but merely indicates the legal system which is competent to provide the rules to be applied. Furthermore, private international law is part of English law and, consequently, it is neither private nor international. Private international law operates indirectly, by providing a technique which is used to solve multi-State problems; it is not a system of independent substantive rules. As Voltaire said, the 'Holy Roman Empire' was not holy, nor Roman, nor was it an empire. Nevertheless, we still use the term.

Three successive stages can be distinguished when an English court is faced with a claim that contains a foreign element. First, it must decide whether it has jurisdiction over the parties and the cause of action. At the jurisdictional stage, an English court has to decide whether the trial should take place in England. In this respect, two sets of rules may be invoked: the traditional common law rules with the accompanying *forum non conveniens* discretion; and the new conventional rules, set out in the 1968 Brussels Convention on Jurisdiction and Enforcement of Foreign Judgments in Civil and Commercial Matters (as amended). Once the court decides that England is an appropriate forum for trial, it has to select the choice of law rule which will indicate the law applicable to a multi-State problem. This task is far from easy, as different preliminary problems may arise, such as the question of classification, the incidental question and the *renvoi*. At this stage, the connecting factor, which changes according to the circumstances of the case, will be decisive as to the determination of the law that will be applied to a multi-State dispute.

The second stage involves the actual application of the selected law, which may be English law or foreign law. Indeed, choice of law rules are both bilateral, and may thus lead to the application of the *lex fori* or foreign law, and neutral, as they indicate the competent law, regardless of the content of the selected law. If the *lex fori* is selected, no major problems arise. However, the application of a particular foreign law poses delicate questions. On the one hand, the foreign law, which would otherwise apply according to the ordinary principles of private international law, may be excluded in some circumstances. Indeed, an English court will not enforce and, often, will not even recognise penal, revenue or other public laws of a foreign State. In addition, foreign expropriatory legislation and foreign laws repugnant to English public policy will not be given effect to in England. On the other hand, under English private international law, a foreign law is treated as a question of fact.

Finally, English private international law also deals with the recognition and enforcement of foreign judgments and foreign arbitration awards. At common law, English courts have no jurisdiction to directly enforce foreign judgments. Consequently, the plaintiff has to commence proceedings against the defendant in England and Wales on the judgment debts. His situation is alleviated where the 1968 Brussels Convention, the Foreign Judgments (Reciprocal Enforcement) Act 1933, the Administration of Justice Act 1920 or the 1958 New York Convention on the Recognition and Enforcement of Arbitral Award apply.

Private international law as a branch of English law has been relatively neglected until recently. The new interest is due to many factors: internationalisation of our everyday life; the developments of telecommunications; increasing economic interdependence among States; and the accession of the UK to the European Community. Paradoxically, those factors challenge traditional conflict of law rules. Indeed, now, more than ever, the traditional recourse to choice of law rules which change from State to State, just as the substantive laws vary from forum to forum, emphasise the need to harmonise both. The only way to eliminate the conflict of law rules is by the universal unification of substantive laws. As this is quite impossible to achieve, the need to apply conflict of laws remains, although considerable progress in the unification of substantive and conflict of law rules has been accomplished. The best and most effective attempt at the unification of law has been undertaken within the framework of the European Union. Two conventions are especially important in the context of conflict of laws: the 1968 Brussels Convention on

Recognition and the Enforcement of Judgments in Civil and Commercial Matters; and the 1980 Rome Convention on the Law Applicable to Contractual Obligations, both in force in the UK.

* by Alina Kaczorowska

Table of Cases

TABLE OF STATUTES

Table of Statutory Instruments

Table of EU Legislation

CHAPTER 1

GENERAL INTRODUCTORY ISSUES IN PRIVATE INTERNATIONAL LAW

Introduction

Prior to the actual application of the law selected by the choice of law rules, an English court has to solve various problems. First, it has to determine the judicial nature of the question raised by a multi-State problem. The identification of the correct legal category into which the factual situation falls is known as the 'classification of the cause of action'. Usually, the process of classification poses no major problems, and an English judge automatically, and often unconsciously, assigns the question to a particular legal category. However, it may happen that a foreign law and the *lex fori* differ in their classification of the cause of action. For instance, in the *Maltese Marriage* case (1891), French law classified the factual situation as raising a question of succession, while it was considered under Maltese law to be a question of matrimonial rights. In order to solve the conflict of classification, English private international law adopts a flexible approach. Although the classification of the cause of action is made by reference to the *lex fori*, an English court will not rigidly adhere to the concepts and legal categories of its domestic law.

Furthermore, a second classification relating to a rule of law may also be necessary. Once the applicable law is ascertained on the basis of an appropriate connecting factor, which varies according to particular legal categories, the nature of the rule which governs the matter must be determined. In this respect, the choice is limited, but it is still far from being automatic, as a rule may relate to procedure (and thus be governed by the *lex fori*) or to substance (in which case, the *lex causae* applies). Again, the *lex fori* and the applicable foreign law may have different perceptions of the nature of the selected rule.

Moreover, even if the applicable law to the main question is ascertained, the incidental question may surface. It is an issue which not only profoundly affects the main question but also requires the determination of the applicable law to be different from that which governs the main question. Three conditions must be satisfied for the existence of the incidental question: the main question must be governed by a foreign law which has been chosen by English choice of law rules; the subsidiary question must involve some foreign element which has arisen separately and which has its own independent choice of law rules; and the solution to the subsidiary question reached under the law selected by English conflict of laws rules must be different from the one determined by corresponding rules adopted by the country whose law governs the main question.

On a conceptual level, once the classification is completed, the question of *renvoi* may arise. Indeed, if the applicable law is a foreign law, the forum has to decide whether it refers to the foreign law as a whole, private international law included, or only to its substantive rules. In the case of the first, the problem of *renvoi* emerges, as the foreign private international law may have different choice of law rules regarding the solution of a particular multi-State problem. Consequently, it may refer the question back to the sending forum (called the 'remissicn') or indicate a law of a third country as the *lex causae* (known as the 'transmission').

There are two forms of *renvoi*: single (or partial) *renvoi*; and double (or total) *renvoi*. In England, the doctrine of total *renvoi* is recognised. As a result, when an English court refers the matter to a foreign law, it has to decide as if it were a court seised with the matter in a foreign country. There are many general objections to the doctrine of *renvoi*, and particular objections to the doctrine of total *renvoi*, the most important being that this doctrine is only workable if it is recognised in one of the countries concerned and rejected in the other. Furthermore, the doctrine of total *renvoi* is difficult to apply in practice, as it requires an English court to ascertain the position of a foreign law vis à vis the doctrine of *renvoi*. In this respect, it may be that, in the light of lower courts' conflicting decisions, contradictory legal opinions and no ruling from the Supreme Court on this point, an English court is faced with insurmountable difficulty (this occurred in *Re Duke of Wellington*). In addition, the doctrine of *renvoi* requires that the

English court must assess what is meant by national law of the *propositus* under the law of the country in which the English judge is presumed to sit, which raises many difficulties in the context of legal systems which comprise several territorial laws, such as the UK or the US. Additionally, the doctrine of *renvoi* does not necessarily lead to uniformity of solutions.

The actual application of a foreign law selected by English choice of law rules may be excluded if it is penal or revenue in nature. In addition, an English court will exclude the application of other public laws which are 'enforced as assertations of the authority of central or local government' of a foreign State. The classification of the nature of the foreign law is left to the *lex fori*, which is not bound by the classification adopted by the foreign country concerned. As to foreign expropriatory legislation, it will be recognised in England only if the affected property is situated within the jurisdiction of a foreign State at the time of the foreign decree of expropriation, even though the property may have subsequently been brought to England before or during the proceedings there. An English court will also refuse the application of a foreign law which is repugnant to English public policy.

Finally, unless a foreign law is pleaded and proven by the party, an English court will determine a multi-State problem as if it were a purely domestic dispute, since, according to English private international law, a foreign law is treated as a question of fact. The only exception relates to Scottish law before the House of Lords. Being the final court of appeal in civil matters for both England and Scotland, their Lordships have judicial knowledge of Scottish law.

Checklist

Students should be familiar with the following areas and concepts:

- nature and scope of private international law;
- proof of foreign law;
- exclusion of foreign law;
- role of public policy;
- sovereign and diplomatic rights;

- the distinction between substance and procedure;
- *renvoi;*
- characterisation;
- the incidental question;
- the time factor;
- theories and methodology applied in private international law;
- the progressive unification of the rules of private international law.

Question 1

Distinguish the theory of double *renvoi* from the theory of simple or partial *renvoi*. Comment on the total *renvoi* doctrine as applied by English courts.

Answer plan

The question of *renvoi* is a popular examination topic, especially in the context of formal validity of wills. The student must be able to distinguish between double and single *renvoi*. An understanding of the context within which the doctrines have been formulated and applied is particularly useful.

The problem of *renvoi* usually arises where the court has characterised the matter in dispute but the private international law rules of the *lex causae* suggest that the law of the *lex fori* should be used. To alleviate this problem, the courts in different jurisdictions have adopted various solutions, including single and double *renvoi*; or they may simply ignore the issue entirely. It is imperative to set out this context in answering a question of this nature, which seeks to examine the student's understanding of the overall perspective.

Cases that should be alluded to include: *Re Annesley* (1926); *Collier v Rivaz* (1841); *Re O'Keefe* (1940); and *R v Brentwood Superintendent Registrar of Marriages* (1968). Bear in mind that a pure recitation of the facts without any commentary is of little merit.

Answer

The term *renvoi* is used to define the practice where the law of more than one country may be applicable in the choice of law question. It is to the effect that, if a judge is seised of a case in one country, X, whose law requires him to apply the law of another country, Y; and the rules of private international law in Y refer to the laws of X, then the judge is to apply the law of country X. The alternative to this is the English doctrine of *renvoi*, also known as the 'foreign court theory'. According to this theory, an English judge who is referred by English law to a foreign legal system must apply whatever law a court in that foreign system would apply. Naturally, this depends on whether or not that foreign legal system recognises the doctrine of *renvoi*.

In the mid-19th century, the continental doctrine of single or partial *renvoi* was primarily confined to the area of formal validity of wills. The situation was that, under the then English rule,[1] compliance with one form alone was required of wills. On the other hand, under continental law, compliance with the forms permitted by the testator's personal law or the law of the place where the will was made is deemed sufficient. In view of the stricture expected under English law, the probate court in *Collier v Rivaz* (1841) admitted the doctrine of single *renvoi* in order to admit the codicils in question. The codicils were opposed on the basis that, while they conformed with the English forum, they should have been made consistent with the Belgian form, since the testator died domiciled in Belgium and, hence, only Belgian law should be used to test formal validity. Sir Herbert Jenner admitted the codicils by stating that Belgian law would have referred the validity of the codicils to the law of the testator's original country of nationality. Where the conflict rules of the foreign State identified by the English forum would have referred the matter back to the English forum, acceptance of the *renvoi* constitutes the application of the doctrine of single *renvoi*.

This status of the *renvoi* doctrine remained until 1926, when Russell J in *Re Annesley* (1926) introduced the double *renvoi* doctrine into English law. This doctrine necessitates not only reference to the conflict rules of the chosen system, but reference to that system's *renvoi* rules as well. In *Re Annesley*, according to English law, the testator had died domiciled in France, but, according to French law, he was domiciled in England. The distinction was fundamental since, under French law, the testator could not bequeath more than one-third of her property because she had surviving children. This would have been possible under English law. The probate court held that, as a French judge hearing the case was bound to turn to English law as the applicable law but subsequently would have to accept the *renvoi* back to French domestic law, French law should apply.

A few points of interest can be raised in this case. First, no authority was cited for making such an introduction into English law as it stood then. Secondly, the judge presumably took a 'common sense' approach and applied French domestic law as the law of the domicile, on the basis that the French court would have arrived at the same result. Thirdly, it is noteworthy that Russell J's *dicta* suggest that a more direct reference or route is preferred, but his Lordship nevertheless applied the doctrine of double *renvoi* without giving any reason.

A case applying the doctrine but arriving at a different conclusion is *Re Ross* (1930), where the court found that, although the testator was domiciled in Italy under English law, it was proved that the Italian court would not have accepted the *renvoi,* following its rules of private international law; hence, the probate court could apply English law. This evidences the dependency that the doctrine of double *renvoi* has on proof of how the foreign court would respond to the *renvoi.*

In *Re Duke of Wellington* (1948), it was remarked that, where there exists a difference in opinion and conflicting decisions on the *renvoi* in the foreign system, application of the doctrine would lack certainty and might lead to injustice. The practice of the foreign court becomes a fact in issue, which counsels will attempt to prove exists when it is patently clear that there is no consistency of practice within the foreign system. The English court is under a duty to make a finding of fact at the conclusion of arguments, and this could very well be contrary to subsequent practice of the foreign system. This was seen in *Re O'Keefe* (1940). In that case, the intestate had lived in Italy for the last 47 years of her life and was clearly domiciled there. Under the *renvoi* doctrine, however, movable property had to be distributed according to the domestic law of the Irish Free State. She was not a citizen of the Irish Free State and had never visited the country, except for a short holiday 60 years before her death. Yet, according to Crossman J, her nationality was crucial under Italian choice of law and, therefore, the law must refer to the country where her father was domiciled at the time of her birth.

On the issue of nationality, the problem caused by authorities like *Re O'Keefe* in the application of the foreign court theory doctrine is that the law of the nationality is frequently referred to by the foreign choice of law system. As far as the British subject is concerned, this raises the absurdity of having to apply 'British' law, which is non-existent. On the other hand, there is no such thing as English nationality. The assumption adopted by the courts in *Re O'Keefe* and *Re Johnson* (1903) was that the national law of a British subject meant the law of his domicile of origin, without any evidence of foreign law. On the other hand, in *Re Ross* (1930), expert evidence was adduced to the effect that the foreign court in question would determine the case on the footing that the English law applicable is that part of the law which would be applicable to a British national domiciled in England. From these cases, it may be argued that there are no guidelines as to the application of the doctrine in cases of nationality and domicile of origin. The English court's assessment of how the foreign court would decide is not necessarily the way that the foreign court would respond.

There is yet another difficulty, as pointed out by the Private International Law Committee.[2] Successful invocation of the doctrine relies on the foreign court rejecting the *renvoi* or adopting only the doctrine of single *renvoi*. Where the foreign court also adopts the doctrine of double *renvoi*, the *renvoi* will move to and from that system, leading to no solution at all.

Finally, it is foreseeable that, in the application of the doctrine of double *renvoi*, the conflict rules of the *lex causae* (the foreign system in question) may refer the case to a third system of law. In *R v Brentwood Superintendent Registrar of Marriages ex p Arias* (1968), the Italian choice of law rules referred to the *lex patriae* of the French national who was domiciled in Italy, the *lex patriae* in this case being French law. The English court could choose to apply French law and, by doing so, it would achieve some form of consistency with the Italian court. However, the problem is the question of where the transmission ends. It seems to be the suggestion of jurists that, where the foreign court and the English court would both turn to a third system, then, for the sake of consistency and practicality, that third system should be given effect to. Where there is no consistency, however, the *renvoi* should be rejected and ignored. This position on transmission is still not entirely clear, and a reading of *R v Brentwood* does not produce a coherent theme as to the logic of the application.

While the problem is undesirably uncertain and, in some cases, severely applied, it is to be noted that the *renvoi* has not been extended beyond the area of succession of property and legitimacy. Further, the area of formal validity of wills is now covered by legislation, the Wills Act 1963.[3] In the area of contract law within the EC, the application of the doctrine is expressly excluded by Art 15 of the Rome Convention 1980. There is opinion to suggest, however, that questions of formal validity of instruments and other (non-contractual) arrangements may still be subject to the doctrine.

Notes

1 The law preceding the Wills Acts 1861 and 1963.
2 See the *First Report,* Cmd 9068, 1954, para 23, for a full account of the proposition.
3 Note, in particular, ss 2(1)(b) and 6(1).

Question 2

> Laws do not remain stagnant. Hence, although conflict rules may refer to a particular system of law, the problem still remains that changes may have occurred to the connecting factor or to the *lex causae* itself.

Comment on how English judges have responded to such an observation.

Answer plan

This is an area of growing importance amongst English lawyers. The time factor is one which private international law rules cannot afford to disregard indefinitely, although the courts have approached the matter on a piecemeal basis in many situations.

The student may expect questions in this area to deal with any of the following three situations:

- changes in the forum's private international law rules;
- changes in the connecting factor in a rule of conflict of laws;
- changes in the *lex causae*.

The student should be able to present the difficulties created by these changes (if any) and assess how the courts have responded to them. An understanding of the court's judgment in *Lynch v Provisional Government of Paraguay* (1871) is especially helpful in setting out the common sense approach. Policy considerations should not be omitted, and perhaps equally important is the English court's manner of addressing issues of policy.

Answer

The situations identified, that is, the changes in the connecting factor and the content of the *lex causae*, form two of the three areas where the time factor may be of particular importance in conflict of laws. The third area is where there has been change to the conflict rule of the forum. For the purposes of this essay, the third area shall be excluded from discussion.

With regard to the possibility of changes made to the content of the connecting factor, it is foreseeable that, while English conflict rules may refer to a particular connecting factor, the character of the connecting factor may be such that it is time dependent. This is to say that the connecting factor is 'variable', rather than constant. A good illustration may be found in the legitimation of children. The conflict rule is that a child's legitimation is dependent on the law of his father's domicile. In this connection, it is crucial for the law to identify the time at which the father's domicile becomes relevant, since the father's domicile could change according to his intention and *de facto* residence. Section 3 of the Legitimacy Act 1976 provides that the father's relevant domicile is his domicile at the time of his marriage.

On the other hand, changes could also occur to the *lex causae*. Problems become exacerbated when these changes purportedly have retrospective effect.

How have the English courts taken to these intervening factors when it comes to determination of the choice of law? The first point to note with reference to the first situation is that, while the courts will always initially endeavour to secure some certainty, this is not always possible. Professor McLean finds that there is, in fact, no general principle identifiable from judicial authority.[1] The reason is simple – the diversity of cases are such that it is impossible to discern how one case on, say, legitimacy, may provide any rational guidance for the resolution of a case on property. It is not easy to locate any discernible trend of judicial thought that is general enough to accommodate situations involving a different subject matter.

In any event, the starting point with most cases is the determination of whether there is any statutory provision that may offer some kind of direction. Where statutes provide a solution, the matter quite speedily resolves itself.

In more vexing cases, however, there is unfortunately no consistency in practice, as highlighted earlier. Grodecki suggests that the better approach is to resolve the problem at hand by framing the most convenient and fair conflict rule and not to be swayed by the time factor.[2] The lack of a metanarrative in resolving the matter is seen in the tremulous decisions on formal validity of wills. In *Coppin v Coppin* (1752), we are reminded of the old common law which states that a will of immovable property must conform to the formalities set out by the *lex situs*. This old rule is perhaps one that has frequently given cause for concern as regards the time factor. In *In bonis Lacroix* (1877), for example, hardship and inconvenience could have resulted if the testator changed his domicile after executing his will. The court in that case purportedly gave recognition to the time factor by admitting to probate wills which met the formalities required by either the domestic law of the testator's last domicile or the domestic law of any system of law identified by the conflict rules of that law.[3]

Still on the matter of wills, a 'worse' scenario is found in the area of construction of wills. The law is that a will of movable property must be construed according to the provisions of the law intended by the testator. As pointed out in *Anstruther v Chalmer* (1826), which was later affirmed in *Re Cunnington* (1924), the court will generally apply the law of testator's domicile at the time the will was made and, contrary to certain views, not at the time of his death. This is, however, only a presumption, and a rebuttable one at that. What is interesting for our purposes is that any change in the testator's domicile is not relevant, according to s 4 of the Wills Act 1963. The qualification is that this is only operative once the presumption has been activated. Where it is proved that the testator intended a different system of law to govern the construction issue, then that intention will be given effect to, whether the intention was expressed at the time of the making of the will or afterwards.

In this case, two matters are pellucid. First, where the time factor is treated as relevant, the position seems to be that which coincides with common sense and convenience. Secondly, it provides support for Grodecki's argument that the time factor is not a relevant factor at all. All the court has to do is to formulate the conflict issue according to the essence of the subject matter. Accordingly, in the above cited case, there was a will and its construction was in issue; as with all construction of deeds, the intention of the maker is fundamental and, hence, the conflict rule should be applied consistent with that intention.

Other areas of dispute have produced similar results, in that there is no uniformity of application of the time factor issue and, in many situations, the time factor has been presumed or ignored in the light of the citation of a wider conflict rule.

With reference to the second situation, it is here where some of the most important problems of the time factor have surfaced, especially when the change necessitates the retrospective effect. Broadly speaking, the forum should apply the *lex causae* in its entirety, and this would naturally include all transitional rules. The qualifier must be that there is a real distinction between constant and variable connecting factors. Where the connecting factor is a constant, the application of the *lex causae* in its entirety would raise few objections. Where the connecting factor is not constant but changes from time to time, the formulation of the applicable conflict rule has to be made more precise.

The main issue for the courts is whether subsequent changes in the *lex causae* should be applied or simply ignored. The problem is aggravated by the fact that policy in this country has always been to treat retrospective laws with some degree of circumspection and apprehension. There is little authority directly on this issue, but the vacuum may be treated like all matters in private international law concerning public policy. As a paradigm, the courts are slow to find a public policy cause and will apply severe tests as to whether judicial notice should be taken of the existence of the alleged public policy. Finally, the courts will only apply it as an exception to the rule.

On the issue of applying the *lex causae* in its entirety, it may be useful to turn to a few cases that have purportedly grappled with the question within the context of public policy. In *Lynch v Provisional Government of Paraguay* (1871), two months after the death of the testator, who was domiciled in Paraguay, there was a revolution in that country. The new government passed a law declaring that the testator's property, wherever situated, 'shall be the property of the State; and the decree will apply as at the time of the testator's death'. This affected the beneficiary plaintiff, who was entitled to the deceased's property in England. Lord Penzance granted probate to the plaintiff, on the basis that English law adopts the law of the domicile as it stands at the time of the testator's death. Any subsequent retrospective change in that law cannot be given effect to.

Two points may be raised here. First, Lord Penzance's formulation of the conflict rule; and secondly, the common sense perception of justice and convenience which His Lordship applied. On the first, Professor FA Mann's criticism is that such a formulation does not take into account any transitional rules of the *lex causae* and, therefore, derogates from the practice of applying the *lex causae* in its entirety.[4] There is also cause for concern that this judgment does not consider the content of the transitional rule. Professor McLean cites the example of where the will had been defective in point of form at the time of death but had subsequently been validated by retrospective legislation in Paraguay: '... it is hard to suppose that Lord Penzance would have thought it "inconvenient and unjust" to give effect to that legislation.'[5]

On the second issue, it could be submitted that a better approach to the resolution of that which is perceived to be ostensibly 'inconvenient and unjust' is not simply to rely on the technical formulation of the conflict rule alone but to place the application of that rule in the context of policy considerations of the highest eminence. This contextual approach is probably a suitably effective compromise, following the House of Lords' recognition of the *Lynch* principle as the 'correct principle' in *Adams v National Bank of Greece* (1961). In that case, the House of Lords refused to apply a retrospective Greek law which would otherwise have freed a Greek bank from its existing contractual liability. It was held unanimously that the principle in *Lynch* was correct. While only Lord Tucker relied squarely on that case to refuse the Greek bank's defence, it was quite obvious that, in the formulation of the conflict question, the House found that the Greek law was not the *lex causae* and should therefore be of no relevance.

This is not to suggest, however, that there is complete consistency in the application of the rule in *Lynch*. The House of Lords in *Starkowski v AG* (1954) had to decide whether the law of the place where a marriage was celebrated, as it stood at the time of the marriage or as it stood when the problem of validity arose, should be applied. The House distinguished *Lynch* on various grounds, *inter alia*, that the case was of an entirely different subject matter. Taking this case and the problems faced by the House of Lords, it is opined that the major difficulty is attempting to find some semblance of congruity in the quagmire of policy considerations. Predictably represented in this legal perplexity is the tussle between flexibility and certainty.

Notes

1 McLean, *Morris – The Conflict of Laws*, 4th edn, 1993, p 431.
2 Grodecki (1959) 35 BYIL 58.
3 See, also, *Collier v Rivaz* (1841).
4 Mann (1954) 31 BYIL 217.
5 *Ibid*, McLean, note 1, p 433.

Question 3

> ... As has often been said, private international law is really a branch of municipal law and obviously there can be no branch of municipal law in which the general policy of such law can be properly ignored [*Dynamit AG v Rio Tinto Zinc Co* (1918), *per* Lord Parker].

Examine the role that the English courts have given public policy in the application of private international law.

Answer plan

The emphasis in this question is on the role of public policy in private international law. The starting point, as suggested in the quote, is the definition of private international law as a branch of municipal law. The chief implication of this proposition is that it is thus subject to the operation of English public policy, regardless of the *lex causae*.

Students attempting a question like this must be familiar with the labour exerted in defining and arguing for a set of coherent rules concerning the application of public policy rules. The cases that deal with penal foreign rules, discriminatory measures in status, the importance of natural justice and fraud, to name a few, are useful in revealing, on the one hand, the lack of consistency, and, on the other, the serious difficulties involved. The good student should highlight the general approach taken by the English courts in this connection.

It would also be of value to refer to the importance of policy applied, not only in the common law, but also through the Brussels and Rome Conventions.

Answer

As is clear from Lord Parker's observation, private international law, unlike public international law, is very much a part of the domestic law of this country. Public international law arguably stands on a different footing: rules of public international law, as found in custom, State practice and treaties, are not usually subject to public policy concerns in the same manner. The application of any rule of conflict of laws must consequently meet the demands of public policy, as understood, construed and applied within the domestic system. Scarman J in *Re Fuld's Estate (No 3)* (1968) said in no uncertain terms that an English court will refuse to apply a law which outrages its sense of justice and decency. There is, however, a qualifier, in that, before the court refuses to do so on the ground of failure of public policy, it must consider the relevant foreign law as a whole and determine whether proof of that foreign law is consistent with the allegation.

In *Fender v St John Mildmay* (1938), this qualification was explained in the following terms. The doctrine should only be called upon in cases in which it is clear that the harm to the public is substantially incontestable and does not depend on the idiosyncratic inferences of a few judicial minds. This is an important demarcation of the boundaries of public policy. It does not seek to define the exact parameters of public policy but sets out one paradigm, that of certainty. It appears that the premise of this exception to the application of rules of conflict is that the fundamental role of public policy in the municipal system should be clear and unambiguous.

The public policy applied must be clearly identified and then raised in context against the foreign law in question. Abstract or purely esoteric reasons will be regarded as insufficient proof of public policy. For example, where English public policy would have rejected the giving of effect to any foreign law which is penal, that provision which is contended as being so must be obviously penal. A case which has been the subject of criticism on this basis is *Re Selot's Trusts* (1902). A testator domiciled in England gave a legacy to his grandson, a French national who was domiciled in France. The grandson was found under French law to be a prodigal and, as a result, could not execute a charge over the property without proper consent. He charged the property as security for a loan without the requisite consent. It was held by the English court that the charge was valid and that the French rule on consent was bad for transgression of English public policy. It was decided by Farwell J that the French status rule was penal. However, 'penal' was not defined by the judge; therefore, his conclusion in that case is open to criticism on that basis.

There is a distinction between cases which simply require adjudication and enforcement of English law and those which have a significant factual connection with England although they are governed by a foreign system. Where the factual connection between the case and England as a forum is tenuous, English public policy should only be applied to reject the result of the application of the foreign law where that application flies in the face of fundamental principles of English law or basic morality. Where there is a substantial connection with England, policy considerations of a lower degree in the hierarchy of norms may be applied to refuse application of the foreign rule.

A model of this first proposition is perhaps best displayed in *Robinson v Bland* (1760). In that case, the English court felt bound to refuse recognition of a contract of prostitution (which was otherwise valid under the foreign law), even though the contract was not connected with the *lex fori*, because to do otherwise would be to derogate from the basic morality of English law. It would have constituted a fundamental departure from the morality of this country. Lower order policy considerations may include, as in *Grell v Levy* (1864), the rule under English law against the acceptance of contingency fees to maintain litigation. Although it was not a fundamental policy or a rule of basic morality, the court declined in that case to enforce the arrangement because the maintenance of the action was to take place in England, hence providing that substantial connection.

Besides these common law considerations, statutory provisions on enforcement and recognition of foreign law and judgments also make exception of matters contrary to public policy. Under the Administration of Justice Act 1920, for example, the defences to the recognition and enforcement of foreign judgments at common law, such as fraud, denial of natural justice and other grounds of public policy, are directly relevant. Under the Brussels Convention, as ratified and enforced in England by the Civil Jurisdiction and Judgments Act 1982, Art 27 provides that a judgment given by a Contracting State will not be recognised if recognition of the judgment would be contrary to the public policy of the recognising State. The precise scope of application is, however, unclear in the light of Art 28(3), which expressly rules out any public policy objections to the original court's jurisdiction. Further, Art 29 states that under no circumstance may a foreign judgment be reviewed as to its substance. The Jarrad Report takes the view that public policy objections vitiate the act of recognition of the judgment, not the judgment itself. This seems to suggest that, while the nature and substance of the judgment cannot be challenged, recognition and subsequent enforcement could be subject to the test of the recognising State's public policy under Art 27.

Under the Contracts (Applicable Law) Act 1990 and, consequently, the Rome Convention 1980, it is clear from Art 16 that the application of a rule of law otherwise applicable by virtue of the Convention may be refused if its application is manifestly incompatible with the *ordre public* of the forum. It is not entirely clear how the *ordre public* will be construed by the English courts and whether its interpretation will depend on the common law distinction made between cases having a substantial connection with England and those that do not.

Another area where the exclusion of foreign law on the grounds of public policy is relatively rare is where the question of status is involved. In general, according to *Re Metcalfe's Trusts* (1864), the rule is that English courts will not give effect to the implications of any status existing under a foreign law which is penal or discriminatory. The status or incapacity imposed on certain individuals will not be given effect to where to do so would be to act as the foreign State's agent in executing an order contrary to the morality of English law. A distinction was made in *Re Selot's Trusts* (1902) between status which is penal and status which is merely protective or discriminatory. The extent to which this distinction will sway a case either way is not exactly clear from *Re Selot's Trusts*. Further, the issue may be better resolved by considering the *lex causae* or the connection between the facts of the case and the forum. In *Re Selot's Trusts*, the question was whether the legatee petitioner could take under the will of a testator domiciled in England. English law appears to be the *lex causae*, hence the foreign rule on incapacity to claim was not applied. Had the foreign law been the *lex causae*, the result would probably have been quite different.

The role of public policy is particularly stark in the area of matrimonial relations, given the issues of morality and cultural differences. The chief concern is to do justice, not to uphold English standards of morality and decency. This difficult balance is well expressed in *Cheni v Cheni* (1965), where the marriage in question was between an uncle and his niece. The marriage was valid under Egyptian law. The wife, who later emigrated to the UK, sought a decree annulling the marriage, on the basis that that relationship was prohibited by English law and, therefore, the Egyptian marriage was contrary to English public policy. Simon J was concerned that the court should 'seek to exercise common sense, good manners and a reasonable tolerance' in such a situation. The decree was not granted, on the basis that the marriage in itself was not so offensive to the conscience of the English court that it should be de-recognised.

This 'reasonable tolerance' that Simon J referred to demonstrates the general reluctance of the English courts to reject status formed or established under a foreign law.[1] Whether this would manifest itself further in the recognition of homosexual relationships established or recognised under a foreign law has become one of the more recent controversies of our time. The issue is whether an English court would deem a homosexual relationship, recognised under, say, Scandinavian laws on registered relationships, as a valid marriage or as something else.[2] This debate, it would seem, will go on.

The courts have been known to hold that they possess a 'residual discretion' to refuse recognition of foreign status (*Re Langley's Settlement* (1962)) if the recognition would be improper or unjust in the circumstances of the case. It must be submitted that such a position will cause even more uncertainty as to the already watery perimeter of public policy.[3] The exercise of such discretion is clearly irrelevant where the recognition of the status has the effect of contravening public policy in the circumstances of the case.

Public policy may also operate where the litigants raise provisions of foreign public law in the proceedings before the English court. According to *Regazzoni v KC Sethia (1944) Ltd* (1956), the English courts do not act as the executive agents for any foreign sovereign. The courts' traditional position with regard to foreign revenue laws, for example, is that they will not act as the foreign State's tax collectors. Additionally, as was the case in *Rossano v Manufacturers' Life Insurance Co Ltd* (1963), direct or indirect attempts by any party to enforce foreign revenue laws will not be entertained. This is, however, not to say that these laws will never be recognised in every circumstance. In *Re Emery's Investment Trusts* (1959), the English court refused to abet any scheme to evade the operation of foreign revenue law. The clearest observation that may be made, as matters currently stand, is that English courts actively choose to remain neutral, neither enforcing nor ignoring the public laws of foreign States.

A stronger prohibition under public policy is the refusal to permit the recovery of a penalty imposed by a foreign tribunal, *a fortiori* a criminal court of the foreign State. This must be confined to actions at the suit of a foreign State, and not extended to individuals who stand to benefit from such penal provisions (*Huntingdon v Attrill* (1893)). Hence, in *SA Consortium General Textiles v Sun and Sand Agencies Ltd* (1978), a foreign award of exemplary damages was enforced, even though such awards are deemed to be punitive at English law. Here, the position of public policy is clearer, in that, while the English court will actively resist being perceived as the police agency of the foreign State, the matter is entirely different where rights of individuals are concerned. In the latter situation, regardless of nationality or domicile, any litigant who appears before the English court is subject to both the governance and the protection of the court.

In conclusion, it may be said that, while the role of public policy in conflict of laws has always been treated by the courts as a necessity, its application and definition have eluded the best of judicial endeavours. In the 1960s and 1970s, the view of writers was that more precise delineation of the role and operation of public policy was needed. The position has somewhat shifted since, the emphasis now being placed on proving connection between the case in question and the forum. Instead of applying a blanket defence of public policy, this shift healthily suggests a more objective placing of the conflict rule.

Notes

1 See, also, *Re Bozzelli's Settlement* (1902) and *Re Pozot's Settlement* (1952).
2 See Lind (1995) 145 NLJ 1553; Norrie (1994) 43 ICLQ 757.
3 See, eg, Nygh (1964) 13 ICLQ 39.

Question 4

To what extent does an English judge actually 'apply' foreign law? Why should an English judge apply foreign law? Discuss, making reference to relevant decided cases.

Answer plan

This is a fairly straightforward question, although students will need to draw upon cases from different areas of their course in order to demonstrate the need to apply foreign law so as to achieve the most just and pragmatic result. It is not enough simply to say that the judge applies foreign law in order to achieve justice for the parties. Students should be aware that no marks are given for pure rhetoric. Illustration of what constitutes 'justice' should also be given.

As to the second question, this requires the student to mention the vexed issue of whether the English judge is compromising State sovereignty by applying foreign law. It is also vital to explain how foreign law is actually 'applied'; that is, how foreign law is to be proved and, subsequently, used to resolve the dispute.

Answer

In order to address the issue of why foreign law is applied at all, it is useful to turn to some of the problems that are unique to situations which contain an international element. Cases with this international element usually create problems in private international law. As far as the question of foreign law is concerned, the thrust of the problem is usually this – why does the English court not apply English law regardless? After all, litigants have chosen, tacitly or expressly, to have their dispute resolved in England. Indeed, this is particularly true of the common law relating to matrimonial and family matters. The celebrated case of *Zanelli v Zanelli* (1948) might be cited to demonstrate that, once the issue of jurisdiction over the divorce or separation action has been resolved in favour of the English court, that court would inevitably apply English law to determine whether the application for divorce should be granted. Similarly, in the area of adoption of children, while there is some validity in the argument that an adoption order should not be made in relation to a child domiciled abroad unless the adoption is not in breach of the law of the child's domicile, this has been soundly rejected by the Adoption Act 1976.

Nevertheless, in many cases, the courts do actually apply foreign law. This judicial act seems to fall foul of the doctrine of State sovereignty; after all, for an English court to disapply English law in favour of foreign law would seem to be a relinquishment of judicial sovereignty.

This contention is fallacious, because the judge does not in fact 'apply' the foreign law in question. What he does is apply the English rules of conflict of laws, which direct the judge to have recourse to a foreign law in order to resolve the dispute at hand. There is no real application of the foreign law; the English judge turns to an expert in the foreign law concerned and, on the basis of that expert's advice and the circumstances of the case, formulates a factual solution. It is thus ultimately a factual matter, not one of law (*Fremoult v Dedire* (1718); *Mostyn v Fabrigas* (1774)).

As early as the *Sussex Peerage* case (1844), *Nelson v Bridport* (1845) and the *Baron de Bode* case (1845), the prevailing rule has been that foreign law, as a matter of fact, must be proved by expert evidence. Merely adducing foreign statutes, written texts and law reports is not sufficient (*Nelson v Bridport*). The English court will not participate in research into foreign law – that is a task for the lawyers and experts who are representing the litigants.

The law takes a firm stance in requiring English judges not to apply foreign law – in *Buerger v New York Life Assurance Co* (1926) and *Sharif v Azad* (1967), we are reminded that, if an expert's evidence goes unchallenged, an English judge will usually accept and adopt his interpretation as representing the foreign law in question. These cases demonstrate how careful the court will be in order to avoid 'applying or deciding' on the foreign law or treating it as a matter of law.

The common law, however, is not unreasonable. Where the expert's suggestion or interpretation is 'extravagant', 'patently absurd' or 'wholly inconsistent with the rest of his evidence', the rule in *Tallina Laevauhisus A/S v Estonian State SS Line* (1947) is that his evidence can and should be rejected, with the result that the foreign law is not proved. Failure to prove the foreign law means that the court, consistent with the doctrine of State sovereignty, will apply English law in order to resolve dispute. This is a manifestation of the traditional common law axiom that jurisdiction must prevail over choice of law.

This axiom was, perhaps, taken to extremes in *Szechter v Szechter* (1971). In that case, under the relevant conflicts rule, Polish law was the proper law. During trial, the expert witness was hospitalised and unable to give oral evidence in court. As a result, the court disregarded Polish law and gave its judgment in reliance on English law. The basis of this case is that English law will always remain the applicable law, unless and until a relevant foreign law has been successfully pleaded and proved.

There are very few instances where proof of foreign law may be dispensed with. Where this is permitted, it must be sanctioned by statute. A conventional example is s 4(2)–(5) of the Civil Evidence Act 1972: where any question of foreign law has been determined in civil or criminal proceedings at first instance in certain higher courts, then any finding made or decision given on that question is admissible in evidence in any civil proceedings; and the foreign law shall be taken to be in accordance with that finding or decision, unless the contrary is proved. The finding or decision must be reported or recorded in writing in a report, transcript or other document which could be cited as an authority in legal proceedings in England if the question had been one of English law. Another instance is the admissibility of copies of laws made by the legislature of any 'British possession' under the Evidence (Colonial Statutes) Act 1907. In both situations, the emphasis is upon the extent to which judicial notice should be given of the foreign law as a matter of fact.

As a matter of proof, where the parties do not rely on the relevant foreign law in their statements of case, the English court will not of its own accord apply that foreign law. Instead, it will merely apply English law to the dispute. In *Aluminium Industrie Vaassen BV v Romalpa Aluminium Ltd* (1976), the contract contained a clause which stipulated that Dutch law was to apply. However, as neither party pleaded Dutch law, the court proceeded to adjudicate the dispute without taking into account any element of Dutch law at all.

Therefore, the right question to ask is not why foreign law is applied, but why English law on conflict of laws requires that foreign law be used to provide a factual solution to the dispute at hand. An important reason is that English justice requires that the reasonable and legitimate expectations of the parties should be given effect to. For example, where the parties have freely chosen a foreign law to apply to their relationship (for example, a contractual relationship), it would be totally unjust to deny the effect of that agreement between them. That foreign law chosen by them reflects their expectations of each other and of themselves; to use English law to determine their obligations and rights towards each other is to crush those expectations.

Naturally, this rationale of the parties' legitimate or reasonable expectations as to what constitutes their rights and obligations does not operate only in the area of contract law or bilateral relationships. In the area of property and succession, the parties may have certain expectations as to what law should govern the distribution or transfer of their property. It would, therefore, be quite unjust for all parties concerned if the distribution of such assets was to be dealt by English law, as it could not have been within the reasonable contemplation of all interested parties. In *Welch v Tennent* (1891), for example, it was important to decide what law governed the issue of ownership to certain sale proceeds. In that case, a husband and wife were domiciled in Scotland. The wife owned a piece of land in England. She sold the plot of land after marrying and gave her husband the proceeds of the sale. She later claimed under Scots law that the proceeds were rightfully hers. The House of Lords held that, as the land was situated in England, English law should apply. As a result, her claim failed.

In a contrasting case, *Re de Nicols (No 2)* (1900), a man and his wife had married in France. They moved to England and bought property here. The question was whether this piece of property was subject to French law on common or community of property. The court held that the property was subject to the law of the parties' matrimonial domicile because the subject matter related to a tacit agreement between the parties which was best resolved under French law, that law presumably having the closest connection to this aspect of the parties' relationship. These cases demonstrate how difficult it is for the court to decide when to disapply English law in the interests of justice.

Reasonable expectation should not be construed as an absolute determinant in the decision to disapply English law. There are situations where, although the parties concerned might want the English court to apply a foreign law, that application might be inconsistent with public policy. Take, for example, the issue of validity of marriages. Although a particular marital relationship may be lawful in a foreign country, it can be one which is entirely repulsive to English public policy. For example, non-consensual marriages might be refused recognition, even though they would have been valid had the English court applied the relevant foreign law. This is naturally subject to how repugnant that marriage or foreign law is. The tolerance of the courts is remarkable capacious; in *Mohamed v Knott* (1969), the marriage in question, which had taken place in Nigeria and was valid under Nigerian law, was upheld by the English court, even though the wife had not attained the English age of consent when the marriage was consummated and such an act would have constituted a criminal offence in England.

Another reason for the use of foreign law is that, wherever the dispute is litigated, the outcome should be largely the same as the outcomes that the courts of the various countries with jurisdiction to try the case would have reached, applying the relevant foreign law. Theoretically, this would reduce the prevalent practice of shopping for the forum whose law is the most favourable to the claimant. In the area of matrimonial relationships, the prospect of different countries applying different 'foreign' or 'proper' law to the relationship could very well result in the couple being treated as a married couple in some countries and not in others. It should, however, be noted that, while universal uniformity in choice of law rules is frequently cited as noble aim, the truth of the matter is that uniformity cannot be a reality. Because of the many different cultural, social, economic and ethnic characteristics of nations, uniformity in private international law cannot be attained; nor, it is submitted, should it be.

Question 5*

Judge Peirson Hall in *Re Paris Crash* (1974) described the American revolution in conflict of laws as follows:

> The law on 'choice of law' in the various States and in the federal courts is a veritable jungle, which, if the law can be found, leads not to a 'rule of action' but a reign of chaos.

Comment.

Answer plan

In order to answer the question, each important theory should be examined. First, it will be necessary to discuss the points common to all theories, such as the 'rule selection' approach and the determination of the 'true' and 'false' conflict. Once a particular theory is presented, it should be critically assessed. The main theories to be examined are:

- the Restatement (Second) of the conflict of laws, elaborated by Professor Reeds, which contains his theory of the most significant relationship;
- the choice-influencing considerations theory of Leflar;
- the governmental interest analysis theory of Currie;
- the comparative impairment theory of Baxter;
- the principles of preference theory of Cavers;
- the interpretation of forum policy theory of Ehrenzweig.

Answer

The American revolution in conflict of laws has its source in the dissatisfaction with traditional choice of law rules, which were criticised for their excessive rigidity. They were also considered as being too general and an obstacle to the unification of private international law. Indeed, the traditional conflict of law rules, in the terminology of the recent American scholars, are based on the 'jurisdiction selection' approach. This requires that, once the conditions for their application are satisfied, the court has to apply them irrespective of the content of the substantive rules selected by the choice of law as competent to solve the multi-State problem. As a result, the traditional conflict of law rules may produce unjust and unfair solutions, since the substantive rules of the selected law are applied without taking into account the circumstances of a particular case. The objective of traditional conflict of law rules is not to find the best solution in each individual case but to provide a mechanism for solving multi-State problems. The essence of the theories espoused in the US is that, in the search for the best solution to multi-State problems, each case has to be examined individually.

American scholars were hostile to generalisation. However, the concept of the best solution is perhaps as elusive as the concept of happiness. Thus, the American authors provided judges with some guidelines as to how to proceed to find the best solution to each case. This approach is based on the 'rule selection' techniques, which require the court to compare substantive rules of law of two or more apparently involved legal systems and to select the one which would produce the best result in a particular case. In this respect, the American theories can be divided into two categories. The first provides a technique which judges should use in order to select the appropriate law, the best example of this being the 'proper law' approach; and the second requires that some objectives must be achieved by the court, such as the application of the substantive law which has the prevailing legitimate interests in a case, according to Brainerd Currie, or to do justice between the parties on the basis of the 'principles of preference' advocated by David Cavers.

The second feature common to new theories is the distinction between 'true' and 'false' conflicts. A basic assumption of the traditional conflict of law rules is that the substantive laws involved in the dispute always claim their application irrespective of the circumstances of the dispute. The 'rule selection' approach makes a distinction between 'false conflict', in which the analysis of the substantive laws indicate that only one law has a legitimate claim to application and, thus, there is no choice to be made; and 'true conflict', where two or more substantive laws have legitimate interests to be applied. However, it may happen that neither law has a legitimate claim to be applied: thus the third possibility, called a 'no-interest' case, emerges. The classic 'no interest' case arises when the substantive law of the claimant's State in favourable to the defendant and the defendant's State has the substantive law favourable to the claimant. Thus the claimant's State has no interest in protecting the defendant from another State, and the defendant's State is not interested in affording more favourable treatment to the claimant than he would get under the law of his own State.

Most significant relationship

Amongst the various approaches, the theory of the most significant relationship provides a technique under which the applicable law is selected by reference to a variety of choice of law factors. This theory is favoured by the moderate fraction of the American scholars and is based on the English 'proper law' approach, which has been elaborated by Dr Morris. According to him, in multi-State torts, the applicable law should be selected on the grounds of 'the most significant connection' with the particular case and the specific issue posed. Instead of automatically applying the *lex loci delicti*, 'the law of the place of injury to all torts', the court should be more flexible and should take into account other factors, such as the residence of the parties, the relationship between them, etc, in order to determine the law which has the *most* significant connection and which would be the most appropriate to solve a multi-State tort. Furthermore, he advocated that different laws might be applied to different issues.

His theory promotes a more flexible and, according to him, rational approach, to choice of law problems in multi-State torts. The proper law idea served as a foundation for Professor Reeds' theory of 'the most significant relationship', which is explained in the Restatement (Second) of the conflict of laws. He considered that courts should follow the directive of its own State on choice of law but, in the absence of such a directive, they should apply the law which has the most significant relationship to the particular issue. In order to ascertain that law, Professor Reeds provided a list of factors which should be taken into consideration in para 6 of the Restatement. Those factors are: (a) the needs of inter-State and international system; (b) the policies underlying substantive laws of the forum; (c) the interest and policies of other States apparently involved in the dispute; (d) the protection of justified expectations of the parties; (e) certainty, predictability and uniformity of result; and (f) difficulty in application of the selected law.

Thus, Reeds blended the proper law theory with the governmental interest analysis and the principles of preference. However, he did not advocate the abolition of traditional choice of law rules but a technique in determination of the most appropriate law to a multi-State problem. The Restatement (Second) enjoys considerable support from scholars and courts in the US (*Babcock v Jackson* (1963)). The main drawback of his theory is, as Cavers remarked, that 'the factors often point in different directions and carry in themselves no measure of their significance'.

The choice-influencing consideration

A variation of Reeds' theory is the 'choice-influencing consideration' approach advocated by Leflar. He elaborated his own list of factors that should guide the courts in determining the applicable law, and added a factor that is absent in the Restatement (Second): the application of the better rule of law. This new ingredient is quite dangerous, as it may encourage the courts to apply the *lex fori* as a better law.

Governmental interest analysis

With reference to the second category, the most important doctrine is the governmental interest analysis elaborated by Brainerd Currie. Currie advocated the abolition of the traditional conflict of laws rules. He was also against multilateralism. He argued that States have interests in promoting their policies. The role of the judge is to identify and assess the policies and interest of substantive rules apparently involved in a dispute. Currie, like Wachter, considered that courts have a duty to promote forum interest. As a result, the *lex fori* should be applied as a matter of principle, and foreign law should displace local rules only if the forum has no legitimate interest in the case. The distinction between 'true' and 'false' conflict is vital to his theory, as it applies only in the first mentioned case. In a 'no-interest' situation, he suggested the application of the *lex fori*.

In order to ascertain the policies underlying the substantive laws, Currie suggested that courts should use the ordinary process of construction and interpretation. He examined real and hypothetical cases, and almost always deduced the legitimacy of asserting a governmental interest from the fact that one of the party was domiciled in that State. The main characteristic of his theory is that a separate analysis is necessary for each issue raised by a multi-State dispute in order to assess which substantive law claims its application. The personal connection of a party with a State constitutes a base for assuming the interest of the local law and the territorial contact is less important. In case of 'no-interest', the *lex fori* should be applied. Similarly, all doubts should be resolved in favour of the forum.

Currie's theory unfortunately introduces uncertainty and unpredictability of results. Additionally, for judges to assess the policies and interest of the substantive laws, if they are able to do so, taking into account the fact that even Currie had difficulty in doing so, it is only relevant as to the determination of the 'false' and 'true' conflict. It is useless as to the solution of the particular case. Indeed, the theory of governmental interest analysis provides little guidance as to how the interests should be weighted and which should prevail. This is particularly obvious in cases where the forum has no legitimate interest in the application of its substantive law but substantive laws of two or more other States claim such an interest. It is submitted that the theory provides a complicated system to justify the exclusive application of the *lex fori*.

Comparative impairment

The theory of comparative impairment was introduced by Baxter and has been applied by the Supreme Court of California. It diverges from the governmental interest analysis in one respect. In case of a 'true' conflict, the court should not automatically apply the *lex fori* (which would be the practical result of Currie's theory) but should assess the conflicting interest on the basis of 'comparative impairment'; that is, they should determine which of the conflicting States' interests would be more impaired if its interests were substantially subordinated to the interest of the other State. The theory of comparative impairment suffers the same drawbacks as the theory of governmental interest analysis.

Principle of preference

David Cavers, like Aldricus, considered that the substantive law which is 'better' in the individual case should be applied. In order to determine the 'best law' where there is a 'true' conflict, he elaborated seven principles of preference to help the court to determine the applicable law. Five of those principles deal with tort and two with contracts and conveyances. The objective of his system, which he himself admitted was incomplete, was to do justice between the parties in each case. His theory is confined to tort and contract and, as he again admitted, it would be more appropriately applied in the context of federal State when it is necessary to resolve inter-State rather than international conflict. The main criticism is that, as with any 'rule-selection' approach, it introduces uncertainty and unpredictability.

Interpretation of forum policy

Finally, the theory presented by Ehrenzwieg criticises the traditional conflict of law operation and the government interest analysis approach without introducing any substantive innovation in the latter. He considered that the courts should give preference to the *lex fori*. The 'interpretation of forum policy' amounted to the systematic application of the *lex fori*, which, according to him, should be a rule. A foreign law should be applied in exceptional circumstances where the application of the *lex fori* would be unfair to the parties. His theory, if applied, would result in the demise of private international law and, further, the unbridled rise of forum shopping.

It is submitted that the different American theories, instead of *introducing* certainty, predictability and uniformity of solution, sacrifice them. In most cases, they justify the systematic application of the law of the forum, and thus virtually eliminate the application of a foreign law. This approach not only promotes the forum shopping but is fundamentally contrary to the objectives of private international law. In practice, the American revolution in conflict of law produces, as Judge Peirson Hall stated, chaos and confusion. Indeed, the American courts apply whichever theory, alone or in combination with another, suits them best in any one case.

* by Alina Kaczorowska

Question 6

Critically examine the common law rules on proof of foreign law.

Answer plan

This question looks at the general issue of proof of foreign law. Students should be able to state the general principle that foreign law has to be proved as a matter of fact. There should also be an account of the statutory exceptions to the general rule.

It would be useful to comment on the attitude of the common law in determining who an expert witness on foreign law is.

Answer

The starting point is that foreign law, as adduced and pleaded at the common law courts, is asserted as a matter of fact. The burden of proving the fact of the foreign law is with the party who relies his claim or defence (as the case may be) on it (*Dynamit AG v Rio Tinto Zinc Co* (1918)). This issue of proof is mandatory in the light of the rule in *Lloyd v Guilbert* (1865), which states that, if the party provides no or insufficient evidence of foreign law, the court will disregard the plea and only apply English law. This rule is reflective of the oft cited presumption that foreign law is the same as English law until the contrary is proved.

The general rule is that, if a party wishes to rely on a principle of foreign law as being applicable to the cause in action or the defence, he must adduce evidence to prove this, as with all questions of fact. The one exception where judicial notice may be applied is found in the British Law Ascertainment Act 1859, which provides that, where the case is governed by the law of certain British territory, the court may take cognisance of the foreign law, even though the party has not provided evidence in support (see below).

Other attempts to raise foreign law by relying on the doctrine of judicial notice have been unequivocally rejected by the courts. Although in *Saxby v Fulton* (1909), judicial notice was taken with reference to the 'notorious' fact that roulette was lawful in Monte Carlo, this is not indicative of the general approach. The general approach is that foreign law is a matter of fact but does not possess the element of notoriety required for the application of the doctrine of judicial notice. The roulette case may be explained on the basis that the foreign law in question was a notorious fact.

Proof of the foreign law does not naturally arise unless it has first been pleaded by the litigants. Where it is not pleaded, as far as English courts are concerned, the applicable law is English law.

This was confirmed in *Aluminium Industrie Vaassen BV v Romalpa Aluminium Ltd* (1976), where the court ignored the choice of Dutch law clause in the contract and proceeded to apply English law because the parties omitted, quite deliberately, to plead it.

Proof of foreign law being a matter of evidence means that the party adducing it as evidence must rely on 'fresh' evidence in every case. He may not plead that, as the foreign law has been applied in another English case, that foreign law stands as it did then (*Lazard Brothers v Midland Bank* (1933)). While in the past, the jury needed to be convinced of the principle of foreign law as a matter of fact, the Supreme Court Act 1981 (s 69(5)) makes it the duty of the judge alone.

There is one exception to this general approach. The House of Lords (or its alter ego, the Judicial Committee of the Privy Council), which has the power to hear appeals from different countries, may rely on its previous decisions to take judicial notice of the laws of any of the countries when it hears an appeal from them. In these cases, the position is that proof of foreign law becomes a matter of law rather than fact.

The question of foreign law is, however, a question of fact *sui generis*. It is peculiar, in that it must be proved by expert evidence. The adduction of legal literature, whether official or unofficial, before the court, is not considered sufficient without the assistance of an expert witness. The justification for this approach to the adduction of evidence is perhaps the fact that legal materials alone may be subject to different interpretative canons and unique rules of construction. It would not be proper for English lawyers and judges to apply English rules of construction to foreign legal materials. When the legal expert refers to legal materials, an English court may then look at the materials and draw some of its own conclusions from both the texts and the expert evidence.

This begs the question of who is an expert in the foreign law concerned. Under s 4(1) of the Civil Evidence Act 1972, it is declared that, in civil proceedings, a person who is suitably qualified to do so on account of his knowledge or experience is competent to give expert evidence as to foreign law, irrespective of whether he has acted, or is entitled to act, as a legal practitioner in the foreign country. The old rule in *Bristow v Sequeville* (1850), where the person called to testify on foreign law had to be a person qualified to act as a legal practitioner in the foreign country, has been abolished by the Act. It should be borne in mind at this juncture that any legally competent witness need not necessarily be the most suitable. While a person may be suitably qualified, the higher his standing in the legal profession of the foreign country concerned, the more weight his evidence carries.

As regards non-lawyers, the law allows various professionals or persons who, by virtue of their status and office, are in a position to testify on a fact or aspect of foreign law. In *Lacon v Higgins* (1822), a vice consul was held to be suitably qualified to act as an expert witness. Other 19th century cases have permitted ambassadors, notary publics, bishops, merchants and other professionals to act as expert witnesses. It should perhaps be pointed out that, in the light of technological advances and the mobility of legal professionals, whilst the rules should not be made more restrictive, greater weight should be given to testimonies of legal practitioners or academics.

Under the new Civil Procedure Rules 1998, no expert can be called, nor his report put in evidence, without the leave of the court (r 35.4(1)). Furthermore, r 35.5(1) provides that expert evidence shall be restricted to that which is reasonably required to resolve the proceedings. Lord Woolf was also concerned that it should be possible to appoint an expert 'assessor' to assist the court under the new rules (r 35.15). Such assessors are expected to preside over meetings between experts to help them to reach some consensus.

The court will usually accept the evidence of an expert where he is not contradicted, as was the case in *Buerger v New York Life Assurance Co* (1927). The court may, however, reject his evidence where acceptance of it would provide an absurd result. Further, the court held in *Tallina Laevauhisus A/S v Estonian State SS Line* (1947) that, where the expert's evidence is inconsistent overall, it should be rejected on the grounds of lack of credibility.

Where the evidence is challenged, the court may look at the legal texts or sources to confirm and assess the consistency of the testimonies. In this regard, the court will also take into account judgments given by the foreign courts in question. Some considerable importance is usually attached to these judgments, provided that they are clear and unambiguous (*Beatty v Beatty* (1924)).

There are a few situations where the proof of foreign law may be unnecessary. Under the Civil Evidence Act 1972, for example, s 4(2)–(5) provides that, where any question of foreign law has been determined in civil or criminal proceedings at first instance in the High Court, the Crown Court, or in any appeal therefrom, or in the Privy Council on an appeal from any court outside the UK, then any finding of that question may be admissible in evidence in any civil proceedings. Subsequent foreign law issues shall be taken as in accordance with that finding or decision, unless the contrary is proved. The finding or decision as to foreign law must be recorded in writing, in a document which could be cited as an authority in legal proceedings in England if the question had been one of English law.

The second exception comes in s 1(3) of the Evidence (Colonial Statutes) Act 1907. This provision states that copies of laws made by the legislature of any British possession, if purporting to be printed by the government printer of the British possession, can be received in evidence in the UK without proof that the copies were so printed. Whilst the substance of these laws may be admitted under the law without the need of expert evidence, the court may require evidence to the effect that these laws are still in force and have not been repealed.

Finally, under the British Law Ascertainment Act 1859, a court may state a case for the opinion of a court in any other part of Her Majesty's dominions, in order to ascertain the view of that court as to the applicable law of the case in question. This is subject to the condition that the applicable law is vital to the disposal of the case in question. This is a matter left purely to the discretion of the court. The court may or may not state a case, depending on the seriousness of the issue involved, as was held in *Lord v Colvin* (1859). The opinion of the foreign court is binding on the English judge, with the general exception of the House of Lords or the Privy Council, where the foreign jurisdiction relies on either of the two judicial bodies for appeals.

It should be noted that the latter two statutes will still apply to Commonwealth countries which are no longer British dominions or possessions.

CHAPTER 2

DOMICILE

Introduction

No person, natural or legal, may be without a domicile at English law. The concept of domicile determines that person's personal law and refers to the person's civil status. Students should note the distinction between the various types of domicile:

- domicile of origin;
- domicile of dependency;
- domicile of choice.

Domicile of origin is the domicile the person acquires at birth. As a rule, a legitimate child will acquire the domicile of his father at birth, whilst an illegitimate child will acquire the domicile of his mother. The importance of the domicile of origin is seen in *Winans v AG* (1904), where it was held that the character of the domicile of origin is more enduring than other types of domicile and is less easily shaken off. Further, where somebody loses the domicile of choice, his domicile of origin will be operative in lieu until he has acquired another domicile of choice.

The fact that a child's domicile follows that of his father or mother, depending on his legitimacy, is a manifestation of the common law rules on domicile of dependency. Besides children, wives at common law should acquire the domicile of their husbands. These rules have been modified in the Domicile and Matrimonial Proceedings Act 1973.

As far as children are concerned, s 4 of the Act provides that 'a child whose parents are living apart has the same domicile as its mother if he then has a home with her and has no home with his father'. As for married women, they are now entitled to have their own domicile as distinct from their husbands', to be determined 'by reference to the same factors as in the case of any individual capable of having an independent domicile' (s 1(1)).

A domicile of choice is determined by the proof of a person's intention to remain in their place of residence indefinitely and the fact of their residence there. These are elements of fact rather than of law. Residence need not be of a very long duration, as long as it can be proved that the person has the intention of remaining there permanently. Following *Puttick v AG* (1980), however, the law is that the residence must be lawful residence and settlement in a country by an illegal immigrant will not suffice. In respect of proof of intention, the law will take into account almost any act or circumstance, however trivial.

The new concept of 'habitual residence' as a connecting factor, replacing that of 'domicile', should be noted. The habitual residence of a person is now extremely important in determining whether a particular court has jurisdiction over the subject matter and, in some cases, the applicable law of the subject matter. Habitual residence is more than mere physical presence in a particular country; the law as set out by the House of Lords in *R v Barnet LBC ex p Shah* (1983) requires proof of an intention to remain at a place voluntarily and for settled purposes, 'as part of the regular order of ... life for the time being, whether of short or long duration', as well as actual physical presence. The concept has grown much in importance, not only in the area of family and matrimonial cases (other than recognition of marriages) but also in contract law, as is evident in the Contracts (Applicable Law) Act 1990.

Checklist

It is essential to be familiar with the following areas:

- importance of the concept of domicile;
- domicile of origin;
- domicile of dependency and the Domicile and Matrimonial Proceedings Act 1973;
- domicile of choice – proof of residence and intention;
- loss of domicile;
- reform in the area of domicile – Law Commission Working Paper No 88;
- concept of 'habitual residence'.

Question 7

Critically examine the development of the concept of 'habitual residence' as a connecting factor in private international law.

Answer plan

Students should first describe the emergence of 'habitual residence' as a new connecting factor, not only in commercial situations, but also in personal law. Reference should be made to the Hague Conference on Private International Law, at which 'habitual residence' was adopted as a compromise between the use of domicile and the use of nationality as a connecting factor.

The answer should then define 'habitual residence'. The application of the definition should be further illustrated by referring to relevant cases. A good answer should highlight how 'habitual residence' can be acquired and lost. The application of the rules to both adults and children should be considered, particularly by reference to cases involving the Hague Convention on Civil Aspects of International Child Abduction 1980.

Answer

In private international law, it is vital that there are certain connecting factors between the parties or case in question and the foreign law and/or jurisdiction. At common law, the main connecting factor is the domicile of the relevant party. However, in civil law systems, the relevant connecting factor is nationality. This generally means that the most 'proper' or 'applicable' law in matters relating to a citizen's personal relationships shall be the law of his nationality. Nationality has the advantage of certainty over the concept of domicile; it is also usually far more straightforward.

There are, however, some very distinct difficulties in using nationality as a connecting factor. In cases of stateless persons and those with multiple nationality, the use of nationality as a connecting factor must either have to be displaced or qualified, making its use almost discretionary. Persons who have evinced an intention to relinquish their nationality by leaving the country and living somewhere else but have not given up their original nationality are also especially vulnerable if nationality is to be used as a chief connecting factor. Finally, there is also a problem with countries whose constituent States/regions have some degree of autonomy, for example, the US. This makes it all the more difficult to refer to nationality as a connecting factor.

The reliance on domicile too is not without problems. The principal problem is with the proof of intention. The domicile of a person is determined by his residence and intention to remain indefinitely. That latter criterion is not easily established. For example, where the *propositus* chooses to remain in the country of residence until some event occurs, it can be difficult to determine whether this might be presumed as lacking in the intention to remain permanently or indefinitely. This difficulty is described by Scarman J in *Re Fuld's Estate (No 3)* (1968) in the following terms:

> ... if a man intends to return to the land of his birth upon a clearly foreseen and reasonably anticipated contingency, for example, the end of his job, the intention required by law is lacking; but, if he has in mind only a vague possibility, such as making a fortune (a modern example might be winning the football pools), or some sentiment about dying in the land of his fathers, such a state of mind is consistent with the intention required by law.

The test in that case was whether the contingent event was 'clearly foreseen and reasonably anticipated'. However, in *IRC v Bullock* (1976), the Canadian *propositus*, who had lived in England for about 44 years, intended to remain in England unless his wife pre-deceased him. If that occurred, he would return to Canada. It was found that he had not acquired English domicile because there was 'a sufficiently substantial possibility of the contingency happening'. It is immediately obvious that this test is different to that of *Fuld*, thus highlighting the problems attendant to use of domicile as a connecting factor. It is outside the scope of this answer to deal with these problems. It suffices to say that both the nationality and domicile tests have difficulties, and a third solution is needed.

A probable solution is the use of 'habitual residence' as a connecting factor. This concept was first adopted and developed at the Hague Conference on Private International Law, but has now gained acceptance almost universally. In English private international law, the concept has been used in many family and matrimonial matters, including divorce and separation, nullity of marriages, the recognition of foreign divorces, international adoptions and international child abduction. It is also relied on to determine the formal validity of wills, as provided for in s 1 of the Wills Act 1963. As far as applicable law of a contract is concerned, the Rome Convention (as contained in the Contracts (Applicable Law) Act 1990) does refer to 'habitual residence' as a presumed connecting factor when determining the applicable law of the contract in Art 4.

It might first be noted that the 'habitual residence' is to be determined as a matter of fact. This means that the court would have to consider all the relevant circumstances of a case in reaching a decision as to whether the *propositus* is 'habitually resident' in a particular country. 'Habitual residence' as a connecting factor at private international law is to be construed and applied according to English law. In *Re A* (1996), it was specifically stated that it is not open to the claimants to argue that, under the law of the country in which the *propositus* is said to be habitually resident, he is so resident.

Definition of habitual residence

Habitual residence requires two components – physical residence and the intention to reside there for a 'settled purpose'. This was firmly established in *R v Barnet LBC ex p Shah* (1983). The House of Lords was, however, swift to qualify that the mental element is not identical to that required to establish the domicile of a person. Lord Scarman stated that 'habitual residence' does not require an intention to reside in that place indefinitely or permanently. All that is required is an intention to remain there voluntarily and for settled purposes 'as part of the regular order of his life for the time being, whether of short or long duration'.

It was further stated in *ex p Shah* that there may be habitual residence even though the person's presence in the country is uncertain at law. This re-asserts the point that habitual residence is about the fact of residence, not 'residence' as defined by law. In *ex p Shah*, it was stressed, therefore, that, although a person might have no right of abode or leave to remain indefinitely in the country under immigration law, he could nevertheless have habitual residence. Where, however, there is an express prohibition on his presence or purpose of presence, there can be no 'habitual residence'. Habitual residence must be lawful residence.

In *Kapur v Kapur* (1984), therefore, an Indian husband's application for an English divorce was admissible, even though he was in the country for one year (reading for the Bar examinations) and did not have the right of abode or leave to remain in the country indefinitely. The 'settled intention' must be voluntarily adopted. In *ex p Shah*, some examples of involuntary residence were given – these included kidnapping, imprisonment, and other instances where the circumstances are such as 'to negative the will to be where one is'.

Voluntariness can sometimes be a problem in determining the 'settled intention' of the *propositus*. In *Re A* (1996), it was held that a US soldier who was stationed in Iceland could have the requisite 'settled intention' to be habitually resident there, even though the posting to Iceland was compulsory. The court considered that, when he joined the armed forces, he had voluntarily agreed to the possibility of being posted to another country. This tacit agreement was sufficient to constitute a 'settled intention' to remain in Iceland.

There are some *dicta* in the more recent case of *Re J* (1990) that the required mental element is similar to that of domicile. In that case, Lord Brandon stated that a person could only acquire habitual residence after an 'appreciable period of time', and there should be evidence of the intention to take up residence for an 'appreciable period'. This element of the 'settled purpose' has caused some degree of uncertainty in the hitherto straightforward test.

In *Re F* (1992), it was acknowledged that the 'appreciable period' need not be very long, and all depended on the extent of the 'settled purpose'. In that case, the subjects of the dispute were found to be habitually resident in Australia, although they had only been there a month, because it was clear that they had the intention to remain there. A contrasting case might be found in *A v A* (1993), where the court expressed doubt as to whether habitual residence could be established, even though the period of residence was appreciable, namely eight months, because the element of 'settled intention' could not be proved. In *Re B* (1994), the parties had been in Canada for two months, trying to save their marriage. This, according to the court, was not sufficient evidence of a 'settled intention'.

As far as statute is concerned, s 19(2)(b) of the Family Law Act 1996 provides that the court may assume jurisdiction over divorce and separation where either party has been habitually resident in England for one year. The same period applies to an application for nullity (s 5(3)(b) of the Domicile and Matrimonial Proceedings Act 1973).

Proof of habitual residence

It is quickly noticeable that, as in domicile, proof plays an extremely vital role in using 'habitual residence' as a connecting factor to show choice of jurisdiction or law. In *Re R (No 1)* (1992), it was established that the burden of proof is on the person who asserts a change or acquisition of habitual residence. In that case, a mother had failed to prove a change in the habitual residence of her child, even though she and the child had moved to Canada, because there was weighty evidence that her primary motivation for moving to Canada was to extort a better financial settlement from the child's father. She therefore failed to prove what she had asserted.

This burden is, however, different from that to be discharged under the rules relating to domicile, because it is possible for a person to have more than one place of habitual residence, or even none at all. This means that a person is not faced with the hurdle of proving that a former habitual residence had been lost and replaced by another. All he needs to show is the acquisition of a 'new' habitual residence. The proof of intention is also much less heavy an onus; there is no need to demonstrate an intention to remain in a place indefinitely or permanently.

Rules relating to children

As far as children are concerned, there is no concept of habitual residence of dependence as is seen in *Re R (No 1)*, but, as a general rule, the habitual residence of a child is usually predetermined by the habitual residence of the person who has parental responsibility for him. Parental responsibility is therefore the chief cornerstone in determining a child's habitual residence. Where both parents have joint parental responsibility over the child, neither of them can change that without the consent of the other (*Re B (No 2)* (1993)). That consent is absolute and can only be bypassed by a court order made in the interest of the child. Although consent is vital, it can be given either expressly or by implication. It was confirmed in *Re F* (1992) that the court may draw the inference that the parent had consented by not taking any active steps to prevent the child from being moved to a different place.

Where the parents have separated, the child's habitual residence is generally that of the parent with main parental responsibility. There is, however, to be no change in the child's habitual residence unless there is actual change in physical control over the child. In *Re O* (1993), a child who was habitually resident in England was taken to the US for a custody hearing. Custody, which was originally vested in the mother, who was habitually resident in England, was conferred by the American court on the father, who was habitually resident in the US. The mother had then taken the child back to England. The question was whether the child was habitually resident in Nevada or England. The court held that, as there had been no actual transfer of physical control, the child's habitual residence had not changed, regardless of the custody order made by the US court.

It would seem, *a fortiori*, that a decision made by a parent to change the child's habitual residence without change in the physical place of residence of the child is inoperative to alter the habitual residence of a child. In *Re KM* (1996), the child's parents, who where habitually resident in England, sent him to India to live with his grandparents. The arrangement was that the child should live in India until he became an adult. One year after he was sent away, the mother changed her mind and wanted to bring the child back to England. Whether the English court had jurisdiction depended on whether the child was habitually resident in England or India. It was held that her decision to remove the child could not alter the fact that he was in fact habitually resident in India.

The fact of the child's habitual residence also depends on the degree of continuity of residence and intention of the parents. In *V v B* (1991), the child's English father and New Zealander mother had met in New Zealand and lived there for two years, before moving to England for a year. They then moved to New South Wales in Australia and lived there for two months, and then the father removed the child and brought him to England. The child's parents were not married. However, under New South Wales law, they both had custodial rights. The question was whether the child was habitually resident in New South Wales. The High Court held that the parents had provided a sufficient degree of continuity of residence in New South Wales and there was sufficient settled intention to regard the child (and family) as being habitually resident in New South Wales immediately before the child was removed.

Where a child is in the sole lawful custody of a parent, his habitual residence generally follows that of the parent. The lawfulness of that custody will naturally depend on the relevant law. In *Re J* (1990), the child had been living with both parents in Western Australia. The parents were of English origin and were not married to each other. The mother then removed and brought the child to England, with a clear intention of not returning to Australia. Soon afterwards, the father secured a court order in Western Australia, giving him sole custody of the child. As to whether there had been wrongful removal or retention under Art 3 of the Hague Convention on Child Abduction, the House of Lords held that there had been no wrongful removal or retention because, when the child was removed, the father did not have custody rights and, when he was granted custody, the child had ceased to be habitually resident in Western Australia. It might also be noted that, under Western Australian law, a mother of an 'illegitimate' child was entitled to custody and guardianship in the absence of a court order.

Finally, it should be noted that it is possible for a child to be without a 'habitual residence'. This was indeed made clear by

Butler-Sloss LJ in *Re F* (1992). However, he was quick to observe that, under the Hague Convention on Child Abduction, where possible, a child should have a habitual residence. Without habitual residence, a child would lose the protection of the Convention, in that he could be taken and abducted from the country in which he was residing immediately before the removal.

Conclusion

Habitual residence has some advantages over nationality and domicile as a connecting factor. However, where the connection forged by habitual residence is not particularly strong, it should be disregarded, or at least be used only as part of the whole determination exercise. This spirit is evident in the Rome Convention (as enacted by the Contracts (Applicable Law) Act 1990), where Art 4 makes it quite clear that, where habitual residence does not provide a sufficient link between the contract and the foreign law applicable, it should give way to a more thorough fact based approach – namely, the weighing of all relevant circumstances in determining which foreign law has the closest connection with the contract. Again, in matters relating to personal law, domicile sometimes serves as the best connecting factor between the *propositus* and the foreign law or jurisdiction. For example, it could be argued that domicile is a much better determinant of the issue of recognition of foreign marriages because parties could try and evade the application of the most relevant foreign law simply by moving to the 'right' country to tie the knot.

Question 8

Mister and Missus were domiciled in Utopia, where divorce is illegal. They then decided to move to Thailand and were subsequently legally separated under Thai law. This separation is not recognised in Utopia.

Two years after the separation, Mister and Missus moved back to Utopia. Last month, while Missus was on holiday in Colonia, she met Man and decided to marry him.

Utopian law states that the validity of matrimonial relations and separations is to be determined by the law of the domicile of the husband when the marriage was contracted. Colonia is a newly independent country that applies English common law as it stood in 1970. Colonian law recognises the separation made under Thai law. Under Colonian law, bigamy is an offence.

Discuss whether Missus can legally remarry in Colonia, paying specific attention to the issue of the incidental question.

Answer plan

This question is primarily about the incidental question in the area of recognition of divorces and separations obtained abroad, before the passage of the Family Law Act 1986 and the Recognition of Divorces and Legal Separations Act 1971. It should be borne in mind that Colonia is a country that applies the common law as it stood before these two Acts were made law.

It is crucial to define what the incidental question is. This should be followed up with a discussion of the approaches suggested by writers. The application of the rule in *R v Brentwood Registrar of Marriages* (1968) must not only be cited but analysed. Examine how the court approached the matter and discuss whether this is justified. It would also be useful to refer to *Lawrence v Lawrence* (1985), where the court did not make a distinction between the main and incidental questions.

Answer

Since Colonia applies the common law as it stood in 1970, in order to advise Missus it would be useful to refer to rules of the common law in dealing with the incidental question which this case reveals. At common law, the incidental question is one that arises in the course of considering the question in issue, but, because it carries foreign elements, the problem here is whether it should be resolved by referring to the forum's conflict rules or whether the court should use the appropriate conflict rules of the foreign system. Generally, three conditions must be fulfilled before a true incidental question may be said to be in existence.

First, the main question must, by the application of the English (or, in this case, Colonian) conflict rules, be governed by the law of a foreign system. Secondly, a subsidiary question involving foreign elements must be found which is capable of arising in its own right or in other contexts, and for which there is a separate conflict rule. Thirdly, the English (or Colonian) conflict rule for the determination of the subsidiary question must lead to a different result from the corresponding conflict rule of the country whose law governs the main question.

Referring to the problem at hand, the main issue for the Colonian court is whether Missus has the capacity to remarry under the common law as it stood in 1970 (in this regard, the application of the two relevant English statutes – the Family Law Act 1986 and the Recognition of Divorces and Legal Separations Act 1971 – must be excluded). The main question would be referred by the common law (Colonian law) to the law of her domicile. This would presumably be the laws of Utopia, as that is where she is probably domiciled. The incidental question is the validity of the separation obtained in Thailand.

The Colonian court is faced with two options. The first is that the incidental question should be resolved using Colonian conflict rules; the second is to turn to the conflict rules of Missus's domicile, Utopian law. Writers are divided on which option to take.

On the first option, by applying Colonian conflict rules, the court may be compelled to give a decision which is contrary to its notions of public policy. Conversely, by applying the conflict rules of the foreign system or by referring to the *lex causae*, Gotlieb[1] argues that uniformity of decisions can be ensured. Whether the case is tried and heard in Colonia or Utopia, the result will be the same. The main problem with this approach is that extracting the incidental question from the main question is not always a straightforward process. There is no fixed method of identifying the incidental question from the main question. It is not unforeseeable that, in some cases, the incidental question and the main question are inextricably linked.[2] In such a situation, the task of determining the *lex causae* is not free from difficulty. This makes the whole practice of looking to the *lex causae* for assistance highly unreliable. Hence, instead of promoting consistency and international judicial harmony, it can lead to the opposite.

Under the common law before the passage of the 1971 and 1986 Acts, as enunciated in *R v Brentwood Marriage Registrar* (1968), the respondent whose law of domicile refuses to recognise his or her legal separation or divorce may not remarry in England, even though that divorce or separation is recognised in England. The choice of law rules as to capacity to marry prevailed over the rules on the recognition of foreign divorces and legal separations. In that case, the Italian respondent had married a Swiss woman and had later obtained a divorce from her in Switzerland, where they were both domiciled. Under Swiss law, capacity to marry is governed by the law of the nationality of the party concerned, and, since Italian law did not recognise divorces of Italian nationals, Swiss law could not give recognition to that divorce, even though it was obtained in Switzerland. The English court's problem was deciding whether that divorce should be dealt with by the English conflict rule (which would have recognised the divorce) or by the Swiss conflict rule (which would have pointed to Italian law). The Divisional Court applied the conflict rule of Swiss law.[3] It must, however, be said that it was not clear how much attention the court actually gave the incidental question. It appears that the court only applied what seemed to achieve the best harmonisation of decisions between the fora concerned.

In *Lawrence v Lawrence* (1985), Lawrence married a Brazilian national, who had obtained a divorce from her former husband in Las Vegas the day before her marriage to Lawrence. Lawrence was domiciled in England at that time. The question was whether the parties had capacity to marry. The incidental question was whether the domicile was valid according to the relevant choice of law rules. Under Brazilian law, the divorce would be of no effect. The Court of Appeal held that, as the divorce was entitled to recognition in England, 'the plain man's view' that the parties to the divorce were free to remarry was to be applied.[4] This is not the application of the conflict rules of the forum to the incidental question. As a matter of fact, the Court of Appeal in that case did not even make a distinction between the main and incidental questions. It may be observed that there is no strict, principled way of resolving the issue; the imperative seems to predicate on the need to achieve uniformity.[5]

If the approach in *R v Brentwood* is correct, the incidental question in Missus's case would be dealt with by the conflict rule of the law of her domicile. Utopian law, as the *lex causae* to the incidental question, does not recognise the divorce. Thus, if the incidental question is to be separated from the main question, the result at Colonian law would be that Missus is not free to remarry. However, as highlighted in *Lawrence*, the court may perhaps not make a distinction between the incidental and main questions. Where the court takes the 'plain man's view' approach, the result may be quite different.

There are no guidelines as to when the incidental question should be distinguished from the main issue. In general, though, it may be safe to suggest that, where the courts agree to the distinguishing of the incidental question from the main question, then the *lex causae* should normally apply in order to achieve some degree of uniformity. The problem is not simply a choice between applying the *lex causae* or the law of the forum but perhaps the frequently overlooked issue of whether the incidental question can and does exist in its own right.[6]

Notes

1 (1977) 26 ICLQ 734.

2 See *Lawrence v Lawrence* (1985).

3 In England, the judgment should be read in conjunction with s 50 of the Family Law Act 1986, which provides that, where a foreign divorce or nullity decree is recognised in the UK, the fact that the divorce is not recognised elsewhere shall not preclude either party from remarrying in the UK or cause the remarriage of either party to be regarded as invalid in the UK.

4 The 1971 Act had no application because the remarriage was entered into outside the UK.

5 Another interesting case is *Perrini v Perrini* (1979), where a remarriage contracted by an Italian domiciled man with an English woman was valid even though the decree of nullity obtained against him by his former wife was not recognised in Italy.

6 See, for example, Wolff, *Private International Law*, 2nd edn, 1950, ss 196–200; Gotlieb (1955) 33 Canadian Bar Rev 523; Hartley (1967) 16 ICLQ 680.

Question 9*

Compare and contrast the domicile of origin with the domicile of choice.

Answer plan

The importance of domicile as a connecting factor in determining personal status should be emphasised. The fundamental differences between the domicile of origin and the domicile of choice should be examined, as well as the capacity of the domicile of origin to revive. Finally, the Law Commission's suggestions for reform in this area should be discussed.

Answer

English private international law refers to domicile in matters relating to personal status. Thus domicile constitutes the most important connecting factor and, as such, is relevant in determining such diverse issues as, *inter alia*, the essential validity of a marriage, legitimacy, legitimisation, adoption, tax liability, succession, and jurisdiction in matrimonial causes. Lord Westbury said in *Bell v Kennedy* (1868) that 'domicile ... is an idea of law. It is the relation which the law creates between an individual and a particular locality or country'. No person can be without a domicile and a person can have only one domicile at a time (*IRC v Bullock* (1976)). However, in order to acquire a domicile of choice, a person of full capacity must first cast off the domicile of origin which the law ascribes to every person at birth. A legitimate child, born during his father's lifetime, receives the domicile of his father; an illegitimate child or a child born after his father's death has his domicile of origin in the country where his mother is domiciled at the time of birth (*Udny v Udny* (1869)). A foundling is considered to have his domicile of origin in the country in which he is found. The domicile of origin is fixed for all times and cannot be changed. Since no one can make the first choice, a person can only shed the domicile of origin when a domicile of choice is acquired. The burden of proof is on the person who asserts it; and it is an especially heavy burden when a person changes his domicile from that of origin to a domicile of choice (*Cramer v Cramer* (1987)). Thus, if the requirements necessary to establish a domicile of choice are not satisfied, the domicile of origin revives.

The persistence and tenacity of the domicile of origin implies that it returns as a 'boomerang' during one's lifetime, and even after one's death, for example, in succession matters. One of the most spectacular cases in this area is *Poingdestre v Sherman, Re O'Keefe (Dec'd)* (1940), where it was held that Mary Alice O'Keefe, who had spent only three weeks of her life (77 years) in Ireland, had Irish domicile at the time of her death. She was born in India, kept British citizenship all her life, and spent 47 years in Italy, where she died. The only connection she had with Ireland was her three week visit to Ireland and the fact that her father was born in Ennis, Co Clare. Regardless of the fact that her father had acquired a new domicile, through her failure to acquire a new domicile, she was deemed to be a domiciliary of the place where her father was domiciled when she was born. As this case illustrates, there need be no connection whatsoever between a person and the country of his domicile at birth; yet he may still keep that domicile.

The tenacity of the domicile of origin can only be understood in the light of the complexity relating to the acquisition of a domicile of choice. In order to acquire a domicile of choice, not only a mere physical presence is necessary but, more importantly, an intention to remain indefinitely in that country must be shown. The requirement of residence, which is also called the *factum*, is easily established. As Lord Chelmsford said in *Bell v Kennedy*: '... if the intention of permanently residing in a place exists, then the residence in pursuance of the actual presence in a new country is of no importance.' Thus the duration of the actual presence is not decisive. In the American case of *White v Tennant* (1888), one afternoon's presence within the jurisdiction was sufficient to acquire a domicile of choice.

Residence as the factual requisite of domicile is easy to establish, and the only problem which may arise in this context concerns the possible illegality of the residence. However, the second factor, intention, poses more difficulty. There are a few reasons why the determination of the intention to reside permanently in a new country is fundamental. One explanation is that the priority given to intention over residency is based on the unhappy influence of the law of contract over the concept of domicile. However, it seems more convincing to say that there may be a sense that someone's 'Englishness' should not be sacrificed lightly and, consequently, the mere fact that someone is living abroad should not amount to acquisition of a domicile abroad. Indeed, in order to ascertain the intention to reside indefinitely, it is necessary to prove one's state of mind, which is extremely difficult. As Brian CJ said in the 15th century, 'minds or will are not in themselves existing things that we can look at and recognise. We are restricted in our earthly experience to the observation'. Thus, all circumstances, however trivial, must be taken into consideration. As a result, the decision in each case depends upon the weight that the judge attaches to the various factors and future contingencies operating on the *propositus*.

The inquiry into the person's state of mind (in succession matters the person is dead) leads to uncertainty, unpredictability of results and, in many cases, the revival of the domicile of origin. There is no guidance, nor is there an objective test which would indicate whether the *propositus'* intention is sufficient for the acquisition of a domicile of choice. In *Ramsey v Liverpool Royal Infirmary* (1930), George Bowie, a Scot who spent 37 years of his life in England and did not return to Scotland, even for the funeral of his mother, was held to retain his domicile in Scotland.

In *Re Joyce, Corbet v Fagan* (1946), George Joyce, who was born in Galway, was twice confined to mental institutions and spent four years in Canada and 37 years of his life in England, was held to have acquired English domicile. This case clearly shows that Joyce intended nothing at all as to his domicile. In *Winans v AG* (1904), Winans' hatred of England prevented him from acquiring a domicile of choice in England, although he had lived in England for the majority of his last 37 years. In *IRC v Bullock*, it was held that Captain Bullock had not acquired a domicile of choice in England, notwithstanding his long residency there (over 40 years), since he intended to return to his native country on the death of his English wife. However, in *Re Furse* (1980), an American, who had lived in England for 39 years but intended to return to America if his health prevented him from working on a farm in England, was held to acquire a domicile of choice in England.

Upon examination of the case law in this area, it appears that often, more weight is given to a trivial act than one which was of considerable importance to the *propositus* as far as the determination of the intention is concerned. Indeed, the standards are so vague that it cannot be predicted which factor, on the balance of probabilities, will be sufficient to decide that the *propositus* has acquired a domicile of choice in any particular court proceedings. Consequently, very often, the domicile of origin revives.

It is submitted that residence should be considered as the main factor in ascertaining whether a person has acquired a domicile of choice. Thus it should constitute a rebuttable presumption. Additionally, the fact that the *propositus* has, for example, obtained foreign citizenship or established a family or business abroad, should be held as relevant. These facts are perhaps more convincing in determining the acquisition of a domicile of choice than the dreams or desires to return to a native country on the death of a spouse or a mistress who may survive the *propositus*. Furthermore, often, the *propositus* intends nothing at all. It is not for the judge to make psychological speculations in order to determine whether a person shows the necessary degree of intention to constitute a requisite intention for the acquisition of a domicile of choice; the judge should only confirm the facts. In this respect, the emphasis should be put on the residency requirement. Also, the substantial and real connections with a particular place are the best indications of the *propositus*'s intention. This approach has been applied by the English courts in a few decisions.

Finally, as the acquisition of the domicile of choice is difficult to ascertain, revival of the domicile of origin, which remains in the background, ever ready to come back, is likely to occur in many cases. The doctrine of revival has been rejected in the US, New Zealand and Australia. The Law Commission has taken the view that domicile of origin should be abolished. The domicile of children at the time of birth and during their childhood would be ascertained, but no special tenacity would be given to the domicile of origin, and the doctrine of revival would be replaced by the rule that the domicile of choice would continue until an adult acquires another domicile of choice. This would ensure that a person's domicile is determined in conformity with the law of the place with which the *propositus* has or has had some real connection, and also that the ascertainment of the domicile is simplified.

* by Alina Kaczorowska

Question 10*

Anna was born in Germany in 1909 to German parents. In 1929, she married José, whose domicile of origin was Spain. They decided to set up a family home in Italy immediately after their wedding. Their son, Marcello, was born in 1933 in Rome. In 1937, Anna and José decided to settle permanently in Canada. They submitted an application for a permanent visa at the Canadian consulate in Rome.

In January 1938, their visa had still not been granted. José, 'fed up' with waiting, informed the Canadian authorities that he and his family would stay in England until all formalities regarding emigration to Canada were completed.

Two weeks after their arrival in England, José died. During that time, Anna received her Canadian emigration visa. She asked her friend, Paula, to take care of Marcello, intending to return for him once she had set up home in Canada. She boarded a ship at Southampton and arrived in Halifax, Canada – there she decided to stay in a hotel whilst she made up her mind whether to go to Quebec or Manitoba. She died a week later in Halifax.

Trace the domicile of each of the persons mentioned above at English law.

Answer plan

Each person should be examined separately. Events which affect the domicile of one member of the family are not necessarily important in relation to the domicile of the others. For that reason, the following points should be discussed:

Anna
Her marriage to José, the death of her husband; her emigration to Canada.

José
His move to Italy in order to set up a family home; his arrival in England; his death in England.

Marcello
His birth; the change of residence of his parents; the death of his father; the death of his mother.

Answer

Anna's domicile of origin was Germany. In 1929, she married José, who was domiciled in Spain. They set up a family home in Italy. According to the old rule, upon marriage, women acquire the domicile of dependency of the husband and retain it for the duration of the marriage. Anna's domicile changes with the change of domicile of her husband, the person on whom she is dependent. The Domicile and Matrimonial Proceedings Act 1973 abolishes the domicile of dependency of a married woman. Her domicile is ascertained in the same manner as a domicile of any individual who can acquire an independent domicile. However, under s 1(2) of the Domicile and Matrimonial Proceedings Act 1973, which contains the transitional provision regarding women married before 1974, the domicile acquired upon marriage by a woman is considered to be her domicile of choice, provided that it was not her domicile of origin, until it changes by the acquisition of a domicile of choice or the revival of the domicile of origin on or after 1 January 1974. As a result, under the 1973 Act, the domicile of dependency is re-imposed on a woman married before 1974 as a domicile of choice. Therefore, in 1929, Anna acquired the domicile of her husband as a domicile of choice, and her domicile followed changes in the domicile of her husband's domicile until his death (*IRC v Duchess of Portland* (1982)). In 1929, José was domiciled in Italy. Therefore, Anna was also domiciled in Italy.

In 1938, José abandoned his domicile of choice in Italy and moved to England. His Italian domicile ceased and his domicile of origin was revived, and remained attached to him until he acquired a new domicile of choice. He had no intention of setting up a home in England, as he was waiting for his Canadian visa. During this period, he died. Thus, he had his domicile of origin at the time of death. As for Anna, she would have the same domicile as her husband during the duration of their marriage. Even under the old common law rule, a married woman could acquire a domicile of choice if the dependency ended, for example, on the death of the husband (*Re Cooke's Trust* (1887); *Re Scullard, Smith v Brock* (1957)). The application of s 1(2) of the Domicile and Matrimonial Proceedings Act 1973 would lead to the same result. After the death of José, Anna could acquire a domicile of choice. However she was still waiting for a Canadian visa and had no intention to remain permanently in England. As a result, her domicile of origin is revived. At that time, she was domiciled in Germany.

Upon her arrival in Canada, she kept her domicile of origin. Although she intended to live permanently in Canada, she could not decide where to go. In order to acquire a domicile of choice, two elements must concur: residence in the country; and an intention to stay there permanently or indefinitely. Residence is a physical presence in the country. As to the requirement of residence (*factum*), it is less important from the point of view of the acquisition of a domicile of choice, since, as Lord Chelmsford said in *Bell v Kennedy* (1868), 'if the intention of permanently residing in a place exists, then residence in pursuance of that intention, however short, will establish a domicile'. The duration of the actual presence in a new country is of no importance (*White v Tennant* (1888)), and an immigrant can acquire a domicile immediately upon his arrival in the country in which he intends to settle permanently (*Bell v Kennedy*), even if he lives in hotels (*Levene v IRC* (1928); *Matalon v Matalon* (1952)). While it may be argued that Anna was physically 'resident' in Halifax, her intention was not to remain there. In the case of a Federal State, such as a State of Canada or the US, the *propositus* has to establish his home in a particular State of the Federation. A person cannot be domiciled in the US or Canada – only in one of its States or provinces. Consequently, Anna's intention to remain in Canada and her presence there are not sufficient, as she did not decide where to go. Thus the element of residency in a particular province of Canada is missing. During the period of indecision, Anna must be deemed to have retained her domicile of origin; consequently, she died domiciled in Germany.

José's domicile of origin was Spain. He acquired a domicile of choice when he set up a family home in Italy. At that time, both requirements necessary to acquire a domicile of choice were satisfied: he was physically present in Italy; and he had an intention to remain there permanently or for an indefinite period. Once he decided to emigrate, his intention, but not his domicile, ceased. A person abandons a domicile of choice by both ceasing to reside in a country and giving up the intention to reside there permanently. If only one requirement is satisfied, the old domicile of choice remains. By giving up his intention of residing, a person does not abandon his domicile of choice (*The Goods of Raffenel* (1863); *Zanelli v Zanelli* (1948); *IRC v Duchess of Portland* (1982)). As a result, his domicile of origin replaced his Italian domicile upon his arrival in England and remained attached to him until his death.

As to Marcello, he is a legitimate child, born during the lifetime of his father. Thus, his domicile of origin is Italy, the country in which his father was domiciled at the time of his birth. Marcello's domicile of dependency would change according to the changes of his father's domicile, since he was legally dependent on him. On the death of José, Marcello's domicile of dependency changed to that of his mother. He was legally dependent on his mother until her death, and any change in her domicile would affect his domicile. His domicile of dependency would follow the changes in the domicile of his mother. At the time of her death, Marcello was not *sui juris*. He was only five years old and could not acquire a domicile of choice. If there is no person on whom he may depend, his domicile of dependency cannot be changed at all. If Paula is a legal guardian of Marcello, the situation is uncertain. There is no authority on this point, but it seems that the domicile of Marcello cannot be changed by his guardian (see *Potinger v Wightman* (1817) – the guardian was the child's mother). In any event, the principle is that the domicile of a child without living parents cannot be changed.

It is submitted that Anna had her domicile of origin in Germany. She acquired a domicile of choice in Italy when she married José. The transitional provision of s 1(2) of the Domicile and Matrimonial Proceedings Act 1973 applies. Thus, Anna's domicile changed with the domicile of her husband. In 1937, when they decided to emigrate to Canada, they both abandoned their domicile of choice and the domicile of origin was revived. However, under the 1973 Act, the domicile of dependency is re-imposed as a domicile of choice on women married before 1 January 1973. As a result, Anna acquired the domicile of her husband as a domicile of choice, namely Spain. On the death of José, Anna acquired a domicile of choice. However, she had no intention to settle in England permanently or for an indefinite period of time. Since no person can be without a domicile, her domicile of origin would revive and would remain until her death. Indeed, on her arrival in Canada, she cannot decide where to go and, as she dies undecided, her domicile of origin subsists.

José's domicile of origin was Spain. He acquired a domicile of choice in Italy where he set up his family home. His domicile of choice ceased when he arrived in England. From that time, his domicile reverted to his domicile of origin. He consequently died domiciled in Spain.

Marcello's domicile of origin is in Italy. His domicile of dependency would change with the domicile of the person on whom he is legally dependent. After the death of his father, his domicile of dependency was in Germany, since he was legally dependent on his mother. After her death, he should continue to have his domicile of dependency in Germany, since the domicile of dependency of a child without living parents cannot be changed at all.[1]

Notes

1 However, in Australia, the Family Law Act 1975 provides that, for the purposes of certain proceedings, a person is considered to be domiciled in Australia.

* by Alina Kaczorowska

Question 11*

Nirvana Ltd was incorporated in Argentina in 1970, with the object of manufacturing precision sheet metal items in its factories in Southampton (UK) and Sofia (Bulgaria). Nirvana Ltd has registered offices in both Southampton and Sofia, each consisting of one room, on the doors of which the name 'Nirvana Ltd' is posted. One employee has been assigned to each registered office in order to keep necessary documents and to forward mail to the company headquarters in Argentina. Under the company's memorandum of association, the board of directors that controls the company's general management is to meet in Argentina. The majority of directors reside there. The general meeting of shareholders, who are from various European and South American countries, has always been held in Sofia, Bulgaria, where dividends have been declared, although they have been paid in Argentina in US dollars.

In 1998, Nirvana staffed and tooled its factory in Southampton for some specialist work that failed to materialise in the volume anticipated. As a result, Nirvana Ltd experienced severe cashflow problems and, in 1999, the board of directors was advised to liquidate the company. When the managing director of Nirvana Ltd consulted John Greedy, an insolvency practitioner, in respect of the liquidation procedure, Mr Greedy stated that the company was by no means in need of the 'death sentence' of liquidation. After conducting an examination, he advised the board of directors to claim back from the Crown the tax paid on the whole of its profits since the incorporation of Nirvana Ltd. According to Mr Greedy, Nirvana Ltd has never been liable to pay tax in the UK. Taking into account the amount of claimed taxes, as well as the fact that, in Argentina, the tax is symbolic, Nirvana Ltd would be able to overcome the current financial crisis and buy time to find new investors.

Is Mr Greedy correct in his assessment of the position of Nirvana Ltd regarding the UK tax authorities? Should the liquidation proceedings be conducted in England?

Advise the board of directors.

Answer plan

There are a number of connecting factors which may link a corporation with a particular country, such as its presence within the territory of that country, its residence there, its domicile in that country and its nationality. Each of these factors should be examined, taking into account the fact that a corporation is an artificial person and therefore, from the point of view of conflict of laws rules, a different weight is attached to each of them as compared to a natural person.

In order to decide whether or not Nirvana Ltd is liable to tax in England, its residence must be ascertained. In this respect, it is necessary to locate the centre of control of a corporation by applying the test laid down in *Cesena Sulphur Co v Nicholson* (1876) and further explained by the House of Lords in *De Beers Consolidated Mines Ltd v Howe* (1906). However, in certain circumstances, the centre of control may be located in more than one country. In this context, it must be determined in which location substantial control is exercised, taking into account the following cases: *Swedish Central Rail Co Ltd v Thompson* (1925); *Egyptian Land and Investment Co v Todd* (1929).

Answer

It is important to ascertain whether or not a corporation is present within the jurisdiction for jurisdictional purposes. If a corporation is present within the jurisdiction, a claim may be served upon it; otherwise, a claim is to be served out of jurisdiction, either with the leave of the court, granted under RSC Ord 11, or, in relation to claims within the scope of the 1968 Brussels Convention, without leave.

The status of a corporation, that is, all matters relating to its creation and dissolution, is governed by the *lex domicilii*. The place of incorporation of a corporate body is considered to be the place of its domicile (*Lazard Brothers v Midland Bank* (1933)). There are some difficulties in applying the concept of domicile to a corporate body by analogy. First, the concept of domicile was developed in respect of natural persons, before the theory of the separate legal personality of a corporation was established in English law; secondly, a corporation, as an artificial person, cannot marry or have children. Nevertheless, as the *lex domicilii* is suitable to determine the status of natural persons, it is also appropriate to determine the status of legal persons. However, a corporation, unlike a natural person, cannot change its domicile (*AG v Jewish Colonisation Association* (1990)). The place of incorporation is regarded as the place of domicile of a corporate body, from establishment until dissolution.

The 1968 Brussels Convention refers to the concept of domicile of a corporation as a connecting factor in allocating jurisdiction to courts in Contracting States, although its meaning is different from that under English law. Article 53 of the Brussels Convention provides that a corporation is domiciled where it has its 'seat', but leaves the task of determining where a corporation has its seat to national rules of conflict of laws. Section 42(3) of the Civil Jurisdiction and Judgments Act 1982, which implements the Brussels Convention in the UK, provides that a corporation has its seat in the UK if it was incorporated or formed under the law of a part of the UK and has its registered office or some other official office in the UK, or its central management and control is exercised in the UK.

Under English private international law, the domicile of a corporation is regarded as the main connecting factor, not its nationality. Only in the context of an armed conflict does the nationality of a corporation acquire some importance from the point of view of English conflict of laws rules. Nationality is determined by reference to the place of incorporation (*Janson v Driefontein Consolidated Mines Ltd* ((1902)).

In order to answer the question, it is necessary to determine whether Nirvana Ltd is regarded as having its residence in England, since only a company which is resident in England is liability to pay tax there. The leading case in this area is *Cesena Sulphur Co v Nicholson* (1876), where it was held that a corporation is regarded as resident in the country where the centre of control exists, that is, where the 'seat' and directing power of the affairs of a corporation are located. Cesena, a mining company incorporated in England under the Companies Acts 1862 and 1867, carried out all its mining activities in Cesena, Italy. Its managing director was a permanent resident of Cesena; the books of account were kept in Italy; the company was registered in Italy; and two-thirds of its shareholders were resident in Italy. Cesena's products were not sold in England. Factors that connected Cesena with England were that the board of directors and shareholders had meetings in England and the dividends were declared there. Taking into account those facts, the court decided that the centre of control was located in England and, therefore, Cesena was liable to pay tax on the profits, wherever earned, in England.

The test applied in *Cesena* was further explained in *De Beers Consolidated Mines Ltd v Howe* (1906). In this case, the company was incorporated in South Africa, where its profits from mining and disposal of diamonds were made. The directors met in both South Africa and London, although the majority of them resided in London. The court held that the centre of management was in London. Lord Loreburn emphasised that an analogy to individuals should be applied in determining the place of residence of a corporation. He said: '... we ought, therefore, to see where it really keeps house and does business ... the real business is carried on where the central management and control actually abides.' Therefore, in the determination of residence of a corporation, the country where it is controlled in fact, not the country where, in conformity with its constitution, it ought to be controlled, is regarded as the country of its residence (confirmed in *Unit Construction Co Ltd v Bullock* (1960)).

In theory, this principle raises no problem, although, in practice, the determination of the country in which substantial control is exercised may be difficult if different aspects of management are carried on in different countries. In this respect, *Swedish Central Rail Co v Thompson* (1925) is very instructive. In this case, a company was incorporated in England in 1870 with the purpose of building and running a railway in Sweden. In 1900, its articles of association were altered in order to reflect a change, in that it leased its railway in Sweden to another company for 50 years at an annual rent of £33,500, payable in England. The general meeting of shareholders, most of them Swedish nationals residing in Sweden, as well as meetings of the directors, were held in Sweden. Dividends were declared in Sweden. There were, however, some connections with England:

committee meetings were regularly set up in London to deal with share transfers, to draft (and attach the seal to) share certificates and to sign cheques on the London banking account. Furthermore, annual accounts were made and audited in London and the company secretary resided there. The House of Lords held that the company was resident in both England and Sweden.

In *Egyptian Delta Land and Investment Co v Todd* (1929), a company was incorporated in England in 1904 with the object of acquiring and disposing of land served by the Egyptian Delta Railways Ltd. It carried on its business in Egypt, where its central control and management were located. All directors resided in Egypt, meetings took place in Egypt, and the seal, books and bank account were there. In order to comply with the (English) Companies Act 1908, the company opened a registered office in London, employing one man who carried on the business of secretary of public companies. The House of Lords decided that the company resided in Egypt.

Taking into account the above mentioned cases, Professor North argues that, 'if the control is so evenly divided between two or more countries as to preclude the possibility of identifying one place of central control, then the company must be regarded as resident in each country in which to a substantial degree control is in fact exercised'.[1]

In our scenario, Nirvana Ltd has been incorporated in Argentina, its board of directors meets in Argentina and the majority of directors are resident in Argentina. The profit has been made from manufacturing and selling sheet metal items in England and Bulgaria. Another connection with England is a registered office in Southampton, in which only one person is employed. Shareholders' meetings are held in Bulgaria, and dividends have been declared there, although they are paid in Argentina. It seems that the real business of Nirvana Ltd has been carried on in Argentina, since the central control and management are located there. As a result, Nirvana Ltd should be regarded as residing in Argentina for tax purposes.

In summary, it is submitted that Nirvana Ltd is present within the territory of England and, as it has a registered office in Southampton, is subject to the jurisdiction of English courts. Nirvana Ltd is domiciled in Argentina, as it was incorporated under the law of Argentina. It is also of Argentinean nationality. Nirvana Ltd cannot be regarded as residing in England for tax purposes. Mr Greedy is correct is assessing that Nirvana Ltd is not liable to pay tax in England.

Note

1 North and Fawcett, *Private International Law*, 12th edn, 1992, p 174.

* by Alina Kaczorowska

CHAPTER 3

JURISDICTION

Introduction*

When an English court is seised with a dispute containing a foreign element, it must first determine whether it has jurisdiction over the cause of action and the parties involved. This is a preliminary question, to be considered before the issue of conflict of laws. The decision as to where to sue has important consequences for the parties: once the court decides to exercise jurisdiction, rules of English private international law will be applied to the dispute, although, very often, parties will seek to enforce the judgment elsewhere. Furthermore, the assumption of jurisdiction by an English court will result in the application of the *lex fori* to the majority of disputes, since a foreign law is considered to be a question of fact. Thus, the parties have to plead and prove its content.

In England, there are two different schemes of jurisdiction: traditional common law rules on jurisdiction; and the rules created by the 1968 Brussels Convention on Jurisdiction and the Enforcement of Judgements in Civil and Commercial Matters, as amended many times in recent years.

The traditional common law rules on jurisdiction are simple and liberal. An English court has jurisdiction if the defendant is present within the jurisdiction at the time of service of the claim, however short his visit to England may be. The first procedural step in commencing proceedings in England differs according to the legal status of the defendant: 'he' may be an individual, a partnership, a firm or a corporation. The service of the claim when the defendant is present within the jurisdiction must be regular, that is, effected in conformity with the current Supreme Court Practice Rules in this area. If the defendant is present within the jurisdiction but cannot be served personally, the claimant may submit an application to the High Court for an order for substituted service, and that court can order service of the claim in any way it considers appropriate.

Secondly, an English court has jurisdiction if the defendant voluntarily submits to the jurisdiction of that court. Finally, if the defendant is outside the jurisdiction, leave of the court in respect of issue of the claim and its service out of jurisdiction is necessary. The procedure that the claimant should follow is contained in RSC Ord 11 r 1(1). Jurisdiction under this rule is discretionary; thus, the claimant must convince the court that it should exercise its discretion in his favour. Since the application for leave is made without notice, certain requirements must be satisfied if the defendant is to be protected.

First, an English court must be cautious and careful and allow service out of jurisdiction only in proper cases. Any doubt as to the interpretation of RSC Ord 11 r 1(1) must be resolved in favour of the defendant. The claimant must fully disclose all the facts of the case (*Société Générale de Paris v Dreyfus Bros* (1885); *Matall und Rohstoff AG v Donaldson Lufkin and Jenrette Inc* (1990)). If the case is within the letter but outside the spirit of the rule, the service will not be authorised (*Société Générale de Paris v Dreyfus Bros*; *Kroch v Rossell* (1937)).

Secondly, the claimant must show that he has a good arguable case on the merits of his claim; that is, he must show that he has more than a *prima facie* case, but is not required to convince the court beyond reasonable doubt, since it is a preliminary stage of proceedings and, thus, the court will not hear and determine the case. In this area, the guidelines have been laid down in *Seaconsar Far East v Bank Markazi Jomhouri Islami Iran* (1993).

Thirdly, in authorising service out of jurisdiction, an English court applies the doctrine of *forum non conveniens* (see below, Question 20). However, the burden of proof is on the claimant. Consequently, he must show that England is clearly the 'natural forum'. Finally, the claim may be within the scope of more than one of the sub-heads of RSC Ord 11 r 1(1).

The technical side of service out of jurisdiction is contained in RSC Ord 11 rr 5 and 6.

As to the system set up by the Brussels Convention (as amended over the years), this applies in cases where the defendant is domiciled in a Contracting State. If he is domiciled in a non-Contracting State, subject to Art 16 of the Convention (in cases of immovable property, Art 16 confers exclusive jurisdiction on the courts of the Contracting State in which the property is situated), the common law rules of jurisdiction are applicable. In cases within the scope of application of the Convention, that is, in civil and commercial matters, leave is not required. The main ground of jurisdiction under the Convention is domicile. A person domiciled in a Contracting State should be sued before courts of that State (Art 2). The meaning of 'domicile' is to be determined in conformity with the national law of a Contracting State. Special jurisdictional rules are contained in Arts 5–18. In some cases, a court in a Contracting State will have additional grounds of jurisdiction to that of domicile of the defendant (Art 5 in relation to contract, tort, maintenance, etc); in others, its jurisdiction will be excluded (Art 16). These special rules correspond broadly to the grounds on which leave to serve out of jurisdiction may be authorised at present under RSC Ord 11. Special rules are also established for cases regarding insurance and consumer contracts.

Finally, the doctrine of *forum non conveniens* is excluded in cases within the scope of the Convention, although some uncertainty lingers in this respect. However, any uncertainties will surely be conclusively resolved by the ECJ. Indeed, the role of the ECJ is essential to the uniform application of the Convention throughout the European Union. Under the Protocol of 1971 on the interpretation of the Convention, a reference for a preliminary ruling may be made to the ECJ in a very similar manner to references under Art 234 (formerly Art 177) of the EC Treaty. However, only appellate courts are authorised to refer to the Court (Art 2 of the Protocol).

National authorities may request a ruling from the Court 'in the interest of the law' when a conflict of interpretation results from different judgments given in different Contracting States (Art 4 of the Protocol). Schedule 1 to the Civil Jurisdiction and Judgments Act 1982 gives effect to the 1968 Brussels Convention and the 1971 Protocol, as amended by the Convention of 1978, which provides for the accession of Denmark, Ireland and the UK to the European Community. The 1982 Act has been in force since 1987.

The Brussels Convention has been in operation for many years. Its application has certainly established the right to obtain and enforce judgments within the European Union, though the Brussels Convention, like any international convention, is not perfect. The Brussels Convention has been re-examined by the European Commission. As a result, on 14 July 1999, the Commission submitted a proposal for a Council Regulation on Jurisdiction and the Enforcement of Judgments in Civil and Commercial Matters, to replace the Brussels Convention.

The main changes that have been proposed concern the enforcement of judgments. Jurisdictional rules have not been substantially modified: the main change in this area concerns provisional and protective measures which are governed by Art 24 of the Brussels Convention. The ECJ held that provisional measures, including protective measures within the meaning of Art 24 of the Convention, refer to measures which, in matters within the scope of the Convention, are intended to preserve a factual or legal situation so as to safeguard rights, the recognition of which is otherwise sought from the court having jurisdiction as to the substance of the case (*Van Uden Maritime* (1998)). However, Art 24 does not unify the conditions for availability of those measures in the courts of Contracting States. This question is left to domestic laws of Contracting States.

The Commission's proposal introduces two modifications in respect of protective measures. It proposes, first, to set up the minimum requirements for the availability of protective measures and, secondly, to set out a clear rule conferring jurisdiction upon a Member State in which assets are located to provide protection in support of proceedings being conducted before a court in another Member State.

Another interesting development within the European Union is a proposal for a Council Regulation on Jurisdiction and the Recognition and Enforcement of Judgments in Matrimonial Matters and Matters of Parental Responsibility for Joint Children.

In the near future, these two EC Regulations will bring about important changes to the basis upon which an English court will determine whether or not it can exercise its jurisdiction in the areas within the scope of those Regulations.

Checklist

In order to answer the questions contained in this chapter, students should be familiar with the following:

- traditional common law rules on jurisdiction in action *in personam*; service of a claim on a defendant present within the jurisdiction;
- RSC Ord 11 r 1(1): service of a claim on a defendant out of the jurisdiction;
- the doctrine of *forum non conveniens*;
- the Arbitration Act 1975, which gives effect to the New York Convention on the Recognition and Enforcement of Arbitral Awards;
- limitations on jurisdiction, particularly the Diplomatic Privileges Act 1964;
- the Civil Jurisdiction and Judgments Act 1982 (as amended) (the Brussels and San Sebastian Conventions);
- Sched 1 to the Civil Jurisdiction and Judgments Act 1991 (the Lugano Convention);
- the proposal for a Council Regulation on Jurisdiction and the Enforcement of Judgments in Civil and Commercial Matters;
- the proposal for a Council Regulation on Jurisdiction and the Recognition and Enforcement of Judgments in Matrimonial Matters and in Matters of Parental Responsibility for Joint Children.

* by Alina Kaczorowska

Question 12*

The simplicity of the English rules on jurisdiction has been stripped away by the coming into force of the Brussels Convention on Jurisdiction and the Enforcement of Judgments in Civil and Commercial matters.

Discuss.

Answer plan

This is an essay question which requires comparison of the traditional common law rules on jurisdiction with the rules on jurisdiction set out by the 1968 Brussels Convention on Jurisdiction and the Enforcement of Judgments in Civil and Commercial matters (as amended).

The main points that should be covered are:

- common law rules on jurisdiction in actions *in personam* when the defendant is present within the jurisdiction and when the defendant is outside the jurisdiction;
- the main features of the Brussels Convention;
- the relationship between the Convention and the common law rules on jurisdiction;
- the role of the ECJ in interpreting the Brussels Convention.

Answer

Under the Brussels Convention, the San Sebastian Convention, the Lugano Convention and the traditional common law rules on jurisdiction, the claimant commences the proceedings by summoning the defendant.

Traditional common law rules on jurisdiction on actions *in personam* are simple: an English court has jurisdiction if a claim is properly served on the defendant present within the jurisdiction or if the defendant submits to the jurisdiction of an English court. If the defendant is outside the jurisdiction, an English court will exercise its discretion based on RSC Ord 11 r 1(1). In that case, the claimant must apply for leave and, if leave is granted, the claimant may serve the claim upon the defendant outside the jurisdiction.

In order to understand the complexity of the rules on jurisdiction under the system of the Brussels Convention, it is necessary to examine:

- the various versions of the 1968 Brussels Convention;
- its material scope and application;
- the relationship with other conventions on jurisdiction ratified by the UK (Art 57 of the Convention);

- its application to defendants domiciled in non-Contracting States.

The various versions of the 1968 Brussels Convention

The main objective of the 1968 Brussels Convention was to guarantee the right to obtain and enforce judgments throughout the European Community. In order to achieve this objective, it was necessary to unify the law on international jurisdiction in Contracting States, since a *sine qua non* of the enforcement of foreign judgments is the verification by the enforcing court of the jurisdictional competence of a 'decision giving court'. As a result, the 1968 Brussels Convention is very ambitious and regulates two major issues: international jurisdiction of courts in Contracting States; and the recognition and enforcement of judgments rendered in other Contracting States.

As the 'free circulation of judgments' within the European Community greatly contributes to European integration, a condition of membership of the European Community is the ratification by a new Member State of the 1968 Brussels Convention and the Protocol on its interpretation by the ECJ. The original Brussels Convention on the Jurisdiction and Enforcement of Judgments in Civil and Commercial Matters was concluded between France, Germany, Italy, Belgium, the Netherlands and Luxembourg on 27 September 1968.

Each enlargement of the European Community has necessitated changes to the original 1968 Brussels Convention and, at the same time, has provided an opportunity for revising the existing rules. As a result, over the years, the original 1968 Brussels Convention has undergone substantial modifications. At present, there are five versions of the 1968 Brussels Convention.

The first enlargement of the European Community substantially modified the original 1968 Brussels Convention, which, for that reason, is now of little importance. The second version of the 1968 Brussels Convention is contained in the Convention of 1978 providing for the accession of Denmark, Ireland and the UK to the European Community.

In the UK, Sched 1 to the Civil Jurisdiction and Judgments Act 1982 gives effect to the Brussels Convention and the 1971

Protocol, as amended by the Convention of 1978. The Civil Jurisdiction and Judgments Act 1982 came into force in 1987.

The third version, which is incorporated in the Civil Jurisdiction and Judgments Act 1982 (Amendment) Order 1991, takes into account the accession of Greece to the European Community. No substantial changes were made to the Brussels Convention, only its geographical scope of application.

The fourth version of the Brussels Convention is known as the San Sebastian Convention. This Convention not only incorporated Portugal and Spain into the existing scheme but also made substantive changes to the Brussels Convention. The Civil Jurisdiction and Judgments Act 1982 (Amendment) Order 1991 gives effect to the San Sebastian Convention.

The fifth version is contained in the Lugano Convention, a parallel to the Brussels Convention. The Lugano Convention was concluded between the European Community and the European Free Trade Association countries (the EFTA countries: Norway, Iceland, Lichtenstein and Switzerland). The Lugano Convention is very similar to the San Sebastian Convention but gives no interpretive jurisdiction to the ECJ. The Lugano Convention appears as Sched 1 to the Civil Jurisdiction and Judgments Act 1991.

The sixth version of the Brussels Convention is contained in the Accession Convention of 1996.[1] It concerns the extension of its provisions to Austria, Finland and Sweden.[2]

The first difficulty in applying the Brussels Convention is in determining which of its many versions is relevant to the dispute. For that reason, it is always necessary to verify the date at which the proceedings have been commenced, in order to select the version which, at that time, was in force in England (Art 54 of the Brussels Convention: its scope of application *ratione temporis*). The next step consists of determining whether the selected version was in force, at that date, in the other Contracting States.

The material scope of application of the Brussels Convention

The scope of the application of the Brussels Convention *ratione materiae* is defined in Art 1. It provides that the Convention applies in civil and commercial matters. However, the concept of civil and commercial matters should have an 'autonomous meaning'. As a result, a Community definition applies, and thus, what constitutes 'civil and commercial matters' under the Brussels Convention does not necessarily correspond to what is understood under this concept in English law. The ECJ has clarified the meaning of 'civil and commercial matters' in *Netherlands v Rüffer* (1980); *LTU Lufttransport v Eurocontrol* (1976); and *Sonntag v Waidmann* (1993). In *LTU Lufttransport*, the ECJ held that the Convention did not apply where a public authority acted in the exercise of its powers.

The second difficulty in applying the Brussels Convention is in ascertaining whether the dispute is within its material scope of application. Matters excluded from its ambit are to be governed by traditional common law rules. The Brussels Convention expressly excludes:

- revenue, customs or administrative matters (Art 1);
- the status or legal capacity of natural persons and rights in property arising out of a matrimonial relationship and wills and succession (Art 1(1)). However, while maintenance is within its scope of application (Art 5(2)), divorce is not. Also, these matters are not excluded if they are incidental to the main action;
- bankruptcy, proceedings relating to the winding up of insolvent companies or other legal persons, juridical arrangements, and compositions and analogous proceedings (Art 1(2));
- social security (Art 1(3)); and
- arbitration (Art 1(4)).

Brussels Convention in relation to other conventions on jurisdiction – Art 57

Art 57(1) of the Brussels Convention states:

> This Convention shall not affect any conventions to which the Contracting States are or will be parties and which, in relation to particular matters, govern jurisdiction ...

This provision further complicates rules on jurisdiction in England and Wales. It means that, if the subject matter is within the scope of application of the Brussels Convention and an English court exercises its jurisdiction over the parties, it may happen that another convention on jurisdiction will also apply to the dispute. In that case, the Brussels Convention will not override that other convention. However, in *Tatry v Maciej Rataj (The Tatry)* (1995), the ECJ held that the specialised convention prevailed over the Brussels Convention in matters not governed by the latter. Thus, if the specialised convention contains no provision on *lis alibis pendens* or related matters, then Art 21 (*lis alibis pendens*) and Art 22 of the Brussels Convention apply. The conventions within Art 57 are, *inter alia*, the 1952 Arrest Convention, the 1952 Collusion Convention of Maritime Law and the 1929 Warsaw Convention Relating to the Unification of Certain Rules Relating to International Air Carriage.

The application of the Brussels Convention when the defendant is not domiciled in a Contracting State

The fundamental principle of the Brussels Convention on international jurisdiction of courts in Contracting States is *actor sequitur forum rei*, which means that, when the defendant is domiciled in a Contracting State, he is subject to the jurisdiction of the courts of that State and his nationality is irrelevant. This simple rule is subject to many exceptions. Under Art 5, which refers to special jurisdiction in seven specific situations, the claimant may sue a defendant in a different Contracting State from the one in which the defendant is domiciled. However, in certain circumstances, the Brussels Convention will apply to defendants who are not domiciled in a Contracting State, and, in so doing, creates an additional difficulty. In this respect, it is necessary to examine two situations.

The Brussels Convention delegates jurisdiction to an English court and effects one of the following: it authorises the application of common law rules on jurisdiction regardless of the place of domicile of the defendant (Art 4); it assigns exclusive jurisdiction to a Contracting State (Art 16); it permits enforcement of the agreement on jurisdiction (Art 17); it permits enforcement of the agreement in a matter relating to insurance (Art 12); it permits enforcement of the agreement in a consumer contract (Art 15); or it accepts a submission to the jurisdiction by a defendant not domiciled in a Contracting State (Art 18).

The second situation arises once the proceedings have been commenced in a Contracting State on the basis of traditional national rules on jurisdiction (*The Nordglimt* (1988)) or under the Brussels Convention. Under Art 21, where proceedings involve the same cause of action between the same parties, the first seised court shall, once its jurisdiction is established, try the dispute, and the court seised second must decline jurisdiction in favour of that court. In *Gubisch Maschinenfabrik KG v Palumbo* (1987), the ECJ held that Art 21 should be interpreted broadly. In *Overseas Union Insurance Ltd v New Hampshire Insurance Co* (1991), it was stated that it was not necessary for either party to be domiciled in a Contracting State.

This means in practice that, if the proceedings are commenced in another Contracting State, an English court (although it is authorised under Common law rules to exercise jurisdiction) must decline it on its own motion in favour of the first seised court. Secondly, if the proceedings are commenced in a Contracting State, the claimant is entitled to seek provisional or protective relief from the courts of other Contracting States. Article 24 would include, for example, the freezing injunction (formerly known as the Mareva injunction). In this regard, it is observed that the ECJ held in *CHW v GJH* (1982) that Art 24 applies only to provisional measures which concern matters within the scope of application of the Brussels Convention.

It is submitted that the simplicity of the common law rules on jurisdiction has been largely displaced by the Brussels Convention. An elaborate statutory scheme is now in force in the UK. As a result, when a question of jurisdiction is at issue, the preliminary consideration of the possible applicability of the Brussels Convention is necessary. Furthermore, once it is decided that the Convention applies, the case law of the ECJ relevant to the dispute must be consulted. Although the Brussels Convention governs civil and commercial matters, its impact on common law rules in areas outside its scope of application is considerable. In addition, the doctrine of *forum non conveniens* does not apply and, thus, once the Convention allocates jurisdiction to an English court, it has no discretion but to try the case. However, the advantages offered by the Brussels Convention prevail over the disadvantages. The rules on jurisdiction are identical in all Contracting States, and the enforcement of judgments which, prior to the entry into force of the Brussels Convention, were burdened by excessive procedural formalities, is now speedy and inexpensive. Finally, the controversies, the difficulties as to the interpretation of the Brussels Convention and the risk of divergent interpretation in Contracting States have been minimised, since the ECJ is now competent to make preliminary rulings on the interpretation of the Brussels Convention at the request of courts in Contracting States.

Notes

1 OJ C15, 15.01.1997.

2 For a consolidated version of the Brussels Convention, see OJ C27, 26.01.1998.

* by Alina Kaczorowska

Question 13*

In November 1995, Landex Ltd, an Italian manufacturer of chocolate and ice creams, appointed Andex GmbH, established in Germany, as its commercial agent for the German and Netherlands markets. Under the contract, Andex was entitled to 5% commission as remuneration. Andex was very successful in selling products on behalf of its principal but never received any commission. After unsuccessfully asking Landex for commission on a number of occasions, Andex decided to treat the agreement as terminated and to start proceedings against Landex before a German court for the payment of arrears of commission and compensation in lieu of notice. The German court held that it had jurisdiction over both obligations, namely, to give reasonable notice on termination of a commercial agency agreement and, in default, to pay compensation in lieu, which was to be performed in Germany; and, secondly, to pay commission, which was to be performed in Italy under the principle that debts are payable where the debtor is resident. The German court held that the two obligations were of equal rank, that is, neither was subordinate to the other.

Landex Ltd challenged the jurisdiction of the German court on the ground that it had jurisdiction only in respect of the first obligation, which was to be performed in Germany, not over the whole proceedings.

Answer plan

The question focuses on Art 5(1) of the Brussels Convention. It is necessary to examine the meaning of the concepts 'contractual matters', taking into account *Arcado v Haviland* (1988), and 'obligations in question', as explained in *De Bloos Sprl v Bouyer SA* (1976).

The determination of a principal obligation when an action is based on multiple obligations is to be made on the basis of *Shenavai v Kreischer* (1987). However, if two or more obligations are of equal rank, the decision of the ECJ in *Leathertex Divisione Sintetici SpA v Bodetex BVBA* (1999) should be applied in order to determine whether the German court has jurisdiction over the whole proceedings.

Answer

Article 5 confers special jurisdiction on courts in Contracting States when there is a close connection between the court and the individual case. It constitutes an exception to Art 2 of the Brussels Convention, according to which a person domiciled in a Contracting State should be sued in the court of the Contracting State in which he is domiciled. Article 5(1) confers jurisdiction, 'in matters relating to a contract, in the courts for the place of performance of the obligation in question'.

Article 5(1) applies to contractual matters. The ECJ held in *Peters v Zuid Nederlandse Aannemers Vereniging* (1983) and *Powell Duffryn v Petereit* (1992) that the concept of 'contractual matters' must have an autonomous meaning. As a result, the automatic characterisation of a matter as contractual under English law should be avoided. The concept must have community meaning. A vague definition was provided in *Handte v TMCS* (1992).

In *Arcado v Haviland* (1988), the ECJ held that proceedings seeking compensation for the wrongful repudiation of an independent agency agreement and payment of commission due under such an agreement are contractual obligations within the scope of Art 5(1) of the Brussels Convention.

Applying this case to our scenario, there is no doubt that a contract of agency is within the scope of Art 5(1) of the Brussels Convention.

The term 'obligation in question' also has an autonomous meaning. What constitutes the obligation in question was defined by the ECJ in *De Bloos Sprl v Bouyer SA* (1976) as one which forms the basis of the legal proceedings, that is, the obligation on which the claimant's claim is based. In most cases, the determination of the obligation upon which the claimant bases his claim poses no special difficulties. If the buyer refuses to pay, the obligation is upon the buyer to pay; if the seller fails to deliver, the obligation is upon the seller to deliver. Therefore, the obligation in question refers to the principal, most important obligation among those on which the claimant's action is based. The case law of the ECJ shows that the Court has rejected arguments based on the reference to the obligation which is characteristic of the contract (*Shenavai v Kreischer* (1987)) and to any obligation arising under the contract (*De Bloos Sprl v Bouyer SA*). Moreover, the ECJ in *Custom Made v Stawa* (1994) held that, under Art 5(1) of the Brussels Convention, a national court cannot assert jurisdiction on the ground that the dispute has its closest connection with the territory of that State.

The situation is more complicated in the case of a dispute involving a number of obligations arising under the same contract and forming the bases of the claimant's claim.

In this respect, in *Shenavai v Kreischer*, the ECJ held that, if a dispute arises in relation to a number of obligations, the court should be guided by the maxim *accessorium sequitur principale*; that is, the principal obligation must be identified and the court of the place which has jurisdiction over the principal obligation also has jurisdiction to deal with other obligations.

Usually, national courts have no problem determining which obligation is the principal one. In *Union Transport v Continental Lines* (1992), the claimants argued that they had exchanged telexes with the defendant concerning a charter of a vessel from Florida to Bangladesh. The defendant, a Belgian company, denied the existence of the contract. The claimants sued the Belgian company for breach of two obligations, namely to nominate and to provide a vessel. The House of Lords held that the principal obligation was the obligation to nominate. Therefore, the English court had jurisdiction, since the obligation to nominate the vessel was to be performed in England (that is, it was to be received by the charterer in the place in which the latter resided).

In our scenario, the claimant argues that the defendant was in breach of two obligations: first, to give reasonable notice on termination of a commercial agency agreement and, in default, to pay compensation in lieu, which was to be performed in Germany; and second, to pay commission, which was to be performed in Italy under the principle that debts are payable where the debtor is resident. The German court found that the two obligations were of equal rank. Our case is based on the case *Leathertex Divisione Sintetici SpA v Bodetex BVBA* (1999), in which the ECJ dealt, for the first time, with the question of two obligations of equal rank arising from the same contract. The Court held that, when a national court is seised with a claim alleging breach of two contractual obligations of equal rank, one to be performed in the Contracting State of that court and the other in another Contracting State, that court does not have jurisdiction under Art 5(1) in relation to the obligation to be performed elsewhere. Therefore, the German court will have jurisdiction only over the claim for payment of compensation in lieu of notice on termination of the commercial agency agreement.

In respect of the decision of the ECJ in *Leathertex Divisione Sintetici*, it is interesting to note that, first, the UK had made a submission regarding this case. The UK Government suggested the reformulation of the referred question, as it argued that it was possible to determine the principle obligation and, consequently, to apply the maxim *accessorium sequitur principale*. It stated that the sole reason why Bodetex considered the contract to be terminated without notice was the failure to pay the disputed commission by the defendant. Therefore, compensation in lieu of notice was to be paid only if it was established that the disputed commission was, in fact, due, and the obligation to pay commission formed the principal obligation. The ECJ decided not to deal with that question. It held that it was for national courts to determine the relative importance of the contractual obligations. The ECJ confined itself to the question referred and answered on the basis stated in the order of reference that the obligations were of equal rank.

A second important implication deriving from the decision of the ECJ in *Leathertex Divisione Sintetici* is that, in the case where two or more obligations are of equal rank, jurisdiction will be split between Contracting States. Under Art 5(1) of the Brussels Convention, different courts will deal with different aspects of the same dispute. This solution is regrettable, as it may result in undermining the uniformity of decisions given under the Brussels Convention, but is in line with the ECJ decision in *Handelskwekerij GJ Bier BV v Mines de Potasse d'Alsace* (1976). Indeed, if there are two or more obligations of equal rank arising out of the same dispute, courts in two or more Contracting States may deliver inconsistent decisions. The obvious solution is to sue the defendant under Art 2 of the Brussels Convention, that is, to sue in the courts of the defendant's domicile.

A third important implication deriving from *Leathertex Divisione Sintetici* is that, in the situation were two obligations are of equal rank, a national court cannot base its jurisdiction over the totality of a composite claim on Art 22 of the Brussels Convention. The ECJ emphasised that this provision was intended to establish how related actions brought before courts of different Contracting States should be dealt with, not to confer jurisdiction on a court of a Contracting State over an action which related to another action of which that court was seised on the basis of the Brussels Convention. Furthermore, if two obligations are of equal rank, there is no relation between those two claims.

It is submitted that Landex Ltd will be successful in challenging the jurisdiction of the German court over the whole proceedings, taking into account the decision in *Leathertex Divisione Sintetici SpA v Bodetex*. The German court has jurisdiction only in relation to the claim for payment of compensation in lieu of notice, provided that the two obligations are of equal rank. It is for a national court to assess the relative importance of those contractual obligations. In our case, the German court has already decided that both obligations are of equal rank, neither being subordinate to the other.

* by Alina Kaczorowska

Question 14*

John and his wife, Andrea, both domiciled in England, went to Paris to celebrate their fifth wedding anniversary in style. John booked dîner at *La vie en Rose*, for which he paid £1,000. Both John and Andrea enjoyed dîner. However, the next morning, they felt unwell, and both suffered from severe headaches and nausea. They decided to continue their trip and went to Venice. In Venice, while boarding a gondola, they collapsed. They were transported to the nearest hospital. A blood test and X-ray showed that both had potentially lethal food poisoning. Early diagnoses and appropriate treatment saved their lives, but they are left with permanent debilitating and uncomfortable symptoms such as terrible pains, swollen knuckles, very smelly breath and bloated tummies. As a result, John and Andrea are unable to work.

When John and Andrea decided to sue *La vie en Rose*, they learnt that the cause of their illness was a piece of chicken that they had for their anniversary dîner. The restaurant has always bought 'ready to cook' chicken from its Netherlands caterer, domiciled in Amsterdam. Chickens are supplied to the Dutch caterer by a farm in Germany. After investigation by the German health authorities, it is discovered that chickens at that farm suffer from a rare liver disorder, caused by a viral agent which damages the lining of the human intestine.

John and Andrea want to start proceedings in England, a main reason being that their illness makes travel difficult.

Advise them as to the jurisdictional issues.

Answer plan

The question involves the application of Art 5(3) of the Brussels Convention. The problem with Art 5(3) is that almost every word requires interpretation. Therefore, it is necessary to examine the concept of tort, delict and quasi-delict under the Convention and also to try to clarify the meaning of the second limb of Art 5(3), which refers to 'place where the harmful event occurred'. Indeed, it is sometimes difficult to establish the place of commission of the tort for jurisdictional purposes, as the essential elements of the tort (the act and the damage) may be of a multifarious and complex nature. Thus, the sequence of events giving rise to the tortious liability may embrace two or more events taking place in different countries. Additionally, the damage may be suffered in more than one country. Cases to take into consideration whilst answering this question are: *Bier BV v Mines de Potasse d'Alsace SA* (1976); *Shevill v Presse Alliance* (1995); *Marinari v Lloyds Bank* (1995); and *Réunion Européenne SA* (1998).

Answer

The fundamental principle of the Convention on international jurisdiction of courts in Contracting States is *actor sequitur forum rei*, which means that, where the defendant is domiciled in a Contracting State, he is subject to the jurisdiction of the courts of that State. However, special jurisdiction is provided in Art 5(3), which states:

> A person domiciled in a Contracting State may, in another State, be sued ... in matters relating to tort, delict or quasi-delict, in the courts of the place where the harmful event occurred ...

The concept of tort has an independent Community meaning

The ECJ acknowledged the necessity for independent interpretation of the expression 'tort, delict or quasi-delict' in *Netherlands v Ruffer* (1980). However, the claim in *Ruffer* fell outside the scope of application of Art 1(1) of the Convention, and the opinion of the Court on the subject of independent meaning was provided in *Kalfelis v Schröder, Münchmeyer, Hengst & Co* (1988), where it was stated that the concept of matters relating to tort, delict and quasi-delict must be regarded as an independent concept. In this case it was held that:

> The term 'matters relating to tort, delict or quasi-delict' used in Art 5(3) of the Convention must be regarded as an independent concept, covering all actions which seek to establish the liability of a defendant and which are not related to a 'contract' within the meaning of Art 5(1).

Thus, the ECJ has stated that, in actions which seek to establish a defendant's liability, it is necessary to determine whether the claim is contractual; if it is not, it is *prima facie* within the scope of application of Art 5(3) of the Convention. The mutual exclusivity of claims in tort and contract is based on the French doctrine of non-cumulation of remedies, according to which a claim in contract precludes a parallel remedy in tort. However, the distinction is not obvious. Article 5(1) and (3) of the Convention are interrelated. Indeed, an action may be framed as a claim either in contract or in tort, but, for jurisdictional purposes, the choice must be made. In this respect, in *Handte* (1992), the ECJ held that proceedings brought by a sub-purchaser of goods against the initial manufacturer were not contractual within the meaning of Art 5(1), but did not specify which of the possible bases, that is, Art 2 or Art 5(3), was appropriate. This problem was resolved in *Réunion Européenne SA* (1998), where the ECJ held that, where an action was brought in contract but is subsequently defined by the Court as tortious, jurisdiction should be allocated under Art 5(3) of the Convention.

The decisions of the ECJ regarding the autonomous meanings of 'tort, delict or quasi-delict' in Art 5(3) suggest that, when an action arises from an agreement that the parties have freely entered into, their claim is within the scope of application of Art 5(1). However, an action which arises from the law attaching legal consequences to an act of a party is within Art 5(3).

Our case is simple, as it involves an action in tort. However, determination of the meaning of 'the place where the harmful event occurred' is necessary in order to ascertain the appropriate forum under Art 5(3).

In the light of the second limb of Art 5(3), it seems extremely difficult to define or determine the place of occurrence of the harmful event, since this may be understood as the place where the wrongful event giving rise to the damage occurred. Here, we have a choice between the place where the meal was served (France), the place where chicken was prepared for consumption (the Netherlands) and the place where chickens were reared (Germany). Thus, it is difficult to decide which event in the series of events constituting the tort is determinative from the point of view of the application of Art 5(3).

As to the place where the damage occurred, we have a choice between the place where the damage first occurred (France), the place where the damage became apparent (Italy) and the place where the effect of the injury continues to be suffered (England).

The leading decision of the ECJ as to the meaning of the second limb of Art 5(3) was given in *Bier BV v Mines de Potasse d'Alsace SA* (1976), where it was stated that:

> ... where the place of the happening of the event which may give rise to liability in tort, delict or quasi-delict and the place where that event results in damage are not identical, the expression 'place where the harmful event occurred' in Art 5(3) ... must be understood as being intended to cover both the place where the damage occurred and the place of the event giving rise to it.

As a result, the defendant may be sued, at the claimant's option, either in the courts of the place where the damage occurred or in the courts of the place of the event which gives rise to and is at the origin of that damage.

Does this decision solve our problem? The answer is 'no'. In *Bier*, there was *ab initio* a single *forum damni* (Holland) and a single *locus delicti* (France). In our case, there are multiple *fora damni* and a multiplicity of places in which the wrongful act could be said to have taken place.

The ECJ shed new light on the matter In *Kalfelis v Schröder* (1988). It held that Art 5(3) should be given a restrictive interpretation, since it constitutes the exception to the general rule *actor sequitur forum rei*. It is a general rule of interpretation that exceptions to a principle should be interpreted restrictively, so as not to undermine the principle. In *Kalfelis*, the Court decided that a court in a Contracting State should be prevented from exercising jurisdiction over a claim as a whole when it had the jurisdiction over only a part of a claim. In that case, the court had competence only to deal with the tortious part of the claim.

In *Dumez France SA v Hessische Landesbank* (1990), the ECJ held that, where a parent company was injured as a result of losses suffered by its subsidiary ('ricochet damage'), it could not bring an action in the courts of the place where the parent company discovered that it had sustained damage to its assets.

Furthermore, the restrictive interpretation of Art 5(3) has been confirmed in more recent cases: *Shevill v Presse Alliance* (1995); *Marinari v Lloyds Bank* (1995); and *Réunion Européenne SA* (1998). In *Marinari*, the plaintiff, an Italian domiciliary, lodged promissory notes of an exchange value of US$752,500 with a branch of Lloyds Bank in England. The promissory notes were issued by the Negros Oriental province of the Republic of the Philippines in favour of a company located in Beirut. The staff of Lloyds Bank refused to return the promissory notes and advised the police of their existence and uncertain origin. As a result, the plaintiff was arrested and the promissory notes were sequestrated. The plaintiff, after being released by the English authorities, brought an action against Lloyds Bank in Italy. He sought compensation for refusal to pay the exchange value of the promissory notes, compensation for damage he had suffered as a result of his arrest and compensation for breach of several contracts and damage to his reputation. Lloyds Bank challenged the jurisdiction of the Italian court by claiming that the damage had occurred in England.

The ECJ held that the term 'place where the harmful event occurred':

> ... must be interpreted as not referring to the place where the victim claims to have suffered financial loss consequential upon initial damage arising and suffered by him in another Contracting State.

In *Réunion Européenne,* the ECJ had to determine the place where damage to goods arose in the context of an international transport operation involving, first, carriage of goods by sea from Australia to Rotterdam, and then carriage by land from Rotterdam to Rungis (France), where the consignee had his registered office and where he discovered that goods (peaches) were damaged due to a breakdown in the cooling system. The plaintiffs, the insurer of the consignee, brought proceedings in France against three defendants: the issuer of the bill of landing, Refrigerated Containers Carrier Pty Ltd, whose registered office was in Sydney; the master of the vessel, who resided in The Netherlands, as representative of the vessel's owners and charterers; and, despite not even being mentioned on the bill of lading, Spliethoffs Bevrachtingskantoor BV, which actually carried the goods by sea, whose registered office was in Amsterdam.

In this case, it was impossible to determine the place of the event giving rise to the damage. The ECJ held that, in such circumstances, the proceedings should be brought against the actual maritime carrier in the courts of the place where the damage occurred. However, that place could neither be the place of final delivery (France) nor the place where the damage was ascertained (France). The place of final delivery was ruled out for two reasons: first, that place could be changed mid-voyage; and second, it would be tantamount to allocating jurisdiction to the place of domicile of the plaintiff, which is contrary to the objectives of the Convention. In respect of the place where damage was ascertained, the ECJ held that Art 5(3) could not be construed so extensively as to encompass any place where the adverse consequences could be felt of an event which had already caused damage actually arising elsewhere. Consequently, taking into account the objective of legal certainty pursued by the Convention, the place where damage to goods arose could only be the place where the actual maritime carrier was to deliver the goods.

As is obvious from the following passage from *Bier*, the ECJ favours a restrictive interpretation of Art 5(3):

> ... the defendant may be sued, either in the court for the place where damage occurred or in the courts for the place of the event which gives rise to and is at the origin of that damage ...

This provokes a number of observations in relation to situations where there is a multiplicity of places where the wrongful act was done and a multiplicity of *forum damni*.

It seems that the place of origin of damage is relevant for jurisdictional purposes. In our example, it is the place where chickens were reared (Germany). Similarly, the place where the damage first occurred constitutes a second option for the claimant. In our example, the damage first occurred in France.

It is submitted that Art 5(3) of the Convention should be construed restrictively in relation to the determination of the place where a tort has been committed. As far as the first element of the tort is concerned, the place where the event which originally started the sequence of events and which eventually resulted in the damage, and without which the damage could not have occurred, is relevant for jurisdictional purposes. As to the second element, a particular forum is an appropriate place for trial only if the claimant or his property first became affected by the damage within the territory of that State. The ECJ offered a wider choice of jurisdiction to the plaintiff in *Bier* only for the purposes of convenience of litigation. This means that, in cases where the damage continues to be suffered by the victim in a State other than the one in which the damage first occurred, or if the claimant commences proceedings in a court located in a State other than the one in which the damage occurred, the court of that State must decline jurisdiction.

It is submitted that John and Andrea can sue the defendant in the place of the defendant's domicile under Art 2 of the Convention (France). Under Art 5(3), they can sue the defendant in the place where the chicken came from (Germany). Similarly, the place where the damage occurred at an earlier point in time constitutes a second option for the plaintiffs (France). However, they cannot sue in England the place where the damage continues to be suffered, as the ECJ clearly favours the restrictive interpretation of Art 5(3).

* by Alina Kaczorowska

Question 15*

Horwath Ltd, an American Company located in New York, specialises in mobile phone technology. Its pioneering work concerning the provision of special mobile phone services to the deaf and visually impaired has been of particular interest to Deaf Services France (DSF), a French company. A contract between Horwath Ltd and DSF was concluded orally. The question of exclusive jurisdiction of the English court was mentioned by Horwath Ltd during negotiations, though DSF had never paid any attention to this point and has never raised any objection to it. DSF focussed negotiations around a promise made by Horwath Ltd to revolutionise the way that deaf people communicate with the hearing world and each other.

When the service was installed in France, DSF was very unhappy. It considered that the new system did not live up to the contract specification and that there was nothing revolutionary about it. Horwath Ltd argued that the new system gave online access and was a new tool which enabled deaf people to communicate with society, whilst DSF claimed that, in France, this technology had been in use for many years.

DSF has commenced proceedings in Paris. It claims that there was no agreement on jurisdiction in England, although Horwath Ltd did send a telefax stating 'exclusive jurisdiction England – conform to established usages' during the contract negotiations. The telefax was never answered by DSF, in writing or otherwise. Furthermore, DSF argues that it has never been aware of any particular usage referring to the jurisdiction of English courts in the mobile phone technology sector and that, in any case, Art 17 of the Brussels Convention requires a link between the contract and the court chosen. The legal adviser to Horwath Ltd contests the jurisdiction of the French court.

Advise DSF as to the jurisdictional issues.

Answer plan

The question concerns prorogation of jurisdiction under Art 17 of the Brussels Convention. Article 17 confers exclusive jurisdiction in cases where there is an agreement on jurisdiction between the parties. In order to answer the question, it is necessary to determine, first, the application of Art 17 to a dispute where one of the parties is from a non-Contracting State. Secondly, formal requirements laid down by Art 17 should be examined, especially Art 17(1)(c), which refers to a usage of which the parties are or ought to have been aware and which, in such trade or commerce, is widely known to, and regularly observed by, parties to contracts of the type involved in the particular trade or commerce concerned. In this respect, the judgment of the ECJ in *Trasporti Castelletti Spedizioni Internazionali SpA v Hugo Trumpy SpA* (1999) is of particular interest. The question of limitation of choice of court in the light of Art 17 was also discussed in that case.

Thirdly, the question of what a court in a Contracting State can do if a court in another Contracting State exercises jurisdiction in breach of an express clause conferring jurisdiction upon that court, should be discussed.

Answer

Parties to an international contract are usually from different States and different legal backgrounds. For that reason, it is preferable to leave to the parties themselves the choice of the law applicable to their contract and the selection of the court which is to have exclusive jurisdiction to settle any dispute that arises in connection with their agreement. This principle implies that the parties have equal bargaining power and, thus, the terms of a contract are negotiated *between* them rather than imposed by the party with greater bargaining power.

First, it is necessary to examine whether the Brussels Convention applies to any agreement on jurisdiction made between these parties when one of them is not domiciled in a Contracting State. In this respect, Art 17 of the Convention stipulates that, if at least one of the parties is domiciled in a Contracting State and the parties have conferred jurisdiction upon a court in a Contracting State, that court shall have exclusive jurisdiction. When both parties are domiciled in non-Contracting States, then, according to Art 17, the court selected by the parties will have jurisdiction over the dispute and the courts in a Contracting State may exercise jurisdiction only if the chosen court has declined jurisdiction. In our case, DSF is domiciled in a Contracting State (France) and the court selected is situated in a Contracting State (England). Therefore, the English court may have exclusive jurisdiction and Art 17 may apply, but this would depend upon the construction of the agreement.

Secondly, Art 17 lays down formal and substantive requirements which an agreement conferring jurisdiction must meet in order to be effective. DSF claims that the formal requirements have not been satisfied and, thus, any exclusive jurisdiction agreement is void. The ECJ has stated in many cases that the formal requirements of Art 17 are necessary in order to establish without doubt the existence of a consensus between the parties as to any exclusive jurisdiction agreement (*Salotti v RUWA* (1976); *Segoura v Bonakdarian* (1976); *Custom Made Commercial v Stawa Metallbau* (1994)).

It is interesting to note that the ECJ has substantially changed its approach toward the formal validity of exclusive jurisdiction agreements. In the early cases, the formal requirements were strictly interpreted. In *Salotti v RUWA*, the Court held that a choice of jurisdiction clause printed on the reverse of a contract did not amount to an agreement under Art 17 (see, also, *Galeries Segoura Sprl v Firma Rahim Bonakdarian* (1976)). However, since then, the ECJ has acknowledged that the formal requirements should not be so onerous as to hinder normal commercial practices. As a result, Art 17 was redrafted in the 1989 version of the Brussels Convention. In its new version, it provides that an agreement on jurisdiction must be in writing or evidenced in writing (Art 17(a)); or be in a form which accords with the practices which the parties have established between themselves (Art 17(b)); or be in a form which conforms to a usage in international trade, of which the parties are, or ought to have been, aware and which is widely known and regularly observed by parties to similar contracts in a particular trade or commerce (Art 17(c)).

With respect to our scenario, it is necessary to take into consideration *F Berghoefer v ASA SA* (1985), in which the ECJ held that an oral agreement later confirmed in writing by one party and accepted by the other, although not confirmed in writing by that party, satisfied the formal requirements of Art 17. In *IP Metal Ltd v Route OZ SpA* (1993), the ECJ decided that a telefax subsequent to an oral agreement stating 'law – England; competent forum – London', amounted to a valid agreement within the scope of Art 17, evidenced by the writing of the telex.

In our scenario, the telefax refers to established usages; therefore, Art 17(1)(c) is at issue. In *Mainschiffahrts-Genossenschaft v Les Gravières Rhénanes* (1997), the ECJ provided some clarification regarding the interpretation of Art 17(1)(c). In that case, the defendant, a French company, chartered a river vessel from the plaintiff, a German company located in Würzburg. The charterparty was concluded orally and the reference to the jurisdiction of a German court was contained in a letter of confirmation, sent by the plaintiff to the defendant, which contained a pre-printed term stating that 'the place of performance is Würzburg and the courts for that place have exclusive jurisdiction'. The defendant did not respond to the letter.

When presented with invoices issued by the plaintiff, the defendant paid them without any objection. They, too, contained a pre-printed reference to the jurisdiction of a German court. When the dispute arose and the plaintiff brought proceedings before a German court, the defendant challenged the court's jurisdiction. The ECJ left it to a referring court to ascertain whether there was a particular usage in the area of carriage of goods by river, but emphasised that Art 7(1)(c) would be applicable in the situation where one of the parties did not react to a confirmation letter sent to it by the other party or paid invoices without objection where those documents contained a pre-printed reference to the jurisdiction of a particular court, provided that it was in conformity with the practice in the particular field of international commerce or trade.

In *Trasporti Castelletti* (1999), the ECJ provided important clarification in relation to factors affecting the validity of jurisdictional clauses in the light of Art 7(1)(c). First, in relation to parties' consent to the jurisdictional clause, the ECJ held that consent is presumed to exist where their conduct is consistent with a usage which governs the area of international trade in which the parties operate and of which they are, or ought to have been, aware. In order to assess the parties' actual or presumed awareness of a particular usage, neither their nationality nor any specific form of publicity which might be given in associations or specialised body to the standard forms which contain a clause of jurisdiction is relevant (although it may help to prove the existence of a particular usage). What should be taken into consideration is either the previous dealings between the parties themselves or with other parties engaged in the same businesses, or the fact that, in that sector, a particular course of conduct is sufficiently well known to be generally and regularly observed when a particular type of contract is concluded so as to be regarded as being an established usage. Thirdly, the ECJ indicated that a national court must determine the existence of a particular usage, not by reference to a national law or international trade in general, but by reference to the area of trade in which the parties to the contract operate.

Applying the above judgment to our scenario, if the French court establishes that there is a practice in the sector of international mobile phone technology regarding agreements on jurisdiction which is so widely known to and regularly observed by parties to this type of contract as to constitute an established usage, actual consent or actual knowledge of it by DSF will not be taken into consideration and the normal usage provision will be deemed to be part of the agreement between them.

This conclusion is also justified under the principle of good faith. Indeed, DSF should have contested the telefax immediately, had it disagreed with Horwath Ltd on the exclusive jurisdiction agreement.

As to the limitations imposed on the choice of jurisdiction in *Zelger v Salinitri (No 1)* (1980), the ECJ confirmed that Art 17 does not require there to be any objective link between the parties or the subject matter of the dispute and the territory of the selected court.

Finally, in the context of our case, it is important to examine whether the French court is entitled to determine the formal validity of an exclusive jurisdiction agreement. According to the Schlosser Report,[1] the court seised must decide of its own motion whether Art 17 allows it to have jurisdiction when a party challenges it on the basis of lack of compliance with formal requirements. In order to answer this question, a number of judgments of the ECJ should be examined. In this respect, it was held in *Elefanten Schuh GmbH v Pierre Jacqmain* (1981) that Contracting States are not free to lay down formal requirements as to the validity of an agreement on jurisdiction, other than those contained in Art 17. Consequently, a French and an English court should reach exactly the same decision as to the validity of the agreement between our parties.

If the agreement is valid, then a French court should decline jurisdiction of its own motion. Nevertheless, if, in breach of a valid agreement on jurisdiction, a French court decides to pursue the proceedings, the defendant is not without remedy. In *Continental Bank NA v Aeakos Cia Naviers SA* (1994), where proceedings had been commenced in breach of a jurisdiction clause before a Greek court instead of an English court, it was held that the latter had jurisdiction to enjoin the plaintiff from continuing proceedings in Greece, even though a Greek court had been the first court seised of the matter. The Court of Appeal stated that the construction of the jurisdiction agreement was governed by English law (the proper law was selected by the parties) and decided that the contested jurisdiction clause had conferred exclusive jurisdiction upon an English court.

Consequently, the Greek court should have declined jurisdiction of its own motion. Obviously, if a party pursues proceedings notwithstanding an injunction, he is in contempt of an English court; in these circumstances, a judgment obtained abroad will not be recognised in England.

Note

1 OJ C59/71 (1979).

* by Alina Kaczorowska

Question 16

Mata is a national of Nanosia. He holds 50% of the shares in Brix Co Ltd, a company established and registered in England. He is also a paid employee of the company. The company was commissioned by the Nanosian Ministry of Culture to design the State Opera House.

The designs were personally drawn up by Mata between January 2000 and June 2000, while he was in England.

The designs proved to be seriously flawed. The Opera House collapsed following a minor earthquake, killing 400 people. In fear of prosecution in Nanosia, Mata fled to Spain.

The Nanosian Government has instituted action for damages against Mata in Spain and England. Mata contends that he cannot be sued in England because he is not domiciled there. He argues in the alternative that the action in England should be stayed, at least until the Spanish court has given its judgment.

Discuss how an English court would deal with these issues of jurisdiction.

Answer plan

The following points should be considered:

- establishing the domicile of Mata for the purposes of establishing the jurisdiction of the English court;

- rules relating to *lis alibis pendens* under Arts 21 and 22 of the Brussels Convention;
- Art 30 of the new Draft Regulation on Jurisdiction, Recognition and Enforcement of Judgments in Civil and Commercial Matters.

Answer

There are two main issues in this problem – the first relates to the allocation of jurisdiction between Member States under the Brussels Convention, and the second to the application of Arts 21 and 22 on *lis alibis pendens*. On the first issue, it is also vital to examine the new Art 30 introduced by the Draft Regulation on Jurisdiction, Recognition and Enforcement of Judgments in Civil and Commercial Matters, which is intended to modify and update the Brussels Convention.

In Mata's case, the Brussels Convention on Jurisdiction and the Enforcement of Judgments in Civil and Commercial Matters would apply if Nanosia's action is one which is founded on civil or commercial law. The Convention will not apply where the matter is founded on criminal or public law. Article 1 expressly provides that it shall not extend to revenue, customs or administrative matters. It is, therefore, safe to say that, if the Nanosian Government is based on some State prerogative over contracts entered into with its nationals, the Brussels Convention will not apply. However, the action is very much a civil matter; thus, the action which is intended to take place in the UK and Spain should fall within the remit of the Convention.

Article 2 of the Brussels Convention and Mata's domicile

The general rule is that persons domiciled in a Contracting State shall be sued in the courts of that State, whatever their nationality. This would mean that, regardless of Mata's Nanosian nationality, he could be sued in Spain if it was established that Spain is his place of domicile. In deciding whether it has jurisdiction to hear the matter under the Brussels Convention, the Spanish court would have to satisfy itself either that the defendant, Mata, is domiciled in Spain under Spanish law, or that the action falls within the special jurisdiction rules set out in Arts 5–18 and 24 of the Convention. As far as the company is concerned, the same applies. However, this answer shall be confined to how the English court would respond to the application by the parties.

As far as English courts are concerned, Art 2 needs to be satisfied before jurisdiction might be vested here. This necessitates the determination of Mata's domicile. Domicile under the Convention is based on two factors – where the *propositus* is resident, and whether the nature and circumstances of his residence indicate that he has a substantial connection with that alleged country of domicile.[1] The fact of his residence in Spain, not England, is incontrovertible. This means that, under Art 52, if the English court wishes to decide whether Mata is domiciled in Spain, it must resort to Spanish law. Considering that the Brussels Convention is very much a harmonising endeavour, it seems pellucid that this is the equivalent to s 41 of the Civil Jurisdiction and Judgments Act 1982 in Spanish law.

Although it is clear that Mata fails to satisfy the residence requirement to qualify as an English domiciliary, it is of some worth to explore how the 'substantial connection' element might be resolved. The term in itself seems somewhat meaningless, since there is no guidance as to what 'substantial' implies. As Stone points out, 'substantial' can mean anything from 'total or almost total' to 'more than minimal'.[2]

However, it may be possible to draw an inference from s 41(6), which provides that an individual who is and has for the last three months or more been resident in the UK or a part thereof is rebuttably presumed to have a substantial connection therewith. Therefore, that connection is linked to duration. As far as Mata is concerned, his residence in Spain might be argued to be involuntary. After all, he had fled there under the threat of prosecution from his home country.

It is a truism to say that the concept of domicile under the Convention is different to that rooted in the common law. At common law, the crucial element (other than residence) is the intention to remain in a place indefinitely. Where that criterion is applied to Mata's situation, it could be raised that his intention was not to remain in Spain indefinitely but to return to his home country once the cloud of prosecution was lifted. This raises difficult problems with the test to be applied (for example, whether the test in *Re Fuld's Estate (No 3)* (1968) or that in *IRC v*

Bullock (1976) should apply) and the quantum of proof. However, as has been pointed out, the position under the Convention does not require an assessment of these tests. The test is whether there is substantial connection.

It would seem, therefore, that Mata is indeed not domiciled in England, but this does not mean that the English court is necessarily bereft of jurisdiction. Jurisdiction also depends on the special rules set out in Arts 5–18 and 24 of the Convention. Pertinent to the present case is Art 5(3). Before examining how Art 5(3) might apply in order to subject Mata to English jurisdiction, it is worthwhile to dispense with Art 5(1), which might be considered as a probable alternative.

'Contract' and 'tort' are to be construed as autonomous concepts, according to the ECJ in *SPRL Arcado v SA Haviland* (1988). This requires that any cause of action be construed against the backdrop of the framework and aims of the Brussels and Lugano Conventions, and not in reliance on the *lex fori*. It seems fairly clear, in reliance on the analysis applied by the ECJ in *Kalfelis v Schröder, Münchmeyer, Hengst & Co* (1988), that, as there is no agreement between Mata and Nanosia, the cause of action is not one 'relating to a contract'. Moreover, there can be no significant ground for suggesting that the company and Mata are one.

Article 5(3) provides that a person domiciled in a Contracting State may be sued in matters relating to tort, delict or quasi-delict in the courts of the place where the harmful event occurred (so long as that place is a Contracting State). England could, therefore, be another forum for the action against Mata if it could be established that that was where the harmful event occurred.

It might be recalled that the Jenard Report made no allusion to whether the 'place where the harmful event occurred' referred to the place where the act which initiated the harm took place or the place where the damage finally took effect.[3] The notorious case of *Bier v Mines de Potasse* (1978) is a good starting point. It was held in that case that both places would have jurisdiction. In the present case, the faulty designs were presumably drafted in England and submitted in Nanosia, where the ultimate damage was caused. First, if *Bier* is to be applied, the fault in drawing up defective designs was committed in England and the designs and the damage occurred in Nanosia. This means that English jurisdiction over Mata could be established. A directly relevant illustration of the principle might be had from Court of Appeal's decision in *Hewden Stuart v Gottwald* (1992). There, it was confirmed that the German designers and manufacturers of a faulty crane could be sued either in Germany, where the faulty designs were made, or in England, where the crane had collapsed, causing damage.

It should be added that this does not seem to be a case on pure financial loss, where it seems that modified rules apply.[4]

Application of Arts 21 and 22

On *lis alibis pendens*, the general rule is set out in Art 21. That Article provides that, where proceedings involving the same cause of action between the same parties are brought in the courts of different Contracting States, any court other than the court first seised shall, of its own motion, stay its proceedings until such time as the jurisdiction of the court first seised is established. Where the jurisdiction of the court first seised is established, any court other than the court first seised shall decline jurisdiction in favour of that court. Where the proceedings do not involve the same cause of action but involve merely related causes of action, the relevant provision is Art 22. Actions are deemed to be related where they are so closely connected that it is expedient to hear and determine them together in order to avoid the risk of irreconcilable judgments resulting from separate proceedings. Article 22 makes it a matter of discretion for the court latterly seised to stay proceedings.

Mata assumes that the English court is not the court first seised. His assumption cannot be allowed to pass without challenge, especially as the facts are not clear as to which court was first seised. The issue of 'first seised' was considered in *Zelger v Salinitri* (1984). The ECJ held that the question of whether a court was definitively seised when the claim was issued (filed) or when it was served could only be answered by reference to the law of the forum concerned. This was subsequently manifested in *Dresser v Falcongate* (1992), where the Court of Appeal held that the issue of an English claim does not mean that the English court becomes seised; it is only when the claim has been properly served that the court becomes seised.

It should perhaps be noted that, if the Draft Regulation on Jurisdiction, Recognition and Enforcement of Judgments in Civil and Commercial Matters (which is intended to replace and update the Brussels Convention) comes into effect, there will be a uniform definition as to when a court becomes seised. The uniform rule as set out in Art 30 will state that, in countries where proceedings are served first and filed with the court subsequently, the court becomes seised when they are served. In countries where proceedings are filed first before being served, the date on which they are served is the date when the court becomes seised.

As to whether Art 21 or Art 22 should apply, it would appear that this question depends on the cause of action being raised in both courts and how closely linked they are. However, in the light of the ruling in *Gubisch Maschinenfabrik v Palumbo* (1987), Art 21 has been so greatly extended that it now appears to be significantly less potent. The dispute involved in that case was the sale of a moulding machine. The seller, a German company, brought an action in Germany for payment of the purchase price. At the same time, the buyer, who was domiciled in Italy, instituted an action in Italy, claiming annulment of the contract or, in the alternative, rescission for delay in delivery. It is clear that the causes of action were not identical in form. The ECJ considered that, as the objective is to avoid irreconcilable judgments, it is important to concentrate on the substance of the actions, not the form. The question is whether the actions have similar objects. In that case, both actions were about the enforceability of the contract of sale and, as such, Art 21 applied.

Article 22 refers to related actions. In *Sarrio SA v Kuwait Investment Authority* (1997), the House of Lords, in an attempt to adopt the approach recommended by the ECJ in *Tatry v Maciej Rataj (The Tatry)* (1995), stated that Art 22 should not be confined to cases where there was a potential conflict between 'primary' issues. Rather, the court should apply a wide test which covers a range of circumstances, from cases where matters before the courts were virtually identical, to cases where the connection was close enough to make it expedient for them to be heard and determined together in order to avoid the risk of irreconcilable judgments.

Be that as it may, both Articles may be pleaded concurrently and, under the present circumstances, it would appear that Mata probably has a good case, subject to the issue of which country was actually first seised.

Finally, it is necessary to mention the relevant procedure in applying for a stay of proceedings. The Civil Procedure Rules (CPR) 1998 have now come into effect and regard must be had to those Rules before any application for a stay of proceedings is made. Part 11 of the CPR governs applications challenging the jurisdiction of the English courts, and it seems to follow that it should also govern applications for a stay of proceedings.

Under the old law, an application for a stay of proceedings was not an action in challenge of the court's jurisdiction. It could, therefore, be raised later, usually after the defence had been served and after it had become clear what the evidence and issues for litigation were likely to be. Under the CPR, it would seem that an application for a stay must be made at the same time, and within the same timescale as, a challenge to the court's jurisdiction. This means that the application must be made before the defence is served.

Notes

1 See s 41 of the Civil Jurisdiction and Judgments Act 1982.

2 See Stone, *Conflict of Laws*, 1995, p 132.

3 OJ C59/1 (1979).

4 In cases involving financial loss, application of the principle is seen in *Dumez Bâtiment and Tracona v Hessische Landesbank* (1990). There, a French company was prevented from claiming damages in France against a German bank which had withdrawn certain credits to a property developer in Germany, thereby causing the financial collapse of the French company's subsidiary in Germany. Similarly, in *Marinari v Lloyds Bank* (1995), the claimant, who had suffered financial loss in Italy because the defendant had, it was alleged, wrongfully retained certain promissory notes due to the claimant, was not entitled to sue in Italy. The delictual or tortious act of retaining the promissory notes was, in fact, committed in England and, although the damage (that is, the financial loss) was suffered in Italy, this did not activate the exception in Art 5(3).

Question 17*

Critically analyse Art 18 of the Brussels Convention, taking into account relevant judgments delivered by the ECJ.

Answer plan

Article 18 of the Brussels Convention raises three interesting issues. The first is regarding the meaning of 'submission', in particular, whether the defendant is regarded as having submitted if he enters an appearance and argues in the alternative, that is, he raises not only the issue of jurisdiction but also makes a submission as to the substance of the action. Secondly, there is the question of whether or not Art 18 applies to a defendant not domiciled in a Contracting State. Thirdly, the limitations on submission should be discussed, in particular whether Art 18 overrides Art 17. The judgment of the ECJ in *Elefanten Schuh GmbH v Pierre Jacqmain* (1981) and the decision of the Court of Appeal in *Continental Bank NA v Aeakos Cia Naviera SA* (1994) should be discussed.

Answer

Article 18 of the Brussels Convention (which is identical to Art 18 of the Lugano Convention) deals with submission to jurisdiction. It stipulates that 'a court of a Contracting State before whom a defendant enters an appearance shall have jurisdiction'. However, when a defendant enters an appearance solely to contest the jurisdiction of the court, he does not submit to the jurisdiction by doing so. If a court in one Contracting State has exclusive jurisdiction by virtue of Art 16, the entry of an appearance of the defendant before a court in another Contracting State has no effect on the exclusive competence of the first mentioned court. The idea behind Art 18 is that the defendant's entry of an appearance shall not prejudice his rights to a defence: *volenti non fit injuria*.

The first issue concerns the meaning of 'submission'. There is no definition of 'submission' in the Brussels Convention, but it has the same meaning as the entry of an appearance. The term 'appearance' has an autonomous Community meaning; therefore, the English distinction between entry of an appearance and submission must be disregarded. The Jenard Report states that whether or not a defendant enters an appearance should be ascertain by the law of the court seised of the proceedings.[1] Therefore, the manner in which the defendant actually enters an appearance is to be determined in accordance with procedural rules of the court seised of the proceedings (the question of procedure is outside the scope of the Convention: see *Hagen v Zeehaghe* (1990)).

The divergences of national procedural rules may lead to a race between the defendant and the claimant in commencing proceedings against each other in different Contracting States, because the court which is seised second is bound to decline its jurisdiction under Art 21 of the Convention (see below, Question 18, for *lis alibi pendens*). The defendant must be very careful when challenging jurisdiction.

When the defendant enters an appearance and fights the action on its merits, he submits to the jurisdiction. However, if the defendant argues in the alternative, it is clear that he does not solely contest the jurisdiction and, thus, the strict interpretation of Art 18 may suggest that he would be considered as submitting to jurisdiction. This problem was clarified by the ECJ in *Elefanten Schuh GmbH v Pierre Jacqmain* (1981), where it was held that the objective and spirit of the Convention required a liberal interpretation of Art 18. Thus, when a defendant argues in the alternative, that is, when he challenges both the jurisdiction of the court and the substance of the action, he submits to the jurisdiction 'only if the plaintiff and the court seised of the matter are able to ascertain from the time of the defendant's first defence that it is intended to contest the jurisdiction'.

The result of this is that, if the challenge to the jurisdiction is not preliminary to any defences as to the substance and is made at the first opportunity, the defendant does not submit to jurisdiction. Consequently, when the defendant is taking procedural steps intended to help him to challenge the jurisdiction, for example, seeking discovery of documents in order to evidence lack of jurisdiction of the court seised of the proceedings, he is not submitting to jurisdiction of that court (*Kurz v Stella Musical GmbH* (1992)). However, when he has taken voluntary steps with a view to fighting the case on the merits, he submits to jurisdiction (*Toepfer International GmbH v Molino Boshi Srl* (1996)).

The liberal approach of the ECJ is justified on the basis that, under some national laws, the defendant who raises only the issue of jurisdiction might be barred from making submissions as to the substance if the court rejects his challenge. In *Continental Bank NA v Aeakos Cia Naviera SA* (1994), the defendant had to follow Greek rules of civil procedure, which obliged him to fight the action on its merits, while contesting the jurisdiction of the Greek court. Thus, it would be unjust and contrary to the defendant's right to defend himself if a court was to decide that the defendant had submitted to its jurisdiction under those circumstances.

The second issue that should be examined concerns the application of Art 18 to a defendant domiciled in a non-Contracting State. Some scholars consider that Art 18 should be examined in the light of Arts 3 and 4 of the Brussels Convention. According to Art 4, when a defendant is not domiciled in a Contracting State, then, subject to Art 16 (exclusive jurisdiction), the jurisdiction of a court in a Contracting State should be determined by reference to private international law of that State. Consequently, the question of whether the defendant has submitted to the jurisdiction of that court should be governed by national rules.

In favour of this solution, it may be said that nothing in the wording of Art 18 suggests that it applies regardless of the domicile of the defendant. Furthermore, a defendant not domiciled in a Contracting State is better protected if his submission is governed by national rules. For example, in England, if a defendant contests jurisdiction of an English court, he takes no chances that his action will amount to submission. If he contests jurisdiction, he must follow the procedure set up in RSC Ord 12 r 8(6); that is, he must give notice of his intention to defend and must apply to set aside the proceedings.[2]

There is, however, an important argument against this solution. Both Arts 17 and 18 concern the prorogation of jurisdiction and should thus be construed in the same way (see Darmon AG in *Brenner v Dean Witter Reynolds* (1994)). This approach would ensure the uniform application of the

Convention and would thus conform to the spirit and the objectives of the Brussels Convention.

As to the relationship between Arts 17 and 18, the ECJ held in *Elefanten Schuh* that Art 18 overrides Art 17. This means that Art 18 will apply, even when a court in another Contracting State has exclusive jurisdiction resulting from an agreement designating the court or courts which will be competent to determine existing or potential disputes between the parties. Indeed, as parties to an international contract are allowed to select the competent court in the case of a dispute, they are also allowed to change their agreement. The entry of an appearance within the meaning of Art 18 constitutes a voluntary act on the part of a defendant; thus, there is no reason why a new agreement between the parties should not be respected by a court in a Contracting State.

Notes

1 OJ C59/1 (1979)

2 In *The Sydney Express* (1988), it was held that, when the defendant acknowledges service and applies to set aside the proceedings, he does not submit to the jurisdiction (RSC Ord 12 r 8).

* by Alina Kaczorowska

Question 18*

Salex Ltd, a Brazilian mining company, concluded a charterparty with James van Dal, a Dutch national who owned a vessel known as the *Anaconda*, for carriage by sea of a cargo of ferrochromium. The cargo was insured by Yalex Ltd, a company incorporated in Brazil.

On 4 August 1989, the *Anaconda* foundered in the inland waters of the Netherlands. Alex GmbH, a German insurance company and insurer of the vessel, had it refloated at its own expense and thus salvaged the cargo.

On 1 December 1990, Alex GmbH brought proceedings before a German Commercial Court in Hamburg against Salex Ltd and Yalex Ltd for payment of contribution by both companies to the general average.

Salex Ltd and Yalex Ltd challenged the jurisdiction of the German court. They raised an objection of *lis alibi pendens* on the grounds that they had brought an action on 2 December 1990 against James van Dal before the District Court in Rotterdam, in which they sought to have him declared exclusively liable for the foundering of the *Anaconda*.

Advise Alex Gmbh as to the jurisdictional issues.

Answer plan

The question deals with concurrent proceedings, that is, the situation where proceedings involving the same cause of action and the same parties are brought in the courts of different Contracting States (*lis alibi pendens*). In this situation, Art 21 of the Brussels Convention applies. Under Art 21, the meaning of the terms 'similar actions' and 'same parties' should be determined, taking into account judgments delivered by the ECJ, in particular, *Gubisch v Palumbo* (1987), *The Tatry* (1995) and *Drouot Assurances SA v Consolidated Metallurgical Industries (CMI Industrial Sites)* (1998).

Answer

From the point of view of legal certainty and the proper administration of justice, Art 21 of the Brussels Convention is paramount. It states that, when *lis alibi pendens* occurs, the court first seised of the proceedings asserts jurisdiction and any other court must of its own motion stay its proceedings until the jurisdiction of the court first seised is established. Once jurisdiction is established, any court other than the court first seised must decline jurisdiction in favour of that court. This formula is very simple, as it is based on a test of chronological priority, although its application raises many controversies.

In order to understand the mechanism under Art 21, it is necessary to consider the objectives of that provision. In this respect, the ECJ has held on a number of occasions that Art 21 must be interpreted broadly, so as to preclude 'in so far as possible and from the outset' a possible clash of inconsistent judgments given by courts in Contracting States (*Gubisch v Palumbo* (1987)). Indeed, under the Brussels Convention, there are situations where courts in a number of Contracting States may be concurrently properly seised of the same proceedings between the same parties. In *Freifrau von Horn v Cinnamond* (1997), the ECJ stressed that Art 21 should be construed in such a way as to reinforce the legal protection of persons established in the Community and to facilitate recognition and enforcement of judicial decisions, in particular, by reducing the danger of irreconcilable judgments being delivered.

The ECJ has consistently held that, in order to determine whether a situation of *lis alibis pendens* arises, the terms used in Art 21 must be regarded as being independent. Therefore, all these terms have autonomous Community meanings.

In relation to similar disputes, the ECJ has always favoured a wide approach. The dispute in *Gubisch v Palumbo* concerned the sale of a machine by a German seller to an Italian buyer. The seller brought an action for payment of the price before a German court, while the buyer brought an action for annulment (or alternatively for rescission) of the contract before an Italian court. The ECJ held that Art 21 applied in this situation and, therefore, the court first seised had jurisdiction. In *The Tatry* (1995), the ECJ decided that an action seeking to make the defendant shipowner liable for causing loss and pay damages had the same cause of action as the earlier proceedings brought by the shipowner, in which he sought a declaration that he was not liable for that loss.

For the purposes of our scenario, it seems that the subject matter of the two disputes has some degree of similarity. In the proceedings between Alex GmbH, on the one hand, and Salex Ltd and Yalex Ltd, on the other, the claim concerns the contribution to the general average, whilst, in the second proceedings, Salex Ltd and Yalex Ltd seek to declare James van Dal exclusively liable for the foundering of the *Anaconda*. Alex GmbH, the insurer of the vessel, cannot be held liable for the fault of its insured.

It is submitted that, even under the ECJ's broad interpretation of 'similar actions', it will be difficult to claim that the two proceedings have the same cause of action. In this respect, in *Drouot Assurances* (1998) (a very similar case to the scenario here), which was brought before French courts, the Paris tribunal held that the cause of action was not the same, while the Court of

Appeal in Paris upheld the plea of *lis alibi pendens*. The Cour de Cassation, on appeal, referred the matter to the ECJ, which focused its reasoning on the concept of the 'same party' (see below) but held that only when the interests of an insurer and its insured are identical and indissociable is the subject matter of both actions the same. In *Drouot Assurances*, there was no subrogation and, therefore, the ECJ held that the interests of the insurer of the vessel could not be considered to be identical and indissociable from those of its insured. However, the ECJ left it to the referring court to determine, in the light of the facts of the case, whether its conclusions as to the dissimilarity of interests between the insurer and its insured were correct.

The concept of 'same parties' requires that the same parties are involved in both sets of proceedings. If some but not all of the parties to the second proceedings are the same as the parties to the first proceedings, Art 21 requires that the court second seised declines jurisdiction, but only to the extent to which the parties to the second proceedings are also parties to the first proceedings. This is a complicated rule, as it allows the second proceedings to continue (*The Tatry*). The possibility of applying Art 22, which concerns related actions, may, in certain circumstances, alleviate the problem of fragmentation of proceedings.

The identity of the parties involved in two sets of proceedings in the context of insurance claims was examined by the ECJ in *Drouot Assurances*. It held that, in certain circumstances, the parties to the two actions are identical. This happens in the case of subrogation, where an insurer brings or defends an action in the name of its insured without the latter being in a position to influence the proceedings. In such a situation, a judgment delivered against one of them would have the force of *res judicata* as against the other. Therefore, if the interests of an insurer and its insured are identical and indissociable, they should be regarded as the same parties for the purposes of Art 21. However, this is not the case where an insurer acts in its capacity of direct participant in the refloating of a vessel and takes no interest in the action against its insured on the ground that the insurer cannot be held liable for the fault of its insured. Applying the reasoning of the ECJ in *Drouot Assurances* to our scenario, it is clear that the parties to the two sets of proceedings are not the same for the purposes of Art 21 of the Brussels Convention.

The question of when the court is considered as being seised of the proceedings is of utmost importance for the parties. Under Art 21 of the Brussels Convention, this question is to be determined under the national procedural law of the court seised of the proceedings. Indeed, the procedure is outside the scope of the Brussels Convention (*Hagen v Zeehaghe* (1990)). In *Zelger v Salinitri (No 2)* (1984), the ECJ held that a national court must decline jurisdiction in favour of another court only if it is established that the same proceedings between the same parties are definitely pending before the other court, this matter being determined in conformity with that court's national rules.

This solution, although justified in the light of the Brussels Convention's material scope of application, creates a serious problem for the parties, on account of the divergencies of national rules of the Contracting States in this area. Under English law, proceedings are definitely pending when the claim is served on the defendant (*The Deichland* (1990); *Dresser v Falcongate* (1992); *The Sargasso* (1994)). In the case of multiple defendants, where the proceedings are served on different dates, it seems that the relevant date is the date of service on each defendant and not the date of the first service on any one of the defendants (*Gruppo Torras v Al Sabah* (1996)). For the purposes of our scenario, the determination of which court was first seised will be left to the national procedural rules of Germany and The Netherlands. It seems that, in both countries, the courts will be considered to have been definitely seised when the claim was served on the defendant.

It is submitted that Alex GmbH, the insurer, and James van Dal, its insured, are neither the same parties, nor do they have a similar cause of action for the purposes of Art 21 of the Brussels Convention. Consequently, there is no *lis alibi pendens* and Art 21 is not applicable to our scenario.

* by Alina Kaczorowska

Question 19*

Diego Velodrome, commander of the Revolutionary Armed Forces of Colombia (FARC), controls a territory about the size of Switzerland. The Government of Columbia has handed this territory over to FARC as a conciliatory gesture aimed at luring FARC into peace talks. In this territory, Diego Velodrome has built his vision of a Marxist utopia. In order to finance this mini-State carved from Columbia, FARC imposes taxes on Colombia's most lucrative export, cocaine. FARC has also earned more than £550 million in taxes imposed on drug traffickers for protecting the cocoa leaf cultivation zone and for shooting down anti-narcotics helicopters that try to raid cocaine manufacturing laboratories in the jungle.

Diego Velodrome has built health clinics, schools, etc, and people in this area live in peace and prosperity. The use of drugs for non-medical purposes is prohibited because, according to Diego, cocaine is a cancer imposed on Columbia by the US. In order to ensure that FARC would have had funds, had the Government of Columbia decided to crack down on the rebels, Diego has a number of well endowed bank accounts in his name throughout the world, including, *inter alia*, an account at the Bingo Bank in England.

Recently, the Columbian army attacked the rebels. They were captured, and the territory has been re-incorporated into Columbia. Diego Velodrome managed to escape to Italy and asked for political asylum there.

Now, the Government of Colombia has begun proceedings in Italy against Diego Velodrome in order to recover the FARC funds. It has also applied for a worldwide freezing injunction in the English High Court.

Advise the Government of Columbia as to whether their application for the worldwide freezing injunction will be successful.

Answer plan

The question focuses on provisional measures, in particular, the freezing injunction (formerly known as the Mareva injunction).

The impact of amendments to the Civil Jurisdiction and Judgments Act 1982 effected by the Civil Jurisdiction and Judgments Act 1982 (Interim Relief) Order 1997 on the granting of interim relief under Art 24 of the Brussels Convention should be assessed. In order to determine the circumstances in which the English courts will be prepared to grant interim relief under the 1997 Order, the Court of Appeal's decision in *Credit Suisse v Cuoghi* (1997) should be examined. Moreover, recent decisions of the ECJ regarding provisional measures under Art 24, especially in *Van Uden Maritime* (1998), should be taken into consideration. It is important to note that the proposed revision of the Brussels Convention sets up minimum requirements for the availability of protective measures, as well as conferring jurisdiction upon Contracting States in which assets are located.

Answer

The list of interim measures which an English court may grant is unlimited. It seems that any interim measures which are necessary and reasonable in the context of a particular dispute and which fall within the court's duty of doing justice will be granted (*Astro Excito Navegacion SA v Southland Enterprise Co Ltd* (1982)). The main categories of interim measures encompass:

- an order addressed to the claimant in foreign proceedings, restraining him from continuing to prosecute in another country;
- an order preventing a defendant from moving his assets – the freezing injunction;
- an order requiring that the defendant allow his premises to be searched and property to be removed from them – the Anton Piller order;
- an order for the preservation of property (ss 33 and 34 of the Supreme Court Act 1981 and RSC Ord 29);
- an order in relation to the obtaining of evidence; and
- interlocutory injunctions in general (*American Cyanamid v Ethicon Ltd* (1975)).

However, interim measures are granted at the discretion of the court. Thus, even if an English court has jurisdiction to make a particular order, it may consider it inappropriate to do so in the circumstances.

In this case, the claimant applied for a freezing injunction. The freezing injunction is personal and not proprietary in character; that is, it is made against the defendant. The freezing injunction may include an order to divulge the location of the defendant's assets, an order to freeze some or all of his assets for an indefinite period of time (*PCW (Underwriting Agency) v Dixon* (1983)) or even an order to move his assets from one jurisdiction to another (*Derby v Weldon (No 6)* (1990)). In order to render the freezing injunction effective, the court is empowered to order appropriate measures, such as the discovery of documents and even to administer interrogatories (*A v C* (1980)). If the defendant refuses to comply with the order, he will be in contempt of the English court. Furthermore, a third party (that is, a person not named in the injunction) who consciously interferes with the assets contemplated in the injunction will also be considered to be in contempt of the English court. The freezing injunction neither affects the ownership of the assets (the effect of a dispute regarding the ownership of assets within the scope of the injunction has been discussed in *SCF Finance v Masri* (1985)) nor improves the position of the claimant as against other creditors of the defendant by giving him priority over the assets. The freezing injunction may be granted both before and after judgment.

The claimant who applies for a worldwide freezing injunction must have a good arguable case. He must also show that the English assets are not sufficient to satisfy the likely judgment and that there are assets abroad. Finally, he must demonstrate that there is a risk that those assets will be dissipated or secreted and may thus render nugatory any judgment which he might obtain. Even where these criteria are fulfilled, an English court will grant a worldwide freezing injunction only in exceptional cases.

Under common law rules, the freezing injunction was considered to be an ancillary order which could only be granted if the English courts had jurisdiction over the main action (*The Siskina* (1979)). The application of the traditional approach would deprive Art 24 of the Brussels Convention of any practical importance. Article 24 of the Brussels Convention stipulates that:

> Application may be made to the courts of a Contracting State for such provisional, including protective, measures as may be

> available under the law of that State, even if, under this Convention, the courts of another State have jurisdiction as to the substance of the matter.

Article 24 does not require a court in another Contracting State to grant this remedy and emphasises national law as a source of interim measures. In order to render English law compatible with Art 24 of the Brussels Convention, s 25 the Civil Jurisdiction and Judgments Act 1982 was enacted. Under this section, English courts are empowered to grant interim measures where proceedings have been or are to be commenced in another Contracting State (that is, contracting to the Brussels Convention) and the subject matter of the dispute was within the scope of application of the Convention (*De Cavel v De Cavel* (1979); *CHW v GJH* (1982); *Haiti v Duvalier* (1990)). Section 25(2) was intended to satisfy the requirements of Art 24 of the Brussels Convention by empowering the English courts to grant interim measures even where they had no jurisdiction in relation to the subject matter of the substantive dispute. Section 25(3) of the 1982 Act extended the power of English courts to grant interim relief where the substantive dispute was determined by a court in a non-Contracting State and in respect of all matters, including civil and commercial matters. The Civil Jurisdiction and Judgments Act 1982 (Interim Relief) Order 1997 brings this provision into effect.

In our case, the proceedings have been commenced in another Contracting State to the Brussels Convention. However, this consideration has lost its importance since the entry into force of the 1997 Order. The power of the English High Court to grant interim relief has been greatly expanded both *rationae materiae* (that is, the 1997 Order covers all proceedings and is not limited to those within the scope of Art 1 of the 1968 Brussels Convention) and geographically (in other words, the 1997 Order applies worldwide, not only to proceedings commenced in a Contracting State to the 1968 Brussels or Lugano Conventions or in another part of the UK). Moreover, under the amended Act, there is no reason to exclude non-judicial proceedings, for example, arbitration, although the term 'proceedings' is not defined under the amended Act.

The guidelines for granting worldwide freezing injunctions by English courts under the 1997 amendment of the 1982 Act have been provided by the Court of Appeal in *Credit Suisse v Cuoghi* (1997). In that case, the Court of Appeal emphasised that a worldwide freezing injunction should be granted if:

- it would have been appropriate had the English court been seised of the substantive proceedings;
- the defendant is domiciled or resident in England; and
- there is no risk that granting it would result in obstructing management of the case by the court seised of the substantive proceedings or give rise to confusion in third countries.

It seems that the above mentioned test will make the High Court more reluctant to grant interim relief in relation to proceedings commenced or to be commenced in other Contracting States where the defendant is not domiciled or resident in England.

It is submitted that, under the 1997 Order, the application of the Government of Columbia in the English High Court for the worldwide freezing injunction will not be successful for three reasons. First, the defendant is not domiciled, resident or present in England and, therefore, there can be no effective enforcement of a personal order. Secondly, the High Court will take into account the decision of the French Cour de Cassation in *Republic of Haiti v Duvalier* (1990), where it was held that French courts had no jurisdiction over claims made by a State against its present or former leaders because those claims related to public law. Diego Velodrome has been recognised by the Government of Columbia as being in charge of a substantial part of its territory; therefore, he enters into the category of persons against whom no civil proceedings can be brought in a foreign court. Thirdly, the judgment of the Privy Council in *Mercedes Benz v Leiduck* (1996), which questioned the correctness of decisions given by English courts in *Republic of Haiti v Duvalier* and *X v Y* (1990), will heavily influence the High Court when applying the 1997 Order. This approach will be in line with the case law of the ECJ and the proposed revision of the Brussels Convention.

In *Van Uden Maritime* (1998), the ECJ emphasised that the granting of interim measures depends on, *inter alia*, the existence of a real link between the subject matter of the measures sought and the territorial jurisdiction of the Contracting State of the court before which those measures are sought. Therefore, when the assets subject to the measures sought are located within the territory of a Contracting State, the courts of that State are best located and best able to assess the circumstances which may lead to the grant or refusal of the measures sought. In respect of Art 24 of the Brussels Convention, the European Commission has submitted a proposal for a Council Regulation on Jurisdiction and the Enforcement of Judgments in Civil and Commercial Matters, which will confer jurisdiction upon a Contracting State in which assets are located in order to provide protection in support of proceedings being commenced in the court of another Contracting State.

* by Alina Kaczorowska

Question 20

Mark runs a small computer servicing business in London, England. He enters into a franchise agreement with World Com, an Internet company based in Utopia. Under the agreement, Mark is the franchisee and will sell internet products and services using World Com's name, goodwill and business strategies.

The agreement provides that 'any dispute arising shall be resolved before the Utopian Sessions Court'.

World Com refuses to supply certain manuals on time. Mark claims that this breaches the franchise agreement. However, he is not keen to bring an action in Utopia. It is a well known fact that the Utopian judiciary is not independent and that the director of World Com is the wife of the Head of the Judiciary in Utopia. Furthermore, any legal action may take many years to settle.

Under World Com's franchise agreements, all franchisees are to take turns at representing the company at the London Personal Computer Trade Fair. They are to hand out leaflets which contain information about the business of the franchisees, including the products and services on offer. It is staffed wholly by the different franchisees on a rotation basis. World Com does not, therefore, run the stall in any practical sense.

Mark intends to institute proceedings against World Com by serving a claim form on the stall.

Advise Mark on the jurisdictional issues.

Answer plan

It is clear that Mark does not wish to sue or be sued in Utopia. The first issue is, therefore, whether it is possible for him to institute an action against World Com in England. On the matter of service within jurisdiction, some discussion as to whether the company had a place of business in England is necessary. If it is not possible to serve the claim form at the trade fair in London, students should then consider the possibility of serving the claim out of jurisdiction.

Jurisdiction to grant leave to serve the claim out of jurisdiction is dependent upon whether England is indeed the *forum conveniens*. Students must be able to explain and apply the principles set out by the House of Lords in *Spiliada Maritime v Cansulex* (1987).

Answer

It is vital to ascertain which regime will apply to these facts. It seems obvious that the traditional rules of common law will apply in this case because the defendant, World Com, is not domiciled in a Lugano or Brussels Convention State. Under the common law, an English court can found jurisdiction over a foreign defendant in one of three ways: first, where the defendant was present within jurisdiction when he was served with the claim form; secondly, where he had submitted to jurisdiction either by appearing before the court to defend the claim or by agreeing to an English choice of forum clause; and, thirdly, where he has been properly served outside jurisdiction under the parameters drawn up by Ord 11 r 1(1).

On the first issue of whether World Com was present in the jurisdiction, it might be pointed out that the law is that, as long as the company has a place of business in England, jurisdiction might be assumed. The term 'place of business' has been given a very wide meaning. In *South India Shipping Corp v Export-Import Bank of Korea* (1985), the Court of Appeal held that a publicity office in Central London which was managed and run by the defendant was properly regarded as a place of business of the defendant, at which a claim form could be served.

The issue is, therefore, whether World Com's stall at the trade fair could be properly construed as a 'place of business'. The fact that the stall does little more than hand out leaflets about the company is naturally no defence to the service of a claim form. In *South India Shipping*, the Court of Appeal made it clear that the nature or degree of work done or conducted by the publicity office was immaterial. In that case, the publicity office did little more than provide information about the services of the bank (defendant) and forge relations with other banks.

It would also be open to Mark to rely on the emphasis made in *South India Shipping* that, however slight the connection between the publicity office and the bank, it was there to represent the interests of the bank. The act of representation should be sufficient to provide the nexus between the office and bank, thereby rendering that office a place of business of the bank. It may further be argued that the stall, by representing the business of the franchisees, is, in fact, also representing the interests of World Com.

Additionally, it is clearly set out in *Cleveland Museum of Art v Capricorn Art International SA* (1990) that the representation need not even be overt. In that case, a converted church was used as a warehouse and gallery for works sold by the defendant. That was sufficient for it to be treated as the defendant's place of business, even though there were no overt signs that the gallery was in fact operated by the defendant. It was enough that it was known to the niche art world that the defendant was operating from those premises. In the present case, it would seem that representation of World Com is a great deal more overt than the representation in *Cleveland Museum*, but there remains the issue of control. In both *Cleveland Museum* and *South India Shipping*, the premises were operated by the defendant.

All this seems fairly incontrovertible. However, the issue of whether the stall is a place of business at all when it was not run, managed or controlled directly by the company poses more of a challenge. Whilst the spirit of the two cases cited above is clearly in favour of giving a wide construction to the term 'place of business', both cases dealt with premises run or operated by the defendants. In the present case, this is not so. The defendant has very little day to day control over the stall. Under the contracts, the franchisees are themselves solely responsible for representing the products and services under the franchise at the trade fair. At most, the company has only a remote interest in ensuring that the franchisees perform their part of the contract to run the stall, that interest being to preserve the goodwill of World Com's products and services. It is also the nature of a franchise agreement that the franchisees are not, in fact or law, the agents of the franchisor. This being the case, it would be difficult to argue that World Com was in fact running or controlling the stall as its place of business through their agents. It would seem that this indirect control, as implied in the franchise agreements, may not be sufficient to indicate the presence of the company in England. It remains to be seen how the courts would deal with such a point.

There clearly being no submission to English jurisdiction on World Com's part, the only other alternative to consider is whether Mark could serve the claim out of jurisdiction under RSC Ord 11 r 1(1). The House of Lords in *Seaconsar Far East Ltd v Bank Markazi Jomhouri Islami Iran* (1994) re-affirmed the long held position that three criteria must be met before leave to serve outside jurisdiction will be given.

Serious issue to be tried

First, the claimant must show that there is a serious issue to be tried. In *Seaconsar*, Lord Goff made it clear that the claimant must establish that there is a substantial issue of law or fact to be tried and that there is *bona fide* intention on his part to have that issue adjudicated upon. Although it is uncertain what this '*bona fide*' requirement entails, it is safe to say that the action must not be vexatious; in other words, the dispute must be a genuine dispute.

This was further reinforced in the recent case of *Amoco (UK) Exploration v British American Offshore Ltd* (1999), where the second defendants had applied to set aside leave the company with proceedings out of the jurisdiction under Ord 12 r 8. The claimants wanted to institute proceedings to restrain the second defendants from litigating a contractual dispute between the parties anywhere other than in England. Leave to serve on them abroad had initially been granted by another High Court judge, Burton J, under Ord 11 r 1(1)(b), (d) and/or (c). Langley J agreed with the defendants that leave should be set aside because there was no dispute that the contract action would proceed in

England; hence, the only 'live' claims in these proceedings were the anti-suit injunctions requiring the defendant to litigate the contractual dispute in England. Those claims did not fall within the parameters of Ord 11 r 1(1). They were not proceedings to ascertain and adjudicate substantive rights.

Circumstances to be satisfied under Ord 11 r 1(1)(d) and (e)

Secondly, the claimant will need to establish that his claim is covered by any of the paragraphs in Ord 11 r 1(1). This almost invariably entails a proper interpretation of the paragraphs relied on by the claimant. In Mark's case, he will hope to rely on Ord 11 r 1(1)(d) and (e).

Order 11 r 1(1)(d) refers to matters relating to contract. Under this rule, there are four areas in which English jurisdiction might be established for the purposes of service of a claim outside the jurisdiction:

- where the contract was made in the jurisdiction;
- where the contract was made by or through an agent trading or residing within the jurisdiction;
- where the contract, by its terms or by implication, is to be governed by English law; or
- where there is a term in the contract which provides that the High Court shall have jurisdiction to hear and determine any action in respect of the contract .

There is insufficient information from the facts as to whether Mark's contract with World Com was made under the circumstances described in (a) or (b). As for (d), there is clear information that the contract refers specifically to the Utopian Sessions Court as the principal arbiter in the event of a dispute. That leaves (c) to be examined further.

Very briefly, where there is choice of English law clause in the contract (which is not clear from the facts), Art 3 of the Rome Convention, as contained in the Contracts (Applicable Law) Act 1990, will apply. Article 3(1) states unequivocally that a contract shall be governed by the law chosen by the parties. Hence, if World Com and Mark have inserted a clause in their contract referring to English law as the applicable law, then it would appear that Mark may be able to apply for leave to serve the claim on World Com overseas, that is, in Utopia.

In the absence of an express choice of law agreement, it may be implied from the facts and circumstances of the case that it was the intention of the parties to subject the contract to English law. Normal rules relating to implied terms apply, the central issue being what constitutes the presumed intention of the parties. From the facts, it is not entirely clear that the parties intended English law to be the applicable law. It could, however, be suggested that, as they have both agreed to refer any dispute to the Utopian Sessions Court, the presumed intention must be that they had also intended that court to apply Utopian law.

Under the Rome Convention, where it is not possible to ascertain the presumed intention of the parties either by means of construing an express term or by eliciting an implied term, certain presumptions can be used to determine the law of the country with the closest and most real connection with the contract (Art 4). The problem that Mark might encounter in this respect is that Ord 11 r 1(1)(d) refers only to express or implied selection of English law. There is no reference to a contract which, under the rules of conflict of laws as enshrined in the Contracts (Applicable Law) Act 1990, has the closest and most real connection with England. However, it might be argued that the term 'by implication' in Ord 11 r 1(1)(d) is not merely confined to the tacit selection of the applicable law by the parties but to the whole process of ascertaining the applicable law in accordance with English conflict of laws rules.

If that were the case, the presumptions in Art 4(2) would be relevant. Article 4(2) refers to the party who is to 'effect the performance which is characteristic of the contract'. In a franchise agreement, it is difficult to ascertain what that performance is, because both parties have very explicit and detailed mutual duties to perform. Where the nature of the performance can be determined, the applicable law is that of the country where that party has its place of central administration. Where the contract had been entered into in the course of that party's trade or profession, the relevant country will be the country in which the principal place of business is situated or where, under the terms of the contract, the performance is to be effected through a place of business other than the principal place of business, the country in which that other place of business is situated. If Mark, being the franchisee, is the party who is to effect the performance which is characteristic of the contract and the franchise agreement was made in the course of his trade, it would follow that the applicable law would be English law. However, if World Com is the party who has to effect the performance which is characteristic of the contract, then Utopian law should apply.

It suffices to say that there is little guidance from the Giuliano-Lagarde Report as to what constitutes 'performance which is characteristic of the contract'. Apparently, it is important to place the contract in its socio-economic context in order to decide what that performance is.

Where the performance which is characteristic of the contract cannot be determined, Art 4(5) provides that the circumstances of the case as a whole should be assessed in order to ascertain which country the contract is most closely connected to. It would appear that the factors which the court would consider are similar to those adumbrated at common law in *Amin Rasheed Shipping Corp v Kuwait Insurance Co* (1984). In the present case, the fact that the franchise agreement was to be wholly executed in England would be a vital factor, but then so is the fact that the contract is underpinned by Utopian jurisdiction by virtue of the jurisdiction clause.

The other provision in Ord 11 r 1(1) that should be discussed is sub-r (1)(e), which provides that jurisdiction may be assumed over an overseas defendant where the claim is brought in respect of a breach of contract committed within the jurisdiction. This seems to be the most likely candidate for Mark's application. It would seem that the failure to supply Mark with the necessary manuals was a breach committed in England, as delivery was presumably to have taken place there. Even so, without further information, this argument must be treated with caution.

Forum conveniens

Finally, in order to rely successfully on Ord 11 r 1(1), Mark must demonstrate that the English court concerned is the *forum conveniens*. This is to say that the court will not give leave to serve abroad unless it is satisfied that, in the interests of the parties and justice, the case is most appropriately tried in England. In *Spiliada Maritime v Cansulex* (1987), the House of Lords stated that the test to be applied is similar to that used in deciding on whether proceedings should be stayed on the ground of *forum non conveniens*.

That test is explained in *Amin Rasheed Shipping Corp v Kuwait Insurance* (1984) as encapsulating two stages. First, the court must look at the nature of the dispute and the practical circumstances of the case. The court will thus consider the relevance of the practicalities involved, such as the availability of evidence and witnesses, the relevance of local knowledge to the dispute, the costs, the language and cultural references used in the agreement and the applicable law of the contract. In *Group Action Afrika and Others v Cape plc* (1999), the court held that a change in circumstances could give rise to a stay of proceedings in England on the basis of practical inconvenience. In that case, the number of claimants had grown from five to over 3,000; clearly, trial in South Africa was more practical.

In *The Varna (No 2)* (1994), the court considered that legal and practical convenience must also take into account the likelihood of two (or more) conflicting judgments arising from the single dispute. There is little in the facts of our problem to suggest whether practical convenience would be better served either way. It must, therefore, suffice to say that Mark must observe that these are some of the factors that the English court would consider before leave under Ord 11 r 1(1) is given.

The second stage requires the court to consider at which forum the ends of justice are best served. Therefore, even if it could be established that England is not the *forum conveniens*, leave to serve abroad may still be given if it could be demonstrated that justice would not be forthcoming abroad. In this connection, it might be argued on Mark's behalf that the interests of justice would be better served by proceeding in England rather than Utopia.

In *Oppenheimer v Louis Rosenthal & Co AG* (1937), the court clearly emphasised the point that, unless a fair hearing could be expected abroad, the overseas forum would not be considered to be the *forum conveniens*. In that case, leave was given to the claimant because, as a Jew, it was likely that he would not be given a fair trial from the 1937 German regime. This must be read against the backdrop of *The Abidin Daver* (1984), where it was held that any allegation of poor quality of justice abroad must be properly supported by positive and cogent evidence. Therefore, it is not open to Mark to make unsupported allegations about the quality of justice. Furthermore, the English court would not apply English standards of morality and ethics too strictly in determining the quality of foreign justice. This seems to be consistent with the pronouncement in *Airbus Industrie v Patel* (1998) that judges are to bear in mind the notion of judicial comity when deciding to grant stay of foreign proceedings on the grounds of *forum non conveniens*.

This could mean that the fact that one of judges is married to World Com's director is of little relevance. On the other hand, if it is well known that the judiciary in Utopia is biased, Mark's application for leave should stand every chance of succeeding.

There appears to be a third element for consideration – other than the interest of the parties and the ends of justice – the element of judicial comity. As mentioned above, the House of Lords in *Airbus Industrie v Patel* (1998) held that, in relation to an application for the stay of foreign proceedings (that is, an application for an injunction to prevent the other party from bringing an action before an overseas court), judicial comity requires that there be some nexus between the action and the English forum before stay is granted on the basis of *forum non conveniens*. It is not entirely certain whether cases under Ord 11 r 1(1) should be treated in this way. It might be argued that, in attempting to situate the case within the boundaries of Ord 11 r 1(1), the nexus between the English forum and the dispute at hand has been forged, albeit tacitly.

Question 21

Dvorak, domiciled in Italy, has contracted to act as Elgar's financial advisor. Elgar lives in Birmingham, England. Dvorak was requested by Elgar to advise him on his prospective investment in a multi-national company. Dvorak sent his written advice to Fauré for confirmation before he dispatched it to Elgar. Fauré, who is domiciled in France, added his approval to the advice.

Based on the advice given, Elgar invested heavily in the company. The company subsequently collapsed and Elgar lost £1.2 million. It is Elgar's contention that both advisors had acted negligently in dispensing the advice.

On 1 March, Elgar commences proceedings in England against Dvorak. The claim is issued on 25 March and served on Dvorak whilst he is in London for his sister's wedding. Meanwhile, on 20 March, Dvorak commences action in Italy against Elgar for non-payment under the financial consultancy agreement. The claim is served on Elgar on 31 March.

Elgar wishes to take action in England against Fauré.

Advise Elgar on the jurisdictional issues in relation to his grievances against Dvorak and Fauré.

Answer plan

The student will need to know when the Brussels Convention is applicable and should point out the general rule that the defendant must be sued in the State of his domicile. The properly structured answer should discuss the two possible defendants separately.

The case concerning Dvorak involves two questions of liability: one in contract and one in tort. Recalling the exceptions of special jurisdiction to the general rule in Art 2, the likelihood of Elgar succeeding in relying on these exceptions (for example, Art 5(1) and Art 5(3)) should be raised in the discussion. The issue of determining the connecting factor in tort should be assessed in the light of *Bier v Mines de Potasse* (1976).

Article 21 needs to be discussed next. This involves the concept of *lis alibis pendens* (but note how the concept is applied differently in the Convention as against the common law). On this note, it is important to determine which court was seised with jurisdiction first. How is this to be determined? There are some important cases associated with this issue, including *Kloeckner v Gatoil* (1990) and *Dresser UK Ltd v Falcongate Freight Management* (1992).

Finally, the relationship between Elgar and Fauré, who appears to be outside the contractual relationship, should be discussed. If this is the case, the possible cause of action under

English law would be tort. Thus, it will necessitate a brief re-application of the principles under Art 5(3). Recent developments in case law on Art 5(3) should not be ignored. In particular, students should refer to *Marinari v Lloyds Bank* (1996), where the *Bier* rule on damage is applied slightly differently to cases involving economic or financial loss.

Answer

Elgar wishes to take action against Dvorak and Fauré, both of whom are domiciled in States privy to the Brussels Convention on Jurisdiction and Enforcement of Judgments. The general rule in the Convention, as contained in the Civil Jurisdiction and Judgments Act 1982, is found in Art 2. This provides that persons domiciled in a Contracting State shall, whatever their nationality, be sued in the courts of that State. This rule is, however, subject to other provisions of the Convention which permit concurrent or special jurisdictional powers to be exercised by the courts of another State. It is proposed to consider first the case against Dvorak.

In this cause of action, Elgar alleges that he has suffered a loss as a result of a breach of contract and, perhaps, a tort committed by Dvorak by dispensing him bad advice. Under Art 2 of the Convention, which applies to all civil and commercial matters, Elgar should have sued in Italy. Italy is where Dvorak has his domicile. However, Elgar has instituted action in England. The question is whether he had acted within the rubric of the Brussels Convention. That Convention allows for special jurisdiction where persons domiciled in one Contracting State may be sued in another.

If the matter upon which Elgar wishes to place his claim is that of the contract, he may rely on Art 5(1) of the Convention. Under Art 5(1), a person domiciled in one Contracting State may be sued in the courts of another Contracting State in which the obligation in question was performed. This means that Elgar may sue Dvorak in England if it is proved that the obligation to provide financial advice is to be performed in England. It appears from the facts that the intention of the parties was that Elgar would receive the advice in England, and it was Dvorak's duty to ensure that this advice, which was to be delivered to Elgar in Birmingham, be proper advice. The place of performance of the contract is likely to be England.

It should be noted that the law applicable to determine the place of performance is that of the national court so seised. This was set out in *Tessili v Dunlop AG* (1976). The place of performance must refer to the 'obligation in question'. In Elgar's case, that obligation is the duty to give proper professional advice, not the duty to pay for that advice or other duties (*Custom Made Commercial Ltd v Stawa Metallbau GmbH* (1994)). This seems to point to England as having jurisdiction to hear the case.

Incidentally, it should be noted that, under the draft Regulation on Jurisdiction, Recognition and Enforcement of Judgments in Civil and Commercial Matters, in contracts for the sale of goods or supply of services, the place with jurisdiction under Art 5 will be the place where the goods were to be delivered or the services were to be performed, even if the action is brought by the seller or supplier for the price.

As far as an action against Fauré is concerned, there does not appear to be a contractual relationship between Fauré and Elgar. In the absence of a contractual relationship, Elgar's interests would be best served by an action in tort. In this respect, Art 5(3) provides that a person in a Contracting State may be sued in another Contracting State where that other Contracting State is the place where the harmful event occurred. Article 5(3) could also be relied on in the action against Dvorak, notwithstanding the existence of a claim in contract (see *Kalfelis v Schröder, Münchmeyer, Hengst & Co* (1988)).

Following the ECJ's ruling in *Bier v Mines de Potasse* (1976), this refers not only to the place of the tortious act but also to the place that the damage occurred. In our case, the alleged negligent act was committed in Italy but the damage (that is, the financial loss caused in reliance on the advice) may be said to have occurred in England. However, it is uncertain where the funds for the investment actually emanated from or where they have been transferred to.

Under the common law, in identifying the place of a tort, it is important to apply the *lex fori* to determine the connecting factor. In *Re Martin* (1900), it was held that, in order to determine the connecting factor of domicile, the law of the seat of the forum has to be relied on. In *Distillers Co (Biochemicals) Ltd v Thompson* (1971), the Privy Council held that the right approach was to look back over the series of events constituting the tort and ask where, in substance, the cause of action arose. This has been applied by the Court of Appeal in *Castree v ER Squibb* (1980), where the substance of the tort was held to have taken place in England, even though the machine had been negligently manufactured in Germany, because it was England where the machine was sold and where the plaintiff was injured as a result of the negligent manufacture.

It would not be too tenuous, therefore, to argue that the substance of the tort was in England, since the advice was expected to be delivered to Elgar in England and was to be acted on in a transaction emanating from England. Returning to the Convention, these common law cases should be read in line with the ECJ's pronouncement in *Bier v Mines de Potasse* (1978). In that case, the French defendant was alleged to have polluted the waters of the Rhine in France. The Rhine also flows into Holland, where damage was caused to the Dutch plaintiff's property. The ECJ held that both the French and Dutch courts had jurisdiction.

In the event of a financial loss, as there is in Elgar's case, it is vital to turn also to the ECJ's ruling in *Dumez Bâtiment and Tracona v Hessische Landesbank* (1990). In that case, the company in France was injured as a result of losses suffered by a subsidiary situated in a different Member State. These losses were caused, it was alleged, by a German bank which had withdrawn certain credit facilities from the subsidiary. The subsidiary company was registered in Germany. The ECJ held that the French company could not institute action in the place where it had discovered the consequential financial loss.

This conservative approach was subsequently confirmed in *Marinari v Lloyds Bank* (1996). There, the claimant was an Italian domiciliary. It had lodged some promissory notes with a branch of Lloyds Bank in England. The bank was suspicious of the origin of the notes and informed the police. The claimant was arrested and the notes were seized. The prosecution was later withdrawn and the claimant took action against Lloyds Bank in Italy for wrongful detention of the notes, for consequent damage to his reputation and for financial loss due to his being unable to perform several contracts related to those notes. Lloyds Bank challenged the jurisdiction of the Italian court, arguing that the damage had occurred in the UK, not in Italy. The ECJ stated that the term 'place where the harmful event occurred' must be interpreted as not referring to the place where the victim claims to have suffered financial loss consequent to initial damage, arising and suffered by him in another Contracting State.

As far as Elgar is concerned, though, it would seem to be open to him to argue that the harmful event actually occurred in England, as that was the place where the advice was received and acted upon. This argument is a strong one, in that the advice was intended to be received in England and, until it was received and acted on, it could, at least in theory, be withdrawn by the defendants without any resulting harm.

It might be useful to refer to the rule in *Shevill v Presse Alliance* (1996), where the ECJ held that it is left to the national conflict of laws rules to determine what constitutes harm. It was argued in that case that, as the claimant had merely claimed that harm or damage had occurred in England and had not actually proved it, Art 5(3) could not apply. This was rejected by the House of Lords, following the ECJ's preliminary ruling on the issue. The position is that, since English law (as the law of the court seised with jurisdiction) presumed harm to have occurred following the publication of a defamatory statement, this was sufficient for the claimant's reliance on Art 5(3). In Elgar's case, English law does not presume damage in the negligence action. This implies, therefore, that it must be shown that the harmful event did occur within jurisdiction; otherwise, Art 5(3) could not be relied upon.

The next important question is whether Art 21 will apply, thus compelling either the Italian or the English court (but not both together) to stay proceedings until such time as the jurisdiction of the court first seised with jurisdiction is established. Before Art 21 may be used, a few preliminary points must be satisfied. The first is that both sets of proceedings must involve the same cause of action and must be between the same parties. In the present case, it may be assumed that the cause of action, that is, entitlement and compensation under the contract to provide financial advice, is the same. It does not appear to be relevant that, under the two *lex fori*, the actual labels of the cause of action are different, as long as the subject matter of the dispute is the same. Under Art 21, neither court has any discretion in the matter, unlike in a situation of *lis pendens* under common law (*S & W Berisford plc v New Hampshire Insurance* (1990)).

The final question for consideration is which court is first seised? In *Zelger v Salinitri* (1984), the court that is first seised is the court before which the proceedings first become 'definitely pending'. To determine when the proceedings were definitely pending, the law of the seat of that particular court must be referred to. The original position was stated in *Kloeckner v Gatoil* (1990), where it was held that proceedings on an action *in personam* were 'definitely pending' following the issue of the claim, not when it was finally served. That case was not followed by the Court of Appeal in *Dresser UK Ltd v Falcongate Freight Management* (1992), where it was decided that, as a general rule, an action is only definitely pending after the claim has been served. The exceptions to the general rule do not apply to Elgar; therefore, as far as he is concerned, the action before the English court will only be treated as definitely pending on 25 March. This means that, unless Italian laws take the same stance, it may be that the Italian court was first seised with jurisdiction.

If this is the case, the only way Elgar can insist upon action in England is to show, to the satisfaction of the Italian court, that they do not have jurisdiction. Once this issue has been established successfully, the original action in England can proceed (Art 21).

It should be further noted that, when or if the Draft Regulation on Jurisdiction, Recognition and Enforcement of Judgments in Civil and Commercial Matters (which is intended to replace and update the Brussels Convention) comes into effect, a uniform definition as to when a court becomes seised will apply throughout all Contracting States. The uniform rule, as set out in Art 30, states that, in countries where proceedings are first served and subsequently filed with the court, the court becomes seised when they are served. In States where proceedings are filed first before being served, the date on which they are served is the date that the court becomes seised.

In conclusion, it should be added that the joinder of defendants provision in Art 6(1) does not apply. This is because the relevant court, namely the English court, is not a court of either Dvorak's or Fauré's domicile.

Question 22

Critically examine the English courts' discretion to grant interim remedies under the Lugano and Brussels Conventions, giving special emphasis to the objectives of interim remedies.

Answer plan

Clearly, the starting point for this essay is Art 24 of the Conventions. The essay should deal with the objectives of Art 24. It should then trace the development in case law from *De Cavel v De Cavel (No 1)* (1979) to *Mietz v Intership Yachting Sneek BV* (1999).

Mention should be made to the granting of a freezing injunction under English law. In this regard, students should refer to *The Siskina* (1979).

Another provision that should be discussed is s 26 of the Civil Jurisdiction and Judgments Act 1982 and how that operates in the active promotion of compliance with the two Conventions.

Answer

Article 24 of the Brussels and Lugano Conventions provides that application may be made to the courts of a Contracting State for such provisional measures, including protective measures, as may be available under the law of that State, even if, under these Conventions, the courts of another Contracting State have jurisdiction as to the substance of the matter. As rhetoric, it is immediately obvious that the provisions of Art 24 actively encourage courts in all Contracting States to co-operate in ensuring that the terms and tenor of the Conventions are complied with. On a pragmatic level, provisional or protective measures are necessary to ensure that the parties' positions are preserved pending an outcome under the allocation of jurisdiction between Contracting States, and to ensure that the final judgment would not be defeated by the siphoning of assets out of jurisdiction, continuing damage, etc.

As far as English common law is concerned, where the claimant is bringing an action against the defendant in England, he is clearly entitled to ancillary or provisional relief to prevent the defendant from hurting or undermining the final outcome of his case. Under Art 24, this rule seems to have been extended to cases where the claimant's main action is not within jurisdiction but is in another Contracting State. This essay will examine how this discretion should be exercised, paying special regard to some of the guidelines given by the ECJ in recent cases.

The ECJ held in *Reichert v Dresdner Bank (No 2)* (1992) that Art 24 is confined to measures which preserve the factual or legal position of the parties. The means that the parties' alleged rights or duties are preserved until the case is finally resolved according to the procedure described in the Conventions. That this element of the main proceedings is underpinned by the Conventions is important. It was held on a number of occasions that Art 24 will not apply unless the substantive, main proceedings could be properly defined as being within the material scope of Art 1.

Another issue to be explored is whether the English court may make an order for provisional relief which compels the defendant to do or refrain from doing some particular act in a foreign country. This is evidently a problematic issue in the light of the international law doctrines of State sovereignty and judicial comity.

As far as English law is concerned, there are two main types of provisional relief – an injunction to address continuing damage and an injunction to prevent the removal of assets from a particular place in an attempt to defeat the claimant's entitlement to compensation. Both would fall within the remit of Art 24, as long as they are ancillary or adjunct to main causes of action described in Art 1. It is clear from the Civil Procedure Rules (CPR) 1998 that a claimant may be entitled to measures in support of one of the two main provisional remedies named above for any of the following orders: an order to inspect the defendant's property before commencement of an action (r 25.5); an order calling for the disclosure of documents before proceedings are started (r 31.16); an order for the disclosure of documents against a person who is not party to the proceedings (r 1.17); an order for the taking of a sample of relevant property (r 25.1(1)(c)(iii)); or an order for the carrying out of an experiment on or with relevant property (r 25.1(1)(c)(iv)).

Jurisdiction of the English court

At common law, the prevailing rule is that an English court may not grant interim remedies unless it is properly seised of the substance of the main action or claim. This was pronounced in *The Siskina* (1979). In that case, the claimant had applied for a Mareva injunction, or a freezing injunction, as it is now called under the CPR, to stop the defendant from removing monies paid into an English bank account. Unfortunately for the claimants, the defendant was not domiciled in England and the main action was outside the jurisdiction of the English court. It was held that the grant of the freezing injunction had to be founded on a pre-existing cause of action which was within English jurisdiction. An interlocutory injunction, like a freezing injunction, cannot stand alone.

A change can be detected in the House of Lords' decision in *Channel Tunnel Group Ltd v Balfour Beatty Construction Ltd* (1993). In that case, it was resolutely held that an English court has the power to grant interim remedies to bolster any foreign arbitration or judicial proceedings if it is clear that, under normal conflict of laws, it would have, or indeed has, jurisdiction over the substantive dispute without reliance on an arbitration or choice of forum clause.

As far as statute law is concerned, s 25 of the Civil Jurisdiction and Judgments Act 1982, as amended by the Civil Jurisdiction and Judgments Act 1982 (Interim Relief) Order 1997, provides that the High Court shall have power to grant interim relief in relation to proceedings of the following descriptions: (a) proceedings commenced or to be commenced otherwise than in a Brussels or Lugano Contracting State; and (b) proceedings whose subject matter is not within the scope of the 1968 Convention as determined by Art 1 thereof. The 1997 Order increases the power of the High Court to grant interim relief to assist legal proceedings in other countries. Under the old law, contained in the unamended 1982 Act, such relief could only be granted where the principal proceedings were taking place in a country which was a party to the Brussels or Lugano Conventions and where those proceedings were within the scope of those Conventions. The Order effectively removes those two limitations on the courts' powers.

It seems to be accepted that the position under the Conventions is different, although Art 24 clearly provides that the power to grant provisional relief in support of the allocation of jurisdiction is specifically confined to 'such protective measures as may be available under the [national] law'. Nevertheless, it would seem to be contrary to the spirit of the Convention to limit that power to the boundaries delineated in *The Siskina*.

Incidentally, s 24 provides that an interim remedy can be granted pending trial or appeal, even where the issue to be tried or appealed is in relation to the jurisdiction of the court or where a reference for a preliminary ruling has been made to the ECJ under the 1971 Protocol.

The effect of these provisions in relation to an action being heard in another Contracting State is that an order made by the English High Court which freezes the assets of the defendant can be served abroad without leave of court. The fact that leave is unnecessary demonstrates the co-operative spirit of the Conventions.

Freezing injunction

The more important interim or provisional remedy in support of Convention proceedings is the freezing injunction. This injunction may be more accurately regarded as a protective measure. It is protective because it ensures that the defendant's assets, which could subsequently be used to settle the compensation or damages secured by the claimant, are not dissipated or siphoned away.

Until 1975, it was long settled that English law did not permit an injunction to restrain a person who was alleged to be a debtor from parting with his property in avoidance of a debt (*Robinson v Pickering* (1881)). Under the traditional rules, the claimant had to obtain judgment first (either summarily or after trial) and then attempt execution of the judgment and, where the situation warranted, institute bankruptcy or winding-up proceedings. This 'honourable' method of execution made it easy for the unscrupulous defendant to transfer his assets out of jurisdiction in order to deny the claimant the justice of a judgment.

The law was changed by the Court of Appeal in *Mareva Compania Naviera SA v International Bulk Carriers SA* (1975). In that case, it was held that, where the claimant is able to show a good arguable claim to entitlement to monies from a defendant, and where there is a real risk of the defendant removing the assets from jurisdiction or disposing of them so as to render them unavailable or untraceable, an injunction can be issued. Rule 25.1(1) of the CPR defines the scope of the injunction in these words: '... an order restraining a party from removing from the jurisdiction assets located there; or restraining a party from dealing with any assets, whether located within jurisdiction or not.' It is clear, therefore, that the rule under statutory law is wider than that as originally set out in *Mareva* and accommodates the rule in *Babanaft International Co SA v Bassatne* (1990).

Under r 25.2(1) of the CPR, where the main proceedings are to take place within jurisdiction, the court may grant an interim remedy, including a freezing injunction, before a claim has been made, only if:

- the matter is urgent; or
- it is otherwise desirable to do so in the interests of justice.

These provisions would seem to reinforce the rules surrounding the grant of a freezing injunction both at common law and under the old rules of procedure. A worldwide injunction (namely, one which prevents the defendant from dealing with assets located abroad in such a way as to deny the fruit of the claimant's action) may be sought in support of proceedings taking place within jurisdiction. It was asserted in *Derby & Co Ltd v Weldon (No 6)* (1990), however, that, although the court would be prepared to order a worldwide freezing injunction, it could only be made if the circumstances were so exceptional as to render this encroachment on another State's territorial integrity justifiable in the interests of urgency and justice.

Rule 25.2(1) further provides that an order for an interim remedy may be made at any time. This means that the claimant may apply for an interim order or injunction before proceedings have started abroad and/or after the foreign judgment has been given. However, that rule is subject to any rule, practice direction or other enactment which provides otherwise.

Unless England is the forum for the main proceedings, the *Babanaft* rule requires that a freezing order be confined to assets located within the jurisdiction. Where the proceedings are held abroad, it is only in the most exceptional circumstances that an interim remedy will be made in support of those foreign proceedings. Another condition for the grant of an extraterritorial injunction in these cases is that it should be demonstrated that the defendant does not have sufficient assets within the jurisdiction to satisfy the potential debt.

However, it seems that, at times, a worldwide injunction in support of foreign proceedings might be condign. In *Republic of Haiti v Duvalier* (1990), Haiti had instituted an action in France against the defendants. It was alleged by Haiti that the defendants had embezzled large sums of money belonging to the country. It applied for a worldwide injunction and an order calling for disclosure of the whereabouts of these assets. The Court of Appeal decided that an order should be given, even though the main proceedings were to take place in France and not in England. It might also be recalled that, where proceedings have been commenced in a country other than a Brussels or Lugano Contracting State, the 1997 Interim Relief Order provides that interim relief can be granted in aid of foreign proceedings which fall outside the purview of the Conventions.

This exercise of discretion should necessarily take into account the interests of third parties. As can be seen in Lord Donaldson MR's judgment in *Derby & Co Ltd v Weldon (Nos 3 and 4)* (1990), the grant of a worldwide injunction should contain protective conditions to preserve the interests of banks, guarantors and other third parties.

Rule 25.4(1) of the CPR provides that, where the remedy sought is in relation to proceedings taking place or which will take place outside the jurisdiction or the application is made under s 33 of the Supreme Court Act 1981 (for ancillary orders calling for disclosure, inspection, etc), the application must follow the procedure set out in Pt 23, which, *inter alia*, requires the service of proper notice to the respondent. It would appear that the new procedure does not do away with the rule that a provisional remedy could be served outside the jurisdiction to another Contracting State without leave.

Extraterritoriality under Art 24

The rule in Art 24 of the Conventions makes express reference to remedies as *may* be available under the law of the Contracting State in relation to the order of provisional relief. This phrase was examined in *Mietz v Intership Yachting Sneek BV* (1999), where the ECJ held that the national court has a choice in deciding to whether to grant interim relief, including provisional or protective measures. It was considered that, where the court has jurisdiction over the merits of the case, it should be free to grant any order within its procedural competence at national law. If it does not have substantive or material jurisdiction over the main dispute (as in *Republic of Haiti v Duvalier* (1990)), it can still grant interim remedies in reliance on Art 24, but any such remedy issued must be reversible. This means that it must be possible to neutralise the effects of the remedy if it turns out that it should not have been given in the first place. In *Mietz*, the ECJ said:

> ... a judgment ordering interim payment of contractual consideration, delivered at the end of a procedure such as that provided for under Arts 289–97 of the Netherlands Code of Civil Procedure by a court not having jurisdiction under the 1968 Convention as to the substance of the matter, is not a provisional measure capable of being granted under Art 24 of that Convention, unless repayment to the defendant of the sum awarded is guaranteed if the plaintiff is unsuccessful as regards the substance of his claim and the measure ordered relates only to specific assets of the defendant located within the area of the territorial jurisdiction of the court to which application is made.

Further, and more importantly, it must be in relation to assets within the jurisdiction of the court making the order. The effect of this decision seems to be that a freezing order in relation to assets in another Contracting State (for example, France) could not be properly granted by an English court. Whether there are any exceptions to the rule (as in *Republic of Haiti v Duvalier* (1990)) is unclear.

The ECJ went on to say that, where a court in another Contracting State is asked to enforce such an order, in order to do so, it would have to enquire whether the court making that order was entitled in the first place. This would seem to derogate from the principle of legal certainty.

Conclusion

It is unclear how this construction of Art 24 would impact on the hitherto wide powers of the English courts to grant freezing injunctions over assets held by a defendant in a foreign country even though there is no substantive action taking place in England. *Mietz* therefore emphasises the importance of the element of judicial discretion and comity, but unfortunately fails to take on board the practice of worldwide injunctions as applied in the various Contracting States.

Question 23*

Anna, a British national, and John, an American citizen, were married in 1991. Their two daughters, Brenda and Paula, were born in the US in 1991 and 1992 respectively. Since 1993, John has been working for the US Government. In 1994, he was appointed a cultural attaché to the US Embassy in London and the family moved to the UK.

In 1995, Anna began divorce proceedings in the UK and applied for residence orders in respect of her two daughters, pursuant to the provisions of the Children Act 1989. Those proceedings were set aside on the ground of the diplomatic immunity enjoyed by her husband in the UK. In 1996, John was ordered by the US Government to return to the US with his family. Before they left, Anna issued an originating summons in an English court, seeking a declaration under s 8 of the Child Abduction Act 1985 that the removal of her children from the UK by John was a wrongful removal within the meaning and terms of Art 3 of the Hague Convention on International Child Abduction.

John contests the jurisdiction of the English court on the grounds of both State and diplomatic immunity and seeks the dismissal of the English proceedings.

While John was employed as a cultural attaché, he entered into a contract with Jeremy, a British national, to purchase office equipment, including 10 computers, for the US Embassy. Jeremy has not been paid. John argues that Jeremy cannot bring proceedings against him because he bought all the equipment on behalf of the US Government and the US Government is entitled to rely on the doctrine of State immunity.

Advise Anna and Jeremy.

Answer plan

The question focuses on the limitations on jurisdiction of the English courts and, in particular, on the distinction between State and diplomatic immunity. In order to determine whether John will be successful in challenging the English proceedings, it is necessary to examine the above facts in the light of the scope of both the State Immunity Act 1978 and the Diplomatic Privileges Act 1964. In order to determine whether John can rely on State immunity, it is necessary to examine the concepts of acts *jure imperii* and acts *jure gestionis*. When advising Anna, the judgment in *P v P (Diplomatic Immunity: Jurisdiction)* (1998) should be taken into consideration.

Answer

Under traditional common law rules, there are a number of limitations imposed on the jurisdiction of English courts. The first concerns the subject matter of the dispute. Actions relating to foreign immovables, foreign intellectual property, foreign revenue law, foreign penal law and discovery of documents outside the jurisdiction are beyond the competence of English courts.

The second limitation relates to the kind of relief sought by the parties. In the area affecting the matrimonial status of the parties, the jurisdiction of English courts must be based not only on the service of the claim on the respondent but also on additional connecting factors, such as the domicile or habitual residence of the parties.

The third limitation concerns the persons involved in the dispute. Certain persons, such as alien enemies, cannot invoke the jurisdiction of English courts, whilst others, such as sovereigns and sovereign States, may claim exemption from the jurisdiction.

Finally, there are restrictions based on statutes enacted in England.

Our question involves immunity from the jurisdiction of the English courts, which may be claimed by foreign States, heads of foreign States and diplomatic representatives of foreign States. The extent of immunity enjoyed by a foreign sovereign or sovereign foreign State was set out in the European Convention on State Immunity 1972, which was given effect in the UK by the State Immunity Act 1978. The scope of diplomatic immunity was the subject of the 1961 Vienna Convention on Diplomatic Intercourse and Immunities. The Diplomatic Privileges Act 1964 implements this Convention in the UK.

The scope of State immunity has changed over the centuries. Originating as a concept of absolute immunity, covering all actions of a foreign State and reflecting the medieval personification of a State and its ruler, it has become subject to a number of limitations both *ratione personae* and *rationae materiae*. The concept of absolute immunity was endorsed and explained by Marshall CJ in the US Supreme Court in *Exchange v McFaddon* (1812), in the context of a dispute involving *Exchange*, a ship, whose ownership was claimed by both the Government of France and a number of US nationals. It was held that:

> ... the full and absolute territorial jurisdiction, being like the attribute of every sovereign, and being incapable of conferring extraterritorial power, would not seem to contemplate foreign sovereigns nor their sovereign rights as its objects. One sovereign being in no respect amenable to another; and being bound by obligations of the highest character not to degrade the dignity of his nation, by placing himself or its sovereign rights within the jurisdiction of another ...

The need to impose restrictions on State immunity became apparent with the development of international trade at the end of 19th century. States became increasingly involved in commercial activities. The emergence of Communist States in the 20th century further accentuated this tendency: these States, along with their trading organisations, entered into commercial dealings with foreign individuals and companies. The latter had no remedy under their national laws if a dispute arose, because a foreign State or its trading organisation could rely on the concept of sovereign immunity and thereby claim immunity from judicial process.

The growing pressure toward establishing a more realistic and pragmatic approach led to a distinction between the public acts of a State (acts *jure imperii*) and private acts, such as trading and commercial activities (acts *jure gestionis*). A State could rely on its immunity only in relation to acts *jure imperii*. The Supreme Court of Austria in *Dralle v Republic of Czechoslovakia* (1950) endorsed this distinction. Other States have followed. Under the auspices of the Council of Europe, European States confirmed this restrictive approach to the concept of State immunity in the Convention on State Immunity 1972, which was implemented in the UK by the State Immunity Act 1978. Even before the State Immunity Act 1978 become operational the UK, courts endorsed the new approach in two cases – *The Philippine Admiral* (1977) and *Trendtex Trading Corporation Ltd v Central Bank of Nigeria* (1977). It was re-affirmed by the House of Lords in *Congreso del Partido* (1981), a case concerning the common law pre-1978.

In order to advise Jeremy, it is necessary to examine the scope of the State Immunity Act 1978, taking into account the fact that John purchased office equipment for a governmental office and was therefore acting on behalf of the US. The 1978 Act applies *erga omnes*; that is, it applies to *any* foreign State, not just to a State which is a contracting party to the 1972 European Convention on State Immunity. The fundamental principle of the 1978 Act is that a foreign State is immune from the jurisdiction of the English courts, regardless of whether it appears in the proceedings. There are 10 provisions setting out exceptions to that rule. For our purposes, the most important is s 3 of the 1978 Act, which provides that a foreign State is not immune in respect of proceedings relating to a commercial transaction. Under s 3(3)(a) of that Act, any contract for the supply of goods or services is considered to be a commercial transaction. Therefore, Jeremy may rely on the 1978 State Immunity Act in order to institute proceedings against the US Government.

In respect of Anna, the situation is more complicated. The divorce proceedings that she instituted against John were rightly set aside by an English court on the basis of the diplomatic immunity enjoyed by John. Under the Diplomatic Privileges Act 1964, John, as a cultural attaché, is regarded as a diplomatic agent and is thus exempt from the civil and criminal jurisdiction of the English courts in respect of both his official and private acts. In *Shaw v Shaw* (1979), it was held that 'civil proceedings' include a divorce petition. The question of whether John can rely on his diplomatic status when he removes his children at the end of his diplomatic posting must be assessed in the light of Art 39(2) of the Vienna Convention on Diplomatic Intercourses and Immunities. This provides:

> When the functions of a person enjoying privileges and immunities have come to any end, such privileges and immunities shall normally cease at the moment when he leaves the country, or on expiry of a reasonable period in which to do so, but shall subsist until that time, even in case of armed conflict. However, with respect to acts performed by such a person in exercise of his function as a member of the mission, immunity shall continue to subsist.

John's act of removing his children from the jurisdiction cannot be regarded as an act performed in the exercise of a diplomatic function within the meaning of Art 39(2). As a result, John cannot rely on his diplomatic status to claim exemption from the jurisdiction of the English courts. In *P v P* (1998), Sir Stephen Brown, President of the Family Division, emphasised that diplomatic privileges and immunities were functional in character, aimed at ensuring the efficient performance of the functions of diplomatic missions as representing States, not at benefiting individual diplomats. In the circumstances, which are similar to our scenario, his Lordship held that the removal of children from the UK by a father at the end of his diplomatic posting could not be construed as an act performed in the exercise of a diplomat's functions within the scope of Art 39(2) of the 1961 Vienna Convention on Diplomatic Relations.

However, John has also challenged the jurisdiction of the English courts on the ground of State immunity. John was ordered by the US Government to leave the UK with his family. Therefore, his action was of a governmental nature and accordingly enjoys State immunity from legal proceedings in the UK. As a result, John will be successful in his act of removing his children from the UK.

It is submitted that Anna will fail in her action against John. Although John cannot rely on his diplomatic immunity, he can invoke the concept of State immunity in order to dismiss the English proceedings. His return to the US occurred in compliance with the direct order of his employer, the US Government. It was an act of a governmental nature and, as such, is accorded State immunity from legal proceedings in the UK.

* by Alina Kaczorowska

Question 24*

Critically examine the proposal for a Council Regulation on Jurisdiction and the Recognition and Enforcement of Judgments in Matrimonial Matters and in Matters of Joint Parental Responsibility for Children (599PC0220).

Answer plan

The main features of the proposal should be examined. Particular attention should be paid to its objectives, its scope of application *rationae materiae*, its rules on jurisdiction and the manner in which it deals with *lis alibi pendens* and provisional measures. Furthermore, the necessity of the inclusion of child custody within the scope of the proposal should be assessed in the light of the Hague Convention of 19 October 1996 on Jurisdiction, Applicable Law, Recognition, Enforcement and Co-Operation in Respect of Parental Responsibility and Measures for the Protection of Children.

Answer

The necessity of establishing uniform rules on jurisdiction in matrimonial matters throughout the territory of the European Union (EU) derives from two sources: first, the new perception of the rights of citizens of the EU after entry into force of the Maastricht Treaty; and, secondly, the difficulties arising between Member States of the EU concerning the recognition of divorces, especially between Germany and France, since those countries have no arrangement facilitating mutual recognition of divorces. Indeed, only eight out of the 15 Member States have ratified the Hague Convention of 1 June 1970 on the Recognition of Divorces and Legal Separation. The 1970 Hague Convention is in force in the following Member States: the UK, Italy, the Netherlands, Luxembourg, Portugal, Denmark, Finland and Sweden.

On 28 May 1998, the Council of the European Union, by virtue of Art K.3(2)(c) of the Treaty on European Union, adopted the Convention on Jurisdiction and the Recognition and Enforcement of Judgments in Matrimonial Matters (often referred to as the Brussels II Convention) and a Protocol on its interpretation, conferring upon the ECJ the task of interpreting its provisions. All Member States have signed both instruments. The Brussels II Convention specifies that, before its entry into force, Member States may, by reciprocal declaration, apply the Convention as between themselves. France and Germany have made such a declaration. However, entry into operation of the Treaty of Amsterdam on 1 May 1999 has brought about changes in the manner in which the Brussels II Convention will enter into force. As the Brussels II Convention concerns a very important aspect of the lives of EU citizens, and taking into account the fact that the subject matter covered by that Convention is within the scope of Art 65 of the EC Treaty, the Commission submitted a proposal in 4 May 1999 for a Council Regulation replacing the Brussels II Convention.The substance of the Brussels II Convention was incorporated into the proposal.

Both the proposal and the Brussels II Convention were modelled on the 1968 Brussels Convention. It promulgated uniform Community rules on jurisdiction and the mechanisms for the recognition and enforcement of decisions delivered by national courts in this area. Within its anticipated scope of application were petitions for and decrees of divorce; legal separation of spouses; and annulment of marriages and applications and orders relating to parental responsibility for children of both spouses (but only if ancillary to proceedings for divorce, separation and annulment). The provisions regarding child custody could be seen as hardly necessary in the light of the adoption of the Hague Convention of 19 October 1996 on Jurisdiction, Applicable Law, Recognition, Enforcement and Co-Operation in Respect of Parental Responsibility and Measures for the Protection of Children, which has not yet entered into force, but is regarded as an outstanding international instrument in terms of legal drafting and the solutions it introduces. In order to avoid clashes between the proposal and the Hague Convention, the former mirrors the provisions of the latter.

The most important part of the proposal is the intended rules on jurisdiction. They are, on the one hand, sufficiently flexible to satisfy the expectations of the parties to those proceedings and, on the other hand, realistic enough to ensure that there is a nexus between the court seised of the proceedings and the parties to those proceedings.

The proposal makes a distinction between direct and semi-direct jurisdiction to entertain petitions for divorce, separation and annulment. The provisions regarding direct jurisdiction are based on habitual residence of spouses at the date of the application and apply uniformly in all Contracting States. Semi-direct jurisdiction is based on the concept of nationality or domicile for the UK and Ireland. In addition, the proposal refers to rules of private international law on jurisdiction of each Contracting State where no court of any Member State has jurisdiction under the proposal. This is known as residual jurisdiction.

In relation to direct jurisdiction, there is no hierarchy of rules. There are alternative fora, from which the petitioner is entitled to select the most convenient to his case. On the basis of habitual residence, the courts of the Member State will have jurisdiction if:

- both spouses have their habitual residence in the territory of that State; or

- both spouses had their last common habitual residence in that State, provided one of them still has his habitual residence there; or
- in the case of joint application, either spouse is habitually resident in the forum State; or
- the respondent has his habitual residence in that State; or
- the petitioner has his habitual residence in that State and has resided there for at least one year immediately before the application; or
- the petitioner has resided there for at least six months immediately before the application and is either a national of the forum State or is domiciled there on a long term settled basis.

The notion of 'habitual residence' has not been defined, though the proposal indicates indirectly the period of time necessary to establish it. In this respect, the proposal provides that, in order to commence proceedings in a Member State, the petitioner must have habitually resided there for at least one year immediately before the application.

In seems that the period of one year has been accepted as sufficient for jurisdictional purposes in England and that ordinary residence has been equated with habitual residence. In the context of the Hague Convention on the Civil Aspects of International Child Abduction, the House of Lords held in proceedings for divorce under the Hague Convention that an Indian, domiciled in India, who was ordinary resident in England for one year for educational purposes, should be considered as habitually resident in England for the same period (*Kapur v Kapur* (1984); also *V v B (A Minor) (Abduction)* (1991)).

In relation to semi-direct jurisdiction, nationality (or domicile in the English sense for the UK and Ireland) is regarded as a connecting factor. The proposal allocates jurisdiction to the courts of a Member State of which, at the date of application, both spouses are nationals or, in the case of the UK and Ireland, at the date that both are domiciled there.

When no court of any Member State has jurisdiction, that is, in the case of residual jurisdiction, the Convention has recourse to a Contracting State's domestic rules on jurisdiction. In addition, when jurisdiction is based on the nationality of the petitioner, the principle of equal treatment entitles a petitioner who is a national of a Member State and who is habitually resident within the territory of another Member State to avail himself of the rules of jurisdiction applicable in the State of habitual residence in the same manner as the nationals of that State.

In order to ensure the proper administration of justice, the proposal states that a court which deals with a matrimonial application also has jurisdiction to entertain a matrimonial cross-application, and that a court which has granted a legal separation also has jurisdiction to convert that separation into a divorce.

Jurisdictional rules regarding child custody operate under very restrictive conditions. The proposal allocates jurisdiction to courts in a Member State in cases where:

- a child is a biological or adopted child of both spouses;
- the child resides habitually in that Member State; and
- the custody proceedings are ancillary to matrimonial proceedings commenced under jurisdictional rules laid down by the proposal.

In order to extend jurisdiction of the courts of Member States entertaining petitions for divorce, separation or annulment, the proposal provides that, even if a child is not habitually resident in a State, its courts will have jurisdiction over child custody if the child has his habitual residence in another Member State, at least one of the parents has parental responsibility for the child and such jurisdiction has been accepted by the parents and is in the best interests of the child. There is also a provision requiring a court exercising ancillary custody jurisdiction under the proposal to take into consideration the Hague Convention of 25 October 1980 on Civil Aspects of International Child Abduction. If it has received notice of a wrongful removal or retention of a child to or in its own country, the court must not decide on the merits of custodial rights until it has been decided that the child is not to be returned under the Abduction Convention, or unless an application under the Abduction Convention is not lodged within a reasonable time following receipt of the notice. At present, all Member States (with the exception of Belgium) are contracting parties to the Abduction Convention.

In respect of *lis alibi pendens*, the proposal provides that, when proceedings fall within its material scope of application (including child custody) and involve the same cause of action between the same parties, any court other than the court first seised must, of its own motion, stay its proceedings until such time as the jurisdiction of the court first seised is established. The same rule applies even where proceedings between the same parties do not have the same cause of action (however, matters relating to parental responsibility are excluded). This means that if, for example, one spouse commences divorce proceedings in France and the other later institutes annulment proceedings in Italy in respect of the same marriage, the court in France will have jurisdiction.

Once the jurisdiction of the court first seised is established, any other court must decline jurisdiction of its own motion, even if the respondent has entered an appearance. In this respect, there are different approaches under the 1968 Brussels Convention and the proposal.

Provisional or protective measures may be ordered by any court within the EU when persons or assets are present in that State. Therefore, it is not necessary for that court to have jurisdiction in relation to the merits of the case. However, provisional or protective measures are limited to the territory of the Member State in which those measures have been granted.

In order to ensure uniformity of decisions throughout the EU, its Member States adopted a Protocol on the interpretation of the Brussels II Convention, which conferred power upon the ECJ to interpret it. This Protocol is now redundant. The replacement of the Brussels II Convention by an EC Regulation means that, under Art 234 of the EC Treaty, the ECJ will exercise its jurisdiction in the same manner as in relation to all Community law.

It is submitted that the proposed Regulation incorporating the provisions of the Brussels II Convention constitutes a step forward in the creation of the area of freedom, security and justice for citizens of the European Community. It promotes further development of judicial co-operation among the Member States by unifying rules for jurisdiction, recognition and enforcement of judgments in matrimonial matters. The proposal concerns a very important aspect of the lives of citizens of the Member States and, as such, demonstrates the importance that the EU attaches to its citizens.

* by Alina Kaczorowska

CHAPTER 4

RECOGNITION AND ENFORCEMENT OF FOREIGN JUDGMENTS AND ARBITRAL AWARDS

Introduction

The main issue in this chapter is the extent to which a successful claimant in foreign judicial or arbitral proceedings is entitled to enforce that award in England and Wales. Enforcement is frequently connected with the act of judicial recognition of the award by the English courts.

At common law, the claimant has only one recourse to 'enforce' the foreign award. He must serve a claim on the defendant, instituting an action against him based on the judgment debt in the English court. Where the judgment debt is entitled to recognition and/or enforcement under any one of the Civil Jurisdiction and Judgments Act 1982 (incorporating the Brussels and Lugano Conventions), the Foreign (Reciprocal Enforcement) Act 1933 or the Administration of Justice Act 1920, recourse to the old common law rule is unnecessary.

There is a draft Regulation on Jurisdiction, Recognition and Enforcement of Judgments which attempts to make the enforcement of judgments between Contracting States even more efficient, limiting the various defences that States can use to refuse recognition and enforcement.

In respect of the enforcement and recognition of an international arbitral award, regard must be had to the New York Convention on the Recognition and Enforcement of Foreign Arbitral Awards 1958 (which has been given effect to by the Arbitration Act 1975) and the Geneva Convention 1927.

The general rule on recognition and enforcement of foreign awards is that the English court will enforce a foreign judgment if that court was a competent court so to do under the rules of competency in English law. On the elements of jurisdiction, see Chapter 3.

Once the foreign tribunal's jurisdiction or international competence has been established, it is important to examine the question of whether the defendant is entitled to raise any of the defences recognised by English law. These defences include public policy considerations, the taint of fraud in the judgment obtained, failure of natural justice and the application of the Protection of Trading Interests Act 1980. These defences are similar, regardless of whether the enforcement and recognition exercise is carried out via the statutory framework, the common law or the Brussels Convention. Similar considerations apply in respect of international arbitral awards.

Checklist

Students should have a good understanding of the following:

- enforcement of a judgment debt at common law;
- recognition and enforcement under the Brussels Convention;
- recognition and enforcement under the Administration of Justice Act 1920 and the Foreign (Reciprocal Enforcement) Act 1933;
- rules of jurisdiction and the international competency of the foreign court;
- defences to the recognition and enforcement of foreign judgments and international arbitral awards;
- stay of proceedings under Art 30 of the Brussels Convention;
- operation of the New York Convention on the Recognition and Enforcement of Foreign Arbitral Awards 1958.

Question 25

Quek, who used to live in Atlantis, entered into a contract with Ray to build a factory in Mireland. Ray resides in Mireland.

In 1993, Ray brought an action in Mireland against Quek for breach of contract. The Mirish court gave leave to serve the claim on Quek, who was on holiday in Spain at the time. Quek's lawyer appeared before a Mirish judge to contest the court's jurisdiction. The judge overruled the lawyer's contention and gave judgment in favour of Ray.

Damages of £100,000 were ordered. Also, in accordance with a Mirish statute, a charge of £1,000, payable to the claimant, was imposed on Quek as a litigant who, in the court's opinion, had vexatiously challenged its jurisdiction. Quek intends to appeal against the decision. The appeal is to be heard by the Mirish High Court in the near future.

In the meantime, Ray wishes to enforce the Mirish judgment in England, where Quek now lives (in London). Ray believes that Quek has considerable assets in England.

Advise Ray.

Answer plan

In order to address this question effectively, the student must highlight the following matters:

- the different regimes within which recognition and enforcement may be executed;
- the treatment of jurisdiction of the foreign court under English law;
- the interaction of public policy vis à vis penal damages in the enforcement and recognition procedure;
- the enforceability of damages equivalent to exemplary damages;
- whether the penal award may be severed from the enforceable damages.

Answer

In determining the applicable regime to the resolution of this problem, the first question is whether Mireland, where the judicial award was made, is a Contracting State to the 1968 Brussels Convention. Since it is clear that Mireland, not being an EC Member State, is not privy to the Convention, the issue will have to be dealt with under the common law as may be qualified by the Administration of Justice Act 1920 and the Foreign

Judgments (Reciprocal Enforcement) Act 1933. It should perhaps be noted that, since Mireland is not part of the Commonwealth, it is unlikely that the 1920 Act has any application. Be that as it may, the rules contained in statute and common law are similar in substance.

At common law, the procedure appears to be that laid down in *Grant v Easton* (1853). The judgment creditor intending to enforce the judgment debt may not do so by direct execution of the debt. He must bring an action on the foreign judgment, normally in reliance on RSC Ord 14, on the ground that the defendant has no defence to the debt.

Where, on the other hand, the Foreign Judgments (Reciprocal Enforcement) Act 1933 is to be applied, for example, if it is established that an Order in Council has extended the application of the Act to Mireland (usually as a result of the foreign State's agreement to recognise and enforce a judgment of the English court (s 1)), the claimant is then entitled to register the Mirish judgment as of right. He could then enforce the judgment without further need of proof.

Whether the rules of the common law or the 1933 Act are used, the English court must satisfy itself that the foreign court has jurisdiction according to English rules of private international law. In *Buchanan v Rucker* (1808), the plaintiff attempted to enforce the judgment of a court in Tobago. The defendant had never been in the territory, nor had he submitted to its jurisdiction. Substituted service was executed by way of nailing the claim on the courthouse door. Lord Ellenborough held that such assumed jurisdiction could not bind the hands of the English courts. Jurisdiction of the foreign court must be proper in the eyes of English law.

The bases for jurisdiction were classed by Buckley LJ in *Emanuel v Symon* (1908) as follows:

- the defendant is a subject of the foreign country where the judgment has been obtained;
- the defendant was resident in the foreign country when the action was commenced;
- the defendant had selected the forum as the one in which he would sue, should a cause of action accrue to him;
- the defendant has made voluntary appearance before the foreign court;

- the defendant has contracted to submit himself to the jurisdiction of the foreign court.

With the exception of the first, the above rules may be broadly channelled into two heads of jurisdiction: residence and submission.[1]

On the given facts, it is observed that Quek was not resident in Mireland when the claim was served. Although the temporary presence of the defendant in the forum concerned would have been sufficient to confer on that court jurisdiction under the rule in *Adam v Cape Industries plc* (1990), it is clear that this is not the case here. Quek was no longer a resident in Mireland when the claim was served.

The next issue, therefore, is whether his counsel, by appearing before the Mirish judge to contest the jurisdiction of the court, had entered an appearance, as required under the head of jurisdiction in *Emanuel v Symon*. According to some older authorities (such as *Harris v Taylor* (1951)), a court's indication that an appearance to argue that the court did not have jurisdiction was to be treated as submission. This position has now been replaced by s 33 of the Civil Jurisdiction and Judgments Act 1982. Section 33 provides that the defendant should not be regarded as having submitted to the jurisdiction of a foreign court if he appeared simply to do one of the following:

- contest the jurisdiction of the court; or
- ask the court to dismiss or stay proceedings on the ground that the dispute should be submitted to arbitration or to determination of the courts of another country; or
- protect or obtain the release of property seised or threatened with seizure in the proceedings.

In the light of this, Quek could not be said to have submitted to jurisdiction when his counsel appeared to contest the court's jurisdiction over him. It may be argued, however, that, by appealing to the Mirish High Court against the lower court's decision, Quek is submitting to Mirish jurisdiction. This argument is tenable only if the appeal is on the merits of the first instance judgment. If Quek is appealing only on the basis that the Mirish lower court lacked the jurisdictional power to hear his case, it is unlikely that the appeal will be treated differently to the original contest of jurisdiction.

If it is indeed established that Quek had submitted to the Mirish court's jurisdiction, the ensuing issue is whether Ray could institute proceedings in England for the enforcement of the two judgment awards or debts pending an appeal. It was held in *Nouvion v Freeman* (1889) that the foreign judgment must be 'final and conclusive' before the English courts have power to entertain an action for recognition and/or enforcement. In Lord Herschell's words, the existence of the judgment debt must be '*res judicata* between the parties at the court in which the debt was established'. The principle of *res judicata*, however, still applies even though the matter is subject to an appeal (*Colt Industries Inc v Sarlie (No 2)* (1966)). In s 1(3) of the Foreign Judgments (Reciprocal Enforcement) Act 1933, a judgment shall be deemed to be final and conclusive, notwithstanding that an appeal may be pending against it or that it may still be subject to appeal in the courts of the country of the original court. This being the state of the law, if it is successfully proved that Quek had submitted to the Mirish court's jurisdiction, Ray may seek to enforce the judgment in England subject to the following considerations.

The first consideration is whether Quek may raise any valid defence at common law against the claim lodged by Ray to enforce the judgment. The entrenched rule at common law, as stated in *Sadler v Robins* (1808) and *Russell v Smyth* (1842), is that the judgment to be enforced must be for a debt or a definite sum of money, including damages and costs. On this authority, it is pellucid that the £100,000 would be in *gremio legis* and would be successfully enforced. On the other hand, unless it is shown that the £1,000 is a true reflection of costs and not simply a penalty or tax, then its purported enforcement may be rejected.

It is for the English court to determine whether the foreign statutory provision is penal in nature (*Huntingdon v Attrill* (1893)). The rationale as stated by the Privy Council in that case is that all breaches of public law, punishable by pecuniary penalties or otherwise at the instance of the foreign government, are local, in the sense that they are only cognisable and punishable in the country where they were committed. Any enforcement of these penal provisions by the *lex fori* would be an unwarranted interference with the foreign State's sovereignty. It is submitted that, since the £1,000 is levied as a punishment, it would be penal in nature and, thus, could not be enforced at English law.

Accordingly, in s 1(2) of the 1933 Act, it is stated that a sum payable in respect of taxes or other charges of a like nature or in respect of a fine or other penalty may be enforced.

On the other hand, where the damages awarded are equivalent to the English law award of exemplary damages, they can be enforced. Under the rule laid down in *SA Consortium General Textiles v Sun and Sand Agencies Ltd* (1978), it would be necessary to enquire as to the nature of the £1,000 under Mirish law.

The final question is whether this unenforceable sum (assuming that it is penal) may be severed from the judgment and, consequently, whether Ray would still be entitled to the £100,000. The position in *Raulin v Fischer* (1911) is that it is not *contra bonos mores* to allow the enforcement of the damages where it is clearly severable from the penalty. In our case, the two awards are quite distinct from each other, making it possible for the court to remove one from the other without affecting the overall effect of the awards.

Note

1 See the judgments of the High Court in *Blohn v Desser* (1962); *Rossano v Manufacturers' Life Insurance Co Ltd* (1963); and *Vogel v RA Kohnstamm Ltd* (1973).

Question 26

Critically examine the circumstances in which an English court would refuse to recognise and subsequently enforce a judgment of a foreign court under the Convention on Jurisdiction and Enforcement of Judgments in Civil and Commercial Matters 1968.

Answer plan

This is a relatively straightforward question. There are also very few English cases on the application of Arts 26–30 of the Brussels Convention. There are, however, some European cases on the matter, which the student should take cognisance of.

A comprehensive understanding of the ambit of Art 27 is essential; it is also useful to indicate how the rules are different (if at all and to what extent) from the position at common law. Do not simply reproduce the provisions of Art 27 *et seq*. Some commentary is imperative; the question requires that a critical examination be carried out. This is not easy, as there are so few cases on the subject.

Answer

The scope of the English court's power to refuse to recognise a judgment of a foreign court is dependent on the applicable framework of recognition and enforcement of foreign judicial awards. The recognition and enforcement of foreign judgments is generally covered by the three distinct regimes: the common law rules on enforcing the judgment as a debt; the Civil Jurisdiction and Judgments Act 1982 (incorporating the Brussels and Lugano Conventions); and the two statutes applicable to non-Contracting States – the Foreign Judgments (Reciprocal Enforcement) Act 1933 and the Administration of Justice Act 1920.

The position of the Brussels Convention is founded on the general principle in Art 26, which provides that a 'judgment given in a Contracting State shall be recognised in the other Contracting States without any special procedure being required'. This is quite distinct from the common law process, whereby the defendant has to bring an action on the foreign judgment as a debt against the judgment debtor. There is no right of direct execution.

The Convention is also wider in ambit, as it permits the recognition and enforcement of relief other than money judgments; for example, specific performance and injunctions.

Article 26 is, however, not unqualified. Article 34 states that an application for recognition (and subsequently enforcement) may be refused as long as one of the circumstances in Art 27 exists. Article 27 catalogues six grounds on which a foreign judgment could be legitimately denied enforcement and recognition:

- Article 27(1) provides that, where the recognition of such a judgment is contrary to pubic policy in England, that judgment may be refused. The precise scope of this defence is not clear, as there is little judicial authority based on Art 27(1). Some assistance could perhaps be derived from a common law case, *Re Macartney* (1921), where the court refused to enforce a maintenance order made by the Maltese court. The affiliation order, which was not restricted to the child's minority, was contrary to English public policy. It is obvious from the court's judgment in *SA Consortium General Textiles v Sun and Sand Agencies Ltd* (1978) that the courts will be deliberately slow in finding a rule of public policy for the purposes of private international law.

- If the judgment was given in default of appearance and the defendant was not duly served with the claim in sufficient time to enable him to arrange for his defence (Art 27(2)), this judgment given in defiance of natural justice cannot be enforced in England. It has been held in *Pendy Plastic Products BV v Pluspunkt* (1982) that the notion and meaning of 'duly served' should follow the definition adopted by the law of the original court (that is, the court that issued the judgment), but what constitutes sufficient time is to be construed according to the law of the State in which recognition is sought.
- If the judgment is irreconcilable with a judgment given in a dispute between the same parties in the State where recognition is sought (Art 27(3)), recognition may be denied. In *Hoffman v Krieg* (1988), an attempt to enforce a maintenance order failed because the order would have been inconsistent with the divorce granted in the State where recognition was sought.
- Specific to the enforcement of maintenance claims, if the original court has decided a preliminary question on the status or legal capacity of any natural persons, rights arising out of a matrimonial relationship, or wills or succession, in a way which conflicts with a rule of English private international law, recognition may be refused. The exception is where the same result would have been reached by the application of the rules of private international law of that State.
- Under Art 27(5), if the judgment is irreconcilable with an earlier judgment given in a non-Contracting State involving the same cause of action and between the same parties,

enforcement may again be denied, provided that the earlier judgment concerned is entitled to recognition (and enforcement) in England.

Besides Art 27, the English courts may also refuse to enforce and/or recognise a foreign judgment which conflicts with the jurisdictional provisions of Arts 7–12A (insurance), 13–15 (consumer contracts) or 16 (exclusive jurisdiction). However, according to the ECJ in *LTU v Eurocontrol* (1976), English courts are not entitled to question the findings of fact arrived at by the court of the Contracting State.

An important provision is Art 16, which provides that the courts of a particular Contracting State are to have exclusive jurisdiction based on the nature of the subject matter of the dispute. Where the court of a Contracting State exercises jurisdiction contrary to Art 16, then the judgment it issues cannot be enforced in England. The cases where exclusive jurisdiction accrues in this context are proceedings relating to immovable property and rights *in rem*, the status and validity of corporations, the validity of entries in public registers and the validity and recognition of intellectual property rights.

On whether fraud is a ground for negating enforcement of a foreign judgment under the Convention (as is the case at common law), it is commonly agreed that this defence falls within the remit of Art 27(1) on public policy. In *Kendall v Kendall* (1977), for example, it was expressly stated by the court that a foreign divorce obtained by fraud need not be recognised because to do so would be contrary to public policy.

A less patent defence is that found in Art 59. Where enforcement of the foreign judgment is contrary to an existing agreement or undertaking to a non-Contracting third State, the courts may decline to effect that judgment.

It could perhaps be said that the two additional defences in the Lugano Convention could go some way to enhance and improve the operation of the Brussels Convention. Under Art 54B(3) of the Lugano Convention, the recognising court has the discretion to refuse enforcement or recognition if the grounds of jurisdiction on which the judgment has been made differ from that resulting from the Lugano Convention and the recognition or enforcement is sought against a party who is domiciled in a Contracting State which is not a member of the EC, unless the judgment may otherwise be recognised or enforced under any rule of law in the State addressed. The second specific defence is found in Art 57(4), which grants that, where the jurisdiction was assumed under some other international convention (for example, the Warsaw Convention on International Carriage by Air 1929), enforcement of the judgment must be refused where to do otherwise would be to go against the convention in question.

It seems that, although the new draft Regulation on Jurisdiction, Recognition and Enforcement of Judgments in Civil and Commercial Matters does not do away with these limitations on the mutual recognition of judgments between Contracting States, it does limit the extent to which some of these defences (especially that of public policy) could be raised. The spirit behind the simplification of existing procedures in the enforcement of judgments obtained from other Contracting States is that of co-operation and judicial comity. This spirit requires that these limitations be retained, but that they be exercised in a way which is reasonable and proportionate to the interest(s) to be preserved.

Question 27

Ben was a resident of Philistia between 1993 and 2000. In July 1999, he entered into an agreement with Chen to market Chen's home made cakes in Philistia. Chen was then living in Oland. The agreement was signed at Ben's home in Philistia.

In April 2000, Chen instituted an action for breach of contract against Ben in Philistia. Unfortunately for him, Ben had, by then, gone to England with his new wife, Delia. Chen is also alleging that Ben had stolen some money which was set aside by Chen for advertising purposes.

Under Philistian law, a claimant is not allowed to serve a 'claim' abroad where the defendant is alleged to have committed criminal offences without express leave from the Philistian Supreme Court. Chen applies for leave.

Before leave is given, Ben's attorney appears before the Philistian Supreme Court to contest the court's general jurisdiction over the subject matter. Dispensing with the issue of leave, the Philistian court holds that it has jurisdiction and proceeds to give judgment in default of appearance in Chen's favour. It further orders that Ben should pay compensation in Philistian dollars equivalent to £10,000 and punitive damages to the value of £1,000.

The UK has extended the provisions of the Foreign Judgments (Reciprocal Enforcement) Act 1933 to Philistia.

Chen wishes to enforce the Philistian judgment in England, where Ben now lives.

Advise Chen as to the requirements that must be met before the Philistian judgment can be enforced in England.

Answer plan

The student must first establish whether the Philistian court had jurisdiction over the dispute according to the rules of English law, not those of Philistia. This is in line with the rule that, without appropriate jurisdiction over the substantive issue, the English court will not recognise the foreign judgment and the judgment will not, therefore, be enforced. Jurisdiction under English law can only be satisfied where there is submission to jurisdiction by the defendant, either by agreement or appearance, or where the defendant was indeed present in the foreign jurisdiction when the claim was served.

Other rules will also apply once the issue of jurisdiction is established. The student should refer to the rules on public policy and natural justice in the 1933 Act in this regard.

Answer

The general framework for the recognition and enforcement of judgments delivered and issued by a foreign court may be classified into two main categories – judgments obtained within the EC and judgments obtained without. The fact that Chen's judgment was obtained from a State under which the Foreign Judgments (Reciprocal Enforcement) Act 1933 (the 1933 Act) applies, indicates that this falls within the latter category.

Under the 1933 Act, a judgment may be registered first and then the applicant may apply to have it enforced in this country. Section 4, however, provides that the registration may be set aside if certain conditions are not met.

In particular, under s 4(1)(ii), the court will set the registration aside if it is proved that the courts of the country of the original court had no jurisdiction in the circumstances of the case. The determination of whether the foreign court has jurisdiction over the subject matter is to be assessed on the basis of English law and not under the foreign court's own rules (*Buchanan v Rucker* (1809)). By the same token, however, English courts will not simply recognise the foreign court's competence because the English courts would have had jurisdiction under the same circumstances (*Schibsby v Westenholtz* (1870)); for example, they will not recognise jurisdiction founded on rules similar to the Rules of the Supreme Court, Ord 11 r 1. This is particularly relevant because it might be suggested by Chen that, under Ord 11 r 1(1)(d)(i), the Philistian court would have jurisdiction over contracts made within its jurisdiction. International competence can only be assessed on two grounds: presence in jurisdiction (*Adam v Cape Industries plc* (1990)); or submission to jurisdiction (*Emanuel v Symon* (1908)).

Applying this rule to Chen's claim, it is evident that the Philistian court did not have jurisdiction on the basis of presence, since Ben had already left the country at the material time. Now being limited, therefore, to the second limb, it may be raised in argument that, by instructing his lawyer to appear before the court, Ben has in fact submitted to the court's jurisdiction (assuming that there is no choice of jurisdiction clause between Ben and Chen).

Where the Civil Jurisdiction and Judgments Act 1982 applies, a distinction must be made between appearance to challenge the jurisdiction of the courts and appearance to challenge the merits of the case. If it were the former, s 33 provides that such an act will not be deemed to be submission to the jurisdiction of that court. Under the old rule of the common law, the position is quite the contrary. In *Henry v Geoprosco International Ltd* (1976), the court held that a challenge on the grounds of *forum non conveniens* was in fact submission to jurisdiction. This rule has been superseded by the Civil Jurisdiction and Judgments Act 1982. By merely contesting the jurisdiction of the Philistian court, Ben falls neatly on the spread of s 33(1)(a), which clearly provides that there has been no submission to jurisdiction on his part.

While it is safe to assume that, under English law, the Philistian court has no international competence in the absence of an appropriate jurisdiction clause in the contract, it warrants discussion as to whether there is a case for claiming that the Philistian court was in excess of jurisdiction under Philistian law and how this may affect enforcement in an English court. The position, as set out in *Vanguelin v Bouard* (1863), is that this is a matter for the foreign legal system and, as a matter of judicial comity, it is not open to the English court to discuss the merits of the case, albeit under the foreign law. Any recourse open to the claimant aggrieved by the 'lack of internal competence' must be restricted to claims and appeals within that domestic structure. This would mean that, if Ben is not satisfied with the fact that the Philistian court acts without serving on him a properly executed claim (there being no mention of a claim actually served on him), he cannot take this issue up in the English courts. This factor is irrelevant unless it goes to show a failure of natural justice (discussed below).

In *Castrique v Imrie* (1870), however, the court regarded it as material 'whether the sovereign authority of that State has conferred on the court of jurisdiction to decide as to the disposition of the thing and whether the court has acted within its jurisdiction'. While this case refers to an action *in rem*, it is not certain how far this difference should be taken. Further support for this position is seen in *Macalpine v Macalpine* (1958). In that case, the distinction between a foreign decree's being void or simply voidable for fraud appeared to have been central to the decision. This assessment relied on a consideration of the foreign power-conferring law. Where the foreign judgment is irregular and simply voidable, *dicta* in *SA Consortium General Textiles v Sun and Sand Agencies Ltd* (1978) suggest that the judgment will be held valid in England until it has been properly annulled in the foreign country. In Ben's case, the judgment entered in default of appearance under those circumstances and the failure to take cognisance of leave may be contrary to Philistian law, but, until the matter is properly addressed by Philistian law, it will be hard to apply this defence.

At common law, as stated in *Adam v Cape Industries plc* (1990), the concept of natural justice may be pleaded to impeach a foreign judgment seeking enforcement in this country. The Court of Appeal in *Adam* found that, if the defendant could have applied to the American court to have the judgment in default set aside, then there was no breach of natural justice. In that case, the defendant had neither knowledge of the facts nor the means to find out whether they could apply to set aside the judgment. Therefore, they were not prevented from using the natural justice defence against enforcement. In this context, it may be possible for Ben to argue that he had been denied natural justice, because it would appear from the facts that no leave to serve the claim was actually granted. Even if leave was granted, his case was not heard, since all his lawyer did was to contest jurisdiction and not the merits of the case.

Another defence which may be of relevance is that of public policy. Where the enforcement or recognition of a foreign judgment will contradict the public policy of this country, that foreign judgment may be impeached. In practice, however, this has not been applied very successfully because it is never easy to prove the existence of a principle of public policy. In this case, though, Chen may rely on the inclination of the courts to treat punitive or exemplary damages as being a matter outside the public policy defence (as seen in *SA Consortium*). Unless the punitive order encroaches some rule of fundamental human rights, it is difficult to envisage the courts departing from this inclination to restrict the ambit of what constitutes public policy. This approach was taken by a Canadian court in *Burchell v Burchell* (1926).

Question 28

Comment on the law relating to the recognition and enforcement of foreign arbitral awards under the New York Convention, as referred to by the Arbitration Act 1996.

Answer plan

It is important to explain the fact that a foreign award is recognised or enforced according to whichever regime it falls under. The student should appreciate the rules of the New York Convention on the Recognition and Enforcement of Foreign Arbitral Awards. Awards falling outside the New York Convention will be governed by the old 1950 Act as a result of s 9 of the Arbitration Act 1996. Where neither the New York or Geneva Convention applies, reference should be made to the common law rules on enforcement of a debt obtained in a foreign jurisdiction.

Answer

In order to determine the extent to which a foreign award could be recognised and enforced in England and Wales, it is important, first, to identify whether the New York Convention on the Recognition and Enforcement of Foreign Arbitral Awards 1958 applies to the award concerned. Foreign awards which are deemed non-Convention awards will be governed by the rules of the Geneva Convention 1927 or the common law. This essay will therefore be confined to so called Convention awards.

Section 100(1) of the Arbitration Act (AA) 1996 defines a Convention award as an award pursuant to a written agreement which is made in any Contracting State of the New York Convention other than the UK. An award shall be treated as having been made at the seat of the arbitration, regardless of where it was signed, despatched or delivered. The crucial determining factor is the place where the award was made; other factors are not material to the definition of the term. According to s 101(1) of the AA 1996, the New York Convention award shall be recognised as binding on the persons between whom it was made, who may rely on the award by way of defence, set off or otherwise in any legal proceedings in England and Wales. Further, a New York Convention award could, by leave of the court, be enforced in the same manner as a judgment or order of the court to the same effect. This provision is of vital importance for the party who wishes to reap the benefits of his award in this country. Section 101 applies, making this distinction between foreign and domestic awards inconsequential in terms of recognition and enforcement. Once it is properly constituted under ss 100 and 101, the foreign award has the same effect as a domestic award.

A foreign award may, however, be refused recognition if it is proved that a party to the arbitration agreement was under some incapacity (s 103(2)(a)). Whether there existed such an incapacity depends on the law applicable to that party. This raises the difficulty of whether this law is the party's personal law or the law applicable to the contract he has entered into. Some have argued that it should be the former, so as to prevent the use of commercial agreements to avoid personal law restrictions on matters such as infancy or mental incapacity.

Section 103(2)(b) concerns the chosen law in arbitration agreements. Here, the chosen law refers to that which the parties have agreed to, either expressly or by implication. The choice of law will not be determined according to the rules in the Rome Convention. It should be pointed out that Art 1(2)(d) of the Rome Convention, as enacted in England by the Contracts (Applicable Law) Act 1990, states that the Convention shall not apply to arbitration agreements. Where no choice of law is made, the court will not apply the common law rules on proper law to determine the proper law but will merely look at where the award was made and use the law of that country to determine the validity of the arbitration agreement (s 103(2)(b)). There seems, therefore, to be an irrefutable presumption that, where the parties do not make a choice of law, the law most closely connected with the arbitration agreement will be the law of the seat of the arbitration.

If the respondent or person against whom the enforcement is sought was either not given proper notice of the appointment of the arbitration proceedings or was otherwise unable to present his case, the courts will not recognise that award; this is to ensure that the rules of natural justice are satisfied.

Another ground for refusal of enforcement is that the award contains decisions on matters outside the arbitration's terms of reference (s 103(2)(d)). This rule re-affirms the requirement of *consensus ad idem* in the arbitration and, as a result, it is possible for the applicant to succeed in gaining recognition and enforcement of those decisions which could be separated from the matters not covered by the reference (s 103(4)). That sub-section recognises that an award should be capable of being enforced where it is severable as regards matters properly dealt with by the arbitration agreement.

The element of *consensus ad idem* is also evident in s 103(2)(e). That paragraph states that an award may be refused recognition or enforcement if the composition of the tribunal or arbitral procedure was not in accordance with the agreement of the parties. It is further open to the party to argue that the composition and procedure of the arbitration was contrary to the law of the country where the arbitration took place.

Section 103(2)(f) refers to a very important principle of the recognition and enforcement of arbitration awards – the principle of finality. It provides that the award may be refused recognition or enforcement on the basis that it has not yet become binding on the parties or that it has been set aside or suspended by a competent authority of the country in which the award was made or of the country under whose law the award was made. It is not clear whether this rule has done away with the rule in *Union Nationale des Coopérative Agricoles v Catterall* (1959) (a case on a Geneva Convention award). In that case, it was argued that, in order for a foreign award to be enforced, it must satisfy the requirement imposed on it by its governing law (*lex arbitri*) that it be expressed, first and foremost, in a judgment or decree from the supervising foreign court. The question was whether this rendered the award final and conclusive for the purposes of its enforcement. The court held that, as long as the award was considered to be final under the law governing its proceedings as understood in England, that should suffice. Hence, even though the award was not final, in the sense that it could not be enforced in the foreign country where it was made, it could still be enforced if it was regarded as being final by that law in the English sense. It is unclear how s 103(2)(f) would be construed in the light of *Union Nationale des Cooperative Agricoles v Catterall*, especially since s 104 expressly states that nothing in s 103 affects any right to rely on or to enforce a New York Convention award at common law or under s 66.

Section 104 would also allow an award to be refused recognition or enforcement on the grounds of illegality or public policy. In the recent case of *Soleimany v Soleimany* (1998), it was held that the enforcing court may inquire into the merits of the case where it is clear that the substance and enforcement of foreign awards would be illegal under English law and/or the law of the country of performance. The latter requirement is usually alluded to in the context of the doctrine of judicial comity. However, there is little guidance from English courts as to how this duty is to be discharged.

Conclusion

It should be recalled that, where the New York Convention does not apply, a foreign arbitral award may nonetheless be recognised and enforced under the rules of the Geneva Convention, namely, within the parameters delineated in Pt II of the AA 1950 or the common law. That part of the AA 1950 has not been repealed (s 99 of the AA 1996) and shall continue to apply in relation to foreign awards, subject to the Geneva Protocol on Arbitration Clauses 1923 and the Geneva Convention on the Execution of Foreign Arbitral Awards 1927.

It is also possible for a claimant to claim indirect enforcement of an award using the procedure set out in Pt 24 of the Civil Procedure Rules. Summary judgment will be ordered where the court considers that a claimant has no real prospect of succeeding on the claim or issue and where there is no other reason why the case should be disposed of at a trial. This means that a court will give judgment to a claimant if he has shown a case which, if unanswered, would entitle him to that judgment, and the defendant has not given any reason as to why the claim should be dealt with at trial. The award is proof of the defendant's debt to the claimant. That is usually sufficient to show that the claimant (making the application before the English court for enforcement of that debt) has a case which, if unanswered, would entitle him to that judgment.

CHAPTER 5

CONTRACT

Introduction

At common law, 'party autonomy' means that the parties to a contract are entitled to make a selection of the system of law to govern their contract. This choice of law will be recognised and enforced by the courts unless it is against public policy or the forum's mandatory rules.

The Contracts (Applicable Law) Act 1990, which came into force on 1 April 1991, brought the Rome Convention 1980 into English law. The Convention recognises the principle of party autonomy, in that the parties' express choice of law is taken to be the applicable law of the contract. Where the parties have not expressed a choice of law, the rule in Art 4(1) is that the law with which the contract is most closely connected shall be the applicable law. Article 4(2) provides a presumption that the contract is most closely connected with the country where the party who is to effect the characteristic performance of the contract has his habitual residence at the time of the conclusion of the contract. Where the subject matter is a right in immovable property, then the contract is presumed to be most closely connected with the *lex situs*.

The presumptions set out in Art 4(2), (3) and (4) may be rebutted if it appears that the contract is more closely connected with another country and, with reference to Art 4(2), where the obligation of which performance is characteristic of the contract is indeterminable.

It is also noteworthy that, like the rules of common law, the applicable law must not derogate from mandatory rules of the forum or public policy considerations.

On issues of material and formal validity, the principles are as follows:

- the essential validity of a contract is to be determined by the law which would govern the contract, assuming that it had been validly made;

- in general, the contract is formally valid if it meets the formalities of either the law of the country where either or both of the parties are resident or the applicable law;
- consumer contracts are subject to the formalities of the law of the country where the consumer is resident;
- where the issue of formal validity is concerned, contracts involving immovables and similar rights *in rem* are to be determined by the *lex situs*.

Checklist

To successfully answer questions on contract, students should have a sound knowledge of:

- the principle of party autonomy;
- common law rules on proper law of the contract (*Amin Rasheed Shipping Corp v Kuwait Insurance Co* (1983));
- scope of the Rome Convention as regards party autonomy;
- the rebuttable presumptions in the Rome Convention;
- operation of Art 4(5) of the Rome Convention;
- material and formal validity of contracts;
- matters to be governed by the applicable law and Art 10.

Question 29

In 1999, while living in Xantis, 20 year old Jack agreed to buy some shares in Kicks Corp. Kicks was a company registered in Xantis. Jack paid one-third of the full purchase price.

The contract states that 'Kicks Corp and/or its agents are expressly exempt from liability arising from any pre-contractual statements concerning the state of the company'. The contract also contains a clause stating that, in the event of a dispute, Spanish law will apply. Kicks Corp's holding company is registered in Spain.

According to the law of Xantis, persons under the age of 21 cannot transact or deal in shares. It seems that the position of Spanish law in relation to this issue is unclear.

Jack has now moved back to England to live with his family. He has discovered that one of the representations made to him by Kicks Corp about the financial state of the company was untrue. If he had known the true position, he would never have parted with his money. He now refuses to pay the remainder of the purchase price.

Xantian law provides that misrepresentations made to induce a person into a contractual relationship are unlawful and any contract made on the basis of a misrepresentation is void *ab initio*.

Kicks Corp has instituted proceedings in England against Jack for the payment of the remainder of the purchase price.

Discuss the parties' legal positions under the Contracts (Applicable Law) Act 1990.

Answer plan

A good answer should include the following points:

- capacity to contract under the relevant regime;
- Arts 1(2)(a) and 11 of the Rome Convention;
- Arts 3 and 7 on mandatory rules;
- Art 10(1)(e) on the consequences of nullity of contracts.

Answer

Under Art 1(1) of the Rome Convention, which is enforceable in England by virtue of the Contracts (Applicable Law) Act 1990, all contractual obligations in any situation involving a choice between the laws of different countries are governed by the Convention. This is so even where the other countries involved in the dispute are not contracting parties to the Convention.

The first question that Kicks Corp should consider is whether Jack had the capacity to contract. The starting point is perhaps Art 1(2)(a), which provides that the rules of the Convention are inapplicable to questions involving the status and legal capacity of natural persons. From this perspective, the Rome Convention may not have an impact on the determination of Jack's status or his capacity to contract. However, this view must be subject to the qualifier in Art 11.

Article 11 provides that, in a contract concluded between persons who are in the same country, a natural person who would have capacity under the law of that country may invoke incapacity resulting from another law only if the other party to the contract 'was aware of his incapacity at the time of the conclusion of the contract or was not aware thereof as a result of negligence'. Jack's status will still have to be assessed at common law. Under English law, Jack does not lack capacity. His lack of capacity is only found in Xantian law.

At common law, the general principle is that capacity to contract, being a matter of personal law, must be assessed by the *lex domicilii* (*Sottomayor v De Barros (No 1)* (1877)). The *lex domicilii* should indicate what the personal law is or should be. If Jack is domiciled in England, then, following this rule, Jack's capacity should be measured by English law. Under English law, he would have had the capacity to contract, the age of majority being 18.

It would appear that an application of the putative proper law of the contract is probably the most practical approach. It was held in *Cooper v Cooper* (1888) that this does not mean the law that the parties themselves have chosen for the governance of the contract. The reason for this was perhaps best illustrated by Lord Macnaghten in the following terms: 'It is difficult to suppose that Mrs Cooper could confer capacity on herself by contemplating a different country as the place where the contract was to be fulfilled.' Consequently, the courts will have to determine the proper law of the contract with selective ignorance of the parties' choice of law.

On the facts, it may be suggested that Xantian law is objectively the proper law for the following reasons: the contract was to be performed in Xantis, where the shares are transacted and transferred to Jack; even though the holding company has its place of business in Spain, it is a perfectly conceivable and credible proposition that the shares are those of the Xantis-based company and not those of the holding company; and, under Xantian law, Jack does not have the capacity to contract – this means that the contract is void *ab initio* and Kicks Corp will not be able to demand full payment. Incidentally, it could also be raised that, as can be derived from *Male v Roberts* (1800), the *lex loci contractus* could be used to determine the issue of capacity. If this approach is taken, the same result will be reached, since the contract was entered into in Xantis.

If the contract is valid, the second issue is whether the exclusion of liability clause written into the contract has any legal effect under the choice of law rules in the Rome Convention. Article 3(1) of the Convention states that the parties may choose the applicable law of their contract. On this basis, the selected Spanish law will take priority and will be applied, regardless of the fact that the contract may have no connection with Spain. This is the oft quoted rule of party autonomy.

Article 3(1), however, must be read subject to Art 3(3), which provides that, where all the other elements relevant to the situation at the time the choice was made are connected with one country only, then the mandatory rules of that country may not be derogated from in the application of the chosen law.

Whether or not all the factors relevant to the situation at the time of the choice are connected with one country (here, Xantis) is a question of fact. In the Australian case of *Golden Acres Ltd v Queensland Estates Pty Ltd* (1969), the operation of 'all elements relevant to the situation', whilst it was explored, did not seem capable of any decisive and consistent definition. In that case, the place where the estate agency was based and, indeed, where the domicile of the purchasers were deemed to be elements relevant to the situation, even though in a business context, were of little material relevance. If this type of approach is recommended, it is likely that, since Jack is (presumably) domiciled in England, not all of the elements relevant to the case are connected with one country alone. Whether the seat of the holding company is a relevant factor when it does not seem to be involved at all must be left as a matter for speculation.

Jack may wish to rely on Art 7(1), which specifies that effect may be given to the mandatory rules of the law of a country other than that of a chosen law with which the situation has a close connection, in so far as those rules must be applied whatever the law applicable to the contract. This would entitle Jack to rely on Xantian law, since Xantis is the country very closely connected with the contract. Unfortunately for Jack, the opt-out spelt out in s 2(2) of the 1990 Act is to the effect that Art 7(1) has no application in the UK.

On the issue of whether Jack will be able to recover his part payment, the rules on restitution at common law shall be applicable. Article 10(1)(e), which allows the applicable law to determine the consequences of nullity of the contract, does not apply, since the UK has entered a reservation to the provision. However, there is a view that the proper law at common law should determine the issue of the consequences of nullity of the contract. This would mean that Spanish law would govern, that being the law expressed in the choice of law clause.

Question 30

Over the last 20 years, Mark and Jason Co Ltd, a company based in Luton, England, have conducted various business dealings with each other. In many of these contracts, they have adopted various American statutory provisions and forms as their contractual terms.

Last month, Mark telephoned Jason Co Ltd from Essexia, offering to sell a consignment of rubber balls. Jason Co Ltd accepted the offer. The goods were to be delivered to Jason Co Ltd's subsidiary company in Ireland in three instalments. It was agreed that the first two payments would be made in Sterling and deposited in Mark's bank account in London, and the third in US dollars, to be entered into Mark's account in Essexia.

The shipment of the first instalment has been substantially delayed as a result of the Essexian authorities' refusal to grant a certificate of quality. Mark contends that the contract has been frustrated.

Discuss how the Contracts (Applicable Law) Act 1990 will determine the applicable law to these issues.

Answer plan

The question requires the student to discuss and apply the presumptions in Art 4(2) of the Rome Convention, as incorporated into English law by the Contracts (Applicable Law) Act 1990. There should also be some discussion of the scope of

Art 4(5) in rebutting the presumption and demonstrating how the law most closely connected to the contract is to be identified.

The good answer will then turn to Art 10 of the Convention and discuss how the issue of whether the contract has been frustrated should be posited in the light of the relevant applicable law.

Answer

Applying the general rule under the Contracts (Applicable Law) Act 1990, if it has been expressly agreed between Mark and Jason Co Ltd (henceforth referred to as 'Jason') that a particular country's system of law is to govern the contract, that chosen system will prevail. This is the case even though the contract may have little or no connection with that country.

Where there is no express selection, the courts will have to decide whether there is an implied choice of law from the facts. Article 3(1) provides that the choice must be demonstrated with reasonable certainty by the terms of the contract or the circumstances of the case. It has been suggested that this entails the difficult issue of construction. The Giuliano-Lagarde Report appears to suggest that this is not necessary: all that the court has to do is construe the wording of the contract in the light of the circumstances of the case. In this regard, the courts will analyse relevant trade practice, any previous course of dealings between the parties and whether the parties, in the course of their dealings, have indicated a selection which can be treated as such with reasonable certainty.

In our case, Mark and Jason have relied on American statutory forms and provisions as terms for their business transactions for a number of years. Before any inference may be drawn following the rules in the Rome Convention, it must be mentioned that, where these previous dealings are similar to the transaction in question, the stronger that inference may be made. This goes some distance in showing the consistency of practice so vital to reasonable certainty. Assuming that this element is met, the second point for determination is whether the use of American forms and precedents is an implied selection of American law as the choice of law or simply as a set of terms without that effect. In *Adamastos Shipping Co Ltd v Anglo-Saxon Petroleum Co* (1959), the contract in question was simply a restatement of the statute verbatim. The provisions operated as a set of agreed terms between the parties, not as a statute. The acid test is whether the contract will still be bound by those provisions in question when the statute has been repealed or amended.

If the parties do not make a choice of law, either by express selection or by implication, Art 4(1) will apply, affiliating the contract to the law of the country with which it is most closely connected. Article 4(2) then applies, making a presumption as to the country with which the contract is most closely connected.

Article 4(2) makes reference to the party who is to effect the performance which is characteristic of the contract. According to the Giuliano-Lagarde Report, the obligation characteristic of the contract is that for which monetary consideration is given in exchange, usually the obligation which is linked to the socio-economic environment of the transaction. From the facts, this would be the obligation to deliver the rubber balls. Thus, Mark is the relevant party for the purposes of the presumption.

Subsequent to this, the courts will have to determine whether that party (Mark) performed the contract in the course of his trade or profession. If he did so, as the facts suggest, then the country most closely connected with the contract is Mark's principal place of business. Although Mark made the phone call from Essexia, it is unsafe to conclude that Essexia is his principal place of business without further information.

It may be the case that, as the contract provides that performance is to be effected through Essexia (that is, that the rubber balls are to be exported from Essexia), the location of *that* place of business, rather than the principal place of business, becomes relevant. This means that, even though Essexia is not Mark's principal place of business, it appears to be the place in which the contract is to be performed.

If Mark was not dealing in the course of his trade or profession, the place of his habitual residence at the time of conclusion of the contract will be the country presumed to have a close connection with the contract. On the facts, the contract was concluded instantaneously over the telephone while Mark was in

Essexia. However, we are not told if Essexia was at that time the place where Mark had his habitual residence.

The presumption in Art 4(2) is rebuttable. Article 4(5) rather obliquely spells out that, where the circumstances as a whole reveal that the contract is more closely connected with another country, then the presumption is to be ignored. In this regard, the court may have to resort to the law as set out in *Amin Rasheed Shipping Corp v Kuwait Insurance Co* (1984), a case which pre-dated the Contracts (Applicable Law) Act 1990. According to that case, the factors that the court will take into account include: the places where the contract is to be performed and where the parties are situated; the currency the contract is expressed in; the language and form of the contract; the existence of a choice of forum clause; and other circumstances indicating the parties' intention. In Mark's case, the place of performance could be either Ireland or Essexia, depending on the nature of the relevant contractual term. The place where the contract was made is the place where the acceptance was communicated, namely, Essexia (*Byrne v Van Tienhoven* (1880)). The language and form is similar to American statutory provisions. The currency is in both sterling and US dollars, and part of the payment is to be made in England and the rest in Essexia. The factors seem to be split in both directions. It is difficult to place any extra emphasis on any of the factors mentioned. The paradigm is the presumed intention of the parties. This must be objectively ascertained by the court.

Another possible issue for consideration concerns the delivery of goods by instalments. Although, on the facts, it seems fairly clear that only one contract is in issue, it should perhaps be mentioned that, where there are other contractual relationships closely allied to the contract, Mance J in *Bank of Baroda v Vysya Bank* (1994) considered that closely related contracts should be dealt with under the same applicable law as a matter of general principle and convenience. In that case, the contractual relationships surrounding a letter of credit were held to share the same applicable law, namely, English law. This was so despite the fact that, as far as the sale agreement was concerned, the characteristic obligation of that contract was to be performed in India.

Another issue of particular importance is whether the question of frustration of the contract is to be determined by the applicable law. Article 10 of the Convention specifies that questions of performance, discharge and extinguishing of obligations are to be governed by the applicable law. This is, however, qualified by Art 10(2), which provides that, in relation to the manner of performance and the steps to be taken in the event of defective performance, regard shall be had to the law of the country in which performance takes place. This, according to the Giuliano-Lagarde Report, legitimises the displacement of the first general provision and allows the courts to apply the law of the place of performance where to do so would converge on the justice of the case.

At common law, a similar position is reflected in the Court of Appeal's decision in *Jacobs v Credit Lyonnais* (1884). The court held that the law of the place of performance might regulate the method and manner of performance, but this was not to be extended to matters of detail, especially those matters which do not affect the substance of the obligation. Juxtaposing this with the present case, the law of the place of performance, which is most likely to be Ireland (where Mark is to deliver the goods), will be applicable to determine the issue of frustration. On whether there is a requirement to obtain the certificate of quality, Essexian law is to apply, but Irish law will be used to decide whether this duty is to be imposed on Mark or whether the failure to do so frustrates the contract.

Question 31

Isabelle Co, a Sociologian company, entered into an agreement with Judith Co, a Teacherian company, to purchase Teacherian artefacts. The contract stated that the artefacts were to be shipped on Utopian ships. Payment was to be made in Utopian currency through a bank based in Utopia.

In the meantime, under international pressure, the Sociologian government passed a law banning the import of certain artefacts from States like Teacheria. In reliance on this intervening illegality, Isabelle Co refused to pay and take delivery of the artefacts.

Convinced that they will not get justice in Sociologia, Judith Co institutes an action against Isabelle Co in England by serving a claim on Isabelle Co's office in London. The office is manned only by the typist and the documentation clerk. The office is responsible for collecting mail on behalf of the main offices in Western Europe.

Examine how English courts will determine the question of jurisdiction and the applicable law of contract.

Answer plan

The first issue is that of jurisdiction when the defendant has only a slight presence in the country. The position in *South India Shipping Corp v Import-Export Bank of Korea* (1985) should provide the solution. The other grounds upon which jurisdiction is founded should also be mentioned.

This question then tests the student's ability to apply the rules under the Contracts (Applicable Law) Act 1990, which incorporates the Rome Convention. The Rome Convention systematically sets out the stages that a court should go through to determine the applicable law.

The first stage is to locate a choice of law clause or agreement. It appears that this agreement may be express or implied. The implication of the choice clause is probably based on the traditional common law rules. It should be noted that some academics argue that the implication of a choice of law clause has no place under the Convention. Where the agreement is silent, the courts should move on to applying the presumptions in Art 4. Only where the presumptions fail under Art 4(5) should the courts apply the traditional rules.

The question also requires some treatment of the issue of mandatory rules and material invalidity.

Answer

In determining whether an English court has jurisdiction to hear and entertain the dispute, the relevant set of rules on jurisdiction must first be identified. On matters of jurisdiction, the courts are governed by three different regimes – the Brussels Convention, the Lugano Convention and the traditional Rules of the Supreme Court which purport to represent the common law. In the matter concerning Isabelle Co and Judith Co, the natural conclusion is that the two Conventions will not apply because none of the Contracting States is involved.

The following elements must be present in order to establish jurisdiction:

- the defendant was present in the jurisdiction when the claim was served;
- the defendant has submitted to jurisdiction, either through a choice of jurisdiction clause/agreement or by appearance before the court;
- for proper service of the claim abroad, RSC Ord 11 r 1(1) must apply.

On the facts, Isabelle Co has been served with the claim at their mail collection office in London. The question is whether this amounts to a valid service of the claim, considering the fact that the office is only a publicity office. In *South India Shipping Corp v Import-Export Bank of Korea* (1985), the Court of Appeal held that the claim had been properly served on the Korean Bank's publicity office in the City of London. Although the office was not maintained for trading, as is the case with Isabelle Co, it was held that the defendants had effectively established a place within jurisdiction which was capable of accepting service. On this basis, Judith Co has lawfully instituted action in England against Isabelle Co.

The next question relates to the question of what law the courts will apply to resolve the dispute as presented by the contract.

The court will have to rely on the Contracts (Applicable Law) Act 1990 in order to determine which law is applicable to the contract. The general rule is that, if the parties (Isabelle Co and Judith Co) had pre-agreed on a particular law to govern the contract, under Art 3 the court will apply that law. The choice of law agreement or clause must be demonstrated with reasonable certainty from the terms of the contract or the circumstances of the case. Where the clause is not expressed clearly, extraneous factors may be adduced to construe the ambiguous clause.

If there is no choice of law clause entered into between the parties, the question is whether it is possible to deduce from the facts an implied agreement as to the choice of law. There is some doubt, however, as to whether an implied selection is to be applied before resorting to the presumptions in Art 4 of the Rome Convention. It is submitted that the problem is more apparent than real because, in the event of the party concerned being able to show that, contrary to the presumption in Art 4(2)(3), the contract is more closely connected to another country, that presumption may be rebutted pursuant to Art 4(5). As far as Art 4(5) is concerned, the general view is that the factors under the common law (as illustrated in *Amin Rasheed Shipping Corp v Kuwait Insurance Co* (1984)) are relevant.

For the sake of convenience, the presumptions in Art 4 will be discussed first. Article 4(2) enables the court to presume that the law of the country with which the contract is most closely connected is the law of the place of the party who has to effect 'the performance which is characteristic of the contract'. This would take the place of the party's place of habitual residence or business.

The preliminary issue is, what does 'performance which is characteristic of the contract' mean? The Giuliano-Lagarde Report offers some assistance. It describes the 'characteristic performance' as 'that which links the contract to the social and economic environment of which it will form a part'. The performance which is characteristic of the contract is the performance for which payment is due, as this usually constitutes the 'centre of gravity' and the socio-economic function of the contractual transaction. In the present case, this must necessarily point to the delivery of the artefacts and, since it is Judith Co that has to supply the goods, Judith Co's place of business will be presumed to be the place having the closest connection with the contract. If Judith Co has its place of business in Teacheria, then Teacheria will be the place with which the contract is most closely connected. Where the dispute is about the carriage of goods, the presumption in Art 4(2) does not apply. Instead, the court will, under Art 4(4), hold that the place of the carrier's principal business is the place with which the contract of carriage is most closely connected, if that place is also any of the following:

- the place of loading;
- the place of discharge;
- the principal place where the consignor of the goods has his business. On the facts, it is fairly certain that the claim lodged against Isabelle Co is one based on the agreement of sale rather than the agreement of carriage. Even if the agreement in question is the latter, it is unclear that either of the two named parties is the carrier.

The court will not be able to rely on these presumptions where it is proved successfully that another country is more closely connected with the contract. The factors which the court will apply in exercising its powers under Art 4(5) to reject a presumption are similar to those espoused by the common law.

The approach of the common law has been to assess the situation, relying on circumstances surrounding the contract and the terms of the contract in question. In *Amin Rasheed Shipping Corp v Kuwait Insurance Co* (1983), it was emphasised that the intention of the parties vis à vis the choice of law must be clear from the terms of the contract or from the circumstances surrounding the contract. In respect of the latter issue, the courts may consider pre-contractual negotiations, representations and the previous conduct of the parties. In general, the courts will consider the following points:

- the existence of an exclusive jurisdiction or arbitration clause;
- while the language of the contract is generally not of much significance, it becomes pivotal when it employs certain terminology which is *sui generis* to a particular system of law (*Whitworth Street Est v James Miller* (1970)). In *Amin Rasheed*, the court inferred from the use of the English Marine Insurance Act 1906 that terms in the insurance policy must necessarily mean that the parties intended to interpret the contract of insurance using English law;
- the currency of payment may be useful where it forms one of several factors. As a lone factor, it does not carry much weight, but the courts will not exclude its consideration where

> there are other factors. In *The Assunzione* (1954), by taking the cumulative effect of the evidence that the contract was made in Italy and that freight and demurrage should be paid in Italian currency, the court concluded that the contract was intended to be governed by Italian law. It should be noted that, in that case, the facts were so evenly balanced between French and Italian law that the Court of Appeal held the decisive factor to be the place where performance was to be effected. As indicated by the currency expressed, delivery and payment were to take place in Italy, hence the decision.

The circumstances that the court will have to consider in Judith Co's application include the place where delivery of the artefacts was to take place. The delivery is probably to take place in Sociologia, where the import ban was so relevant. The added aggravation is that the currency of payment and delivery of the goods appear to be connected more with Utopia than either of the two States involved. Upon the caveat in *Amin Rasheed*, these discrete factors must be accommodated with care; it is the task of the court to weigh all such matters together to assess their cumulative effect.

Once the selection of the applicable law has been made, whether through operation of the presumptions or not, it is important to determine whether the Sociologian law banning the import of certain artefacts is protected by the Rome Convention. The Convention recognises the importance of some national rules and provides that the relevant applicable law must not derogate from the mandatory rules as defined by that Convention. It suffices to say that Art 3(3) does not apply in Isabelle Co's situation because the parties have not made a selection of a foreign law. As for Art 7(1), the UK has opted out of its operation.

However, it is pertinent to refer to Art 10(2) which provides that, in relation to the manner of performance, regard shall be had to the law of the country in which performance is to take place. The issue is whether, in applying Teacherian law, the court will have to consider Sociologian law. The Giuliano-Lagarde Report gives somewhat perfunctory treatment to the issue by simply stating that the judge has discretion in every case, but it offered no guidelines as to how this discretion is to be exercised.

Another matter of doubt is found in the phrase 'manner of performance', which is nowhere defined in the Convention. This, too, is not afforded any clarification in the Giuliano-Lagarde report.

The discretion of the judge is, in general, governed by Art 16. That article provides that a rule of the law of any country specified by the Convention may be referred only if such application is manifestly incompatible with the public policy of the forum. This is yet anther element that the applicant should be wary of.

Finally, it is not open to the party concerned to argue that the contract may be invalid under the applicable law; thus, the selection process based on the contract is frustrated. Article 8 addresses the situation by stating that the existence and validity of the agreement shall be determined by the law which would govern it under the Convention if the contract or term were valid. The common law concern, as reflected in rules on putative proper law, is met.

Question 32*

Assess the impact of Art 7(1) of the Rome Convention on the Law Applicable to Contractual Obligations on the principle of party autonomy. Discuss alternative approaches to party autonomy as adopted by some jurisdictions.

Answer plan

In the first part, the traditional approaches to the limitations on party autonomy should be examined: in England, the decision of the House of Lords in *Vita Food Products Inc v Unus Shipping Co Ltd* (1939) is most relevant. As a comparative study, s 1-105(1) of the Uniform Commercial Code of the US and para 187 of the Restatement (Second) of Conflict of Laws could be considered. In the second part, the unlimited freedom of choice of applicable law and the limitations introduced by the internationally binding mandatory rules should be discussed. In this respect, the decision of the Supreme Court of The Netherlands (the Hoge Raad) in *The*

Alnati (1966) and Art 7(1) of the Rome Convention on the Law Applicable to Contractual Obligations provide an illustration as to the meaning of the new approach. Article 7(1) should be analysed in detail.

Answer

Party autonomy is a rule of conflict of laws according to which parties to international transactions are free to choose the law applicable to their contract. The extent of their freedom to select the applicable law is governed by the relevant national law. In England, the House of Lords in *Vita Food Products Inc v Unus Shipping Co Ltd* (1939) recognised the unlimited freedom of choice, with the proviso that it is *bona fide*, legal and not contrary to the public policy. However, this liberal approach has not been followed in many countries. Several limitations have been imposed by national laws in order to restrain parties' choice: the necessity of substantial links between the contract and the selected applicable law; the objective localisation of contract; the 'reasonable connection' requirement; and the mandatory application of the *lex fori* when the contract is to be performed in the territory of that State.

The Uniform Commercial Code of the US (UCC) provides that:

> ... when a transaction bears a reasonable relation to this State and also to another State or nation, the parties may agree that the law either of this State or of such other State or nation shall govern their rights and duties [s 1-105(1)].

Thus, the UCC allows the parties to choose between the law of the seller, the law of the buyer and the law of a third State, provided that the latter has a reasonable link with the transaction. Paragraph 187 of the Restatement (Second) of Conflict of Laws 1971 endorses the UCC's approach. Nowadays, however, such limitations on party autonomy are not particularly favoured. Modern legislation or international conventions in this area prefer the unlimited freedom of choice. For example, the State of New York has rejected the substantial relationship approach advocated by the Restatement. The Assembly Bill 7307-A of 1984, which was implemented as Title 14 of the New York Law of General Obligations, stipulates in s 5-1401 that, when a transaction involves $250,000 or more, no connection between the applicable law and the transaction is needed.

At the European level, Art 3(1) of the Rome Convention on the Law Applicable to Contractual Obligations recognises unlimited freedom of choice. Also, the 1986 Hague Convention on the Law Applicable to Contract for the International Sale of Goods imposes no limits on party autonomy. The reason for this approach is that new limitations have emerged in the form of national and international mandatory rules. Article 7(1) of the Rome Convention provides the best example in this area. The antecedents of Art 7(1) are the judgment of the Hoge Raad in *The Alnati* (1966) and Art 15 of the 1978 Hague Convention on the Law Applicable to Agency. The judgment of the Hoge Raad in *The Alnati* concerned a contract for carriage of potatoes by a Dutch carrier from Antwerp to Rio de Janeiro, under a bill of lading stipulating that Dutch law was to be applicable to the contract. The Hoge Raad decided that no mandatory rules of Dutch or Brazilian law were applicable to the contract. However, it took into consideration the potential application of Art 91 of the Belgian Commercial Code, which incorporated the Hague Rules and, according to which, in cases involving the carriage of goods originating at a Belgian port, Art 91 is directly applicable. Although the Hoge Raad upheld Dutch law as the *lex contractus*, it stated that: '... it may happen that, for a foreign State, the observation of certain of these rules, even outside its own territory, carries such importance that the courts must take them into account.'

Article 7(1) of the Rome Convention incorporates and broadens this idea. It provides that:

> When applying under this Convention the law of the country, effect may be given to the mandatory rules of the law of another country with which the situation has a close connection, if and in so far as, under the law of the latter country, those rules must be applied whatever the law applicable to the contract. In considering whether to give effect to these mandatory rules, regard shall be had to their nature and purposes and to the consequences of their application or non-application.

The definition of mandatory rules is provided in Art 3(3) of the Rome Convention. They are 'rules of the law of a country which cannot be derogated from by contract'.

Article 7(1) poses considerable practical difficulties. Indeed, a national judge is required to assess the interest of a foreign State (or foreign laws) which is neither the *lex fori* nor the *lex contractus*. Thus, the question arises as to the criteria which should guide the judge in determination of the vital and essential priorities of a foreign State. One way of determining whether certain rules are mandatory is to follow the interpretation of the foreign courts of the potentially interested country in respect of the mandatory nature of the rules. Accordingly, if the foreign law itself has decided that the rule at issue is mandatory, then the forum should uphold this characterisation. However, it may happen that even a foreign court is uncertain whether the rule in question is mandatory if, for example, there is no case law or legislation in this respect. The obvious answer is that, if a foreign law is unclear on the matter, then the forum should reject the application of a rule of dubious mandatory nature.

However, it is not that simple. For example, what does a French judge know about essential and vital interests of the law of Venezuela? Logically, the forum can only assess the mandatory nature of foreign rules by reference to its own national law. In this respect, Art 19 of the Swiss Code on Private International Law is more explicit. It provides that the mandatory rules of a law other than the applicable law may be taken into account if interests of a party which are at issue are considered worthy of protection and manifestly preponderant according to the standards of Swiss law.

Furthermore, under Art 7(1), more than one law may be closely connected with the situation. The Giuliano-Lagarde Report explains the necessity of giving wide latitude to the judge, particularly in cases where the judge must make a choice between contradictory mandatory rules of two different countries which both purport to be applicable to the same situation. In this context, the question of the meaning of 'close connection' arises, as the very nature of an international contract implies that it has contacts with various legal systems. Thus, almost any factor can be important: the nationality of the parties; the place of habitual residence of the parties; the place of business; the place of performance of contractual obligations of each party; the place of conclusion of a contract, etc. The Report suggests that, in the determination of the situation which has the close connection required thereunder, the contract 'as a whole' should be taken into consideration.

Kaye argues that this interpretation is unacceptable.[1] He states that the connection between the point in dispute and a particular law applicable to it should prevail. For example, if the dispute concerns the seller's claim that the buyer failed to pay for delivered goods, the question at issue is the forthcoming payments. Mandatory rules of the country for payments would be the most appropriate to apply to this question, not the *lex contractus*, which may be, for example, the law of the seller's place of business. He emphasises that the dismembering of the contract is the inevitable consequence of Art 7(1).

Although this view has some validity, it is submitted that the application of mandatory rules of closely connected laws should be kept within reasonable bounds. Thus, where the applicable law has been chosen by the parties, the search for a closely connected law is justified. However, where the court determines the applicable law on the basis of the choice of law rules set out in the Rome Convention, it seems ludicrous to allow the court to keep looking for another law which is also closely connected with the situation but not as closely connected as the previously selected law. Only the single closest connection should be taken into account. There must be a limit to potentially applicable laws, especially in the absence of choice by the parties. Furthermore, as the Rome Convention recognises the *depeçage*, in some cases a judge will already have several laws to consider, as well as the potential application of several mandatory rules. For example, where parties have selected the *lex contractus*, the judge will have to examine the following laws and their mandatory rules:

- public policy requirements of the forum and its mandatory rules par excellence envisaged by Art 16 of the Rome Convention;
- mandatory rules of the *lex contractus*, since they form an intrinsic part of that law;
- mandatory rules of the closely connected law or laws under Art 7(1) of the Rome Convention;

- mandatory rules of the *lex fori* under Art 7(2) of the Rome Convention;
- in the case of *depeçage*, mandatory rules of the laws applicable to the contract;
- if Art 3(3) of the Rome Convention applies, the mandatory rules of the law with which the contract is entirely connected.

The complexity of Art 7(1) has prompted many countries to refuse its application. As a result, Art 7(1) is inapplicable in the UK, Germany, Ireland and Luxembourg.

It is submitted that mandatory rules of a third country should be taken into consideration only if the parties have selected the *lex contractus* and the selected law is not the one which would be normally applicable in the absence of choice by the parties.

Article 7(1) introduces a new approach to interpreting 'party autonomy'. Indeed, the traditional restrictions on party autonomy have given way to new ones, namely the directly applicable mandatory rules of the forum and the internationally binding mandatory rules of third countries closely connected with the contract.

Note

1 Kaye, *Civil Jurisdiction and Enforcement of Foreign Judgments*, 1987.

* by Alina Kaczorowska

Question 33*

Asbestex GmbH, a German company specialising in removing asbestos from buildings, entered into a contract with an Italian manufacturer, Dorex SpA, which had developed a computerised 'asbestos register', a system for the creation and maintenance of safety registers of asbestos in buildings. The contract was negotiated in Germany, written in German and the price was fixed in German marks. The parties discussed neither the question of jurisdiction nor the applicable law to their contract. Under the terms of the contract, Dorex SpA had to deliver and install computerised asbestos registers at the buyer's (Asbestex Ltd) place of business. Dorex SpA performed its contractual obligations. Asbestex GmbH refused to pay the agreed price, claiming that the computerised asbestos register, which was designed to record four sets of data (survey and safety audit details; test sample results; remedial work required and performed; calibration of instruments), did not record any of them according to the contract specification.

When Dorex SpA commenced proceedings before an Italian court in Rome, Asbestex GmbH contested the jurisdiction of the Italian court.

Advise Dorex SpA.

Answer plan

The relationship between Art 5(1) of the 1968 Brussels Convention on Jurisdiction and the Enforcement of Judgments in Civil and Commercial Matters and Art 4 of the Rome Convention on the Law Applicable to Contractual Obligations should be examined.

If the jurisdiction of a court in a Contracting State is challenged, the court must determine the place of performance of the obligation to pay on the basis of Art 4 of the Rome Convention in order to ascertain the law applicable to the contract. Article 4 of the Rome Convention is crucial to the determination of the law applicable to a contract when the parties have not chosen the *lex contractus* under Art 3(1). Under Art 4(1), the contract is governed by the law of the country with which it is most closely connected. The following case law should be examined:

- *De Bloos Sprl v Bouyer SA* (1976);
- *Custom Made Commercial Ltd v Stawa Metallbau GmbH* (1994);
- *Société Nouvelle des Papéteries de L'Aa SA v BV Machinefabriek BOA* (1992).

Answer

Article 5(1) of the Brussels Convention and Art 4 of the Rome Convention are interrelated. Article 5(1) confers special jurisdiction on courts in Contracting States 'in matters relating to a contract, in the courts of the place of performance of the obligation in question'.

It is necessary to determine whether the transaction in question satisfies the requirement set out in Art 5(1). In our scenario, there is a contract of sale – certainly 'a matter relating to a contract'. There is also no problem in determining 'the obligation in question'. In *De Bloos Sprl v Bouyer SA* (1976), the ECJ held that 'the obligation in question' is the one which forms the basis of the legal proceedings, that is, the obligation on which the claimant's claim is based. In our case, the relevant obligation for the purposes of Art 5(1) is the defendant's obligation to pay.

Next, the place of performance of the obligation must also be determined. In *Tessili v Dunlop* (1976), the ECJ held that it was for the court before which the question had arisen to determine the place of the performance of the contractual obligation on the basis of national conflict of laws rules. This approach was confirmed in *Custom Made Commercial Ltd v Stawa Metallbau GmbH* (1994). In *Custom Made*, the Advocate General suggested the introduction of an autonomous concept of the place of performance of the obligation in question. He stated that, 'as regards each type of contract, the place of performance should be identified according to the factual realities, rather than according to legal niceties'. The reference to national rules of conflict of laws has been strongly criticised. However, with the entry into force of the Rome Convention on the Law Applicable to Contractual Obligations, especially the fact that it applies *erga omnes* and replaces the existing choice of law rules in this area, the risk of divergencies and discrepancies has considerably diminished.

The Rome Convention came into effect in the UK in 1991 under the Contract (Applicable Law) Act 1990. Its basic rule is set out in Art 3, which enshrines the contracting parties' unlimited freedom of choice in respect of the applicable law. However, in the absence of choice, Art 4(1) provides for application of 'the law of the country with which [the contract] is most closely connected'. That country is presumed to be the place of residence or place of business of the party who is to effect the performance which is characteristic of the contract (Art 4(2)).

The concept of characteristic performance is not defined. In the context of international sale of goods, the place where the party is to effect the characteristic performance is where the seller has his place of business. The concept of characteristic performance refers to the centre of gravity of the transaction. The objective of the presumption of characteristic performance is not the determination of the place of the characteristic performance but the determination of the residence or place of business of the party who is to effect the characteristic performance. However, Art 4(5) provides that the presumption is rebuttable and may be eschewed when the characteristic performance cannot be identified or if it appears that the contract is more closely connected with another country than the country where the seller has his place of business.

In our case, an Italian court must determine the law which governs the contract between Dorex SpA and Asbestex GmbH according to Art 4 of the Convention (Italy is a Contracting State to the Rome Convention). In this respect, two possibilities arise: the court may apply Art 4(2), or it may disregard the presumption of characteristic performance on the basis of Art 4(5). In respect of the first option, according to the Report on the Convention by Giuliano and Lagarde,[1] when goods are exchanged for money, the supplying of goods, not the payment, is the characteristic performance. Furthermore, under Italian law, the place of payment of money is, contrary to English law, the place of the creditor's residence. As a result, the presumption clearly indicates that Italian law is the law applicable to the contract.

However, the second option appears to be quite persuasive, taking into account the fact that many factors point to German law as being applicable to the contract: the contract was negotiated in Germany; it was written in German; and the currency in which the price was expressed was German currency. Furthermore, under German law, the place of payment of money is the place of the debtor's residence. If the Italian court disregards Art 4(2) in favour of Art 4(5), the claimant will have to sue under Art 2 of the Brussels Convention; that is, he must sue at the place where the defendant has his place of business. Indeed, the main and only connection to Italian law is the place of business of the seller. In *Société Nouvelle des Papéteries de L'Aa SA v BV Machinefabriek BOA* (1992), the Supreme Court of the Netherlands (the Hoge Raad), when confronted with a similar choice, decided to apply Art 4(2). It held that Art 4(1) contains a general rule and that Art 4(5) is an exception and, as such, should be interpreted restrictively in order to ensure uniformity in the application of the Convention. The presumption in Art 4(2), that is, the presumption of characteristic performance, is the most important connecting factor. Finally, it was stated that, as a rule, the presumption in Art 4(2) should apply unless there is a real and significant connection between the contract and a country other than the country in which the seller has his place of business. As a result, the application of Art 4(2) conferred jurisdiction upon a Dutch court.

Following the Hoge Raad's reasoning in *Société Nouvelle des Papéteries de L'Aa SA v BV Machinefabriek BOA*, it is submitted that the Italian court should have jurisdiction over the dispute.

Note

1 OJ C282/1 (1980)

* by Alina Kaczorowska

CHAPTER 6

TORT*

Introduction

The most exciting recent development in conflict of laws in tort was the entry into force of Pt III of the Private International Law (Miscellaneous Provisions) Act 1995 on 1 May 1996. This Act gives effect to the recommendation of the Law Commission in the area of multi-State torts. It abolishes the common law rules on multi-State torts but does not apply retroactively, that is, in respect of acts or omissions giving rise to claims before its entry into force, nor does it apply to the tort of defamation. Consequently, the common law rules remain relevant in both cases.

The 'double actionability' rule as modified in *Boys v Chaplin* (1971) is done away with. Now, the *lex loci delicti commissi* (the law of the country in which the events constituting the tort occur) generally applies to multi-State torts. However, the *lex loci delicti commissi* is displaced if a more significant connection is established between the law of another country and the tort.

The reform of conflict of laws rules in tort was necessary for many reasons, the most important being the uncertainty and unpredictability of decisions in multi-State torts. On the one hand, there was a rule of double actionability, according to which a tort committed abroad was actionable in England if it satisfied two requirements, namely that it was actionable under the law of the foreign country where it was done and would be actionable as a tort in England (that is, the act would be a tort under English law if it was done in England). This rule originates from a judgment delivered over a hundred years ago in *Phillips v Eyre* (1870).

On the other hand, a more flexible approach was introduced by the doctrine of the 'proper law'. Under this approach, the law applicable to multi-State torts was the law of the country which had the most significant relationship to both the occurrence of the event generating tortious liability and the parties. This doctrine has gained recognition in many States of the US and has become a cornerstone of the American revolution in conflict of laws. A great deal of controversy has lingered since the decision in *Boys v Chaplin*, a leading authority on multi-State torts in England. For some, no *ratio decidendi* could be extracted from the case; for others, the lower courts were entitled to select, from five judgments delivered by their Lordships, the one which they considered appropriate to the dispute at hand.

However, it was certain that the House of Lords in *Boys v Chaplin* had overruled *Machado v Fontes* (1897) and decided that the double actionability rule of *Phillips v Eyre* should be subject to a flexible exception, without specifying what this exception should be based upon. According to Dicey and Morris (*Conflict of Laws*, 12th edn, 1993), it meant that the proper law of tort applied in some 'exceptional circumstances' as a compliment to the traditional rule stated in *Phillips v Eyre*. In practice, English courts applied the doctrine of proper law in numerous cases (see, for example, *Church of Scientology of California v Comr of Police* (1976); *Johnson v Coventry Churchill International Ltd* (1992)), and thus they seemed to accept Lord Wilberforce's judgment in *Boys v Chaplin* as a definitive statement on English choice of law rules in multi-State torts. The complexity was compounded by the 'new' approach taken by the Privy Council in *Red Sea Insurance Co Ltd v Bouygues SA* (1994).

Checklist

To successfully answer questions on conflict of laws rules in tort, the student needs a thorough understanding of:

- traditional common law rules in tort: *Phillips v Eyre; Boys v Chaplin;*
- the proper law of tort;
- the implications of the judgment of the Privy Council in *Red Sea Insurance Co Ltd v Bouygues SA*;
- Pt III of the Private International Law (Miscellaneous Provisions) Act 1995;
- special rules relating to the tort of defamation.

Question 34

James has always loved cars. In May 1994, he acquired a sports version of an Alfa Moretti. According to James, it was the most entertaining driver's car of the century. His new car had a turbocharged engine producing around 340 bhp which out on the road translated to 0–60 mph acceleration in just 4 seconds and 0–100 mph in 10 seconds. James wanted to try out his new car. He invited his friend, Anthony, for a long drive to Malandia. Due to James' negligent driving, they had an accident in Malandia. Anthony was seriously injured. According to the law of Malandia, a gratuitous passenger has no claim against the driver.

Analyse Anthony's situation in the light of English conflict of laws rules in tort. Would his situation be different if he could recover damages under the *lex loci delicti* but had no claim under the *lex fori*?

Answer plan

The accident happened before the entry into force of the Private International Law (Miscellaneous Provisions) Act 1995. For that reason, it is necessary to examine the question in the light of conflict of laws rules prior to the 1995 Act.

In order to answer the question, the rule in *Phillips v Eyre*, as expanded in *Boys v Chaplin* and *Red Sea Insurance Co Ltd v Bouygues SA*, must be examined.

Answer

The fundamental rule of English private international law in tort was formulated in *Phillips v Eyre* (1870). It is contained in the *dictum* of Willes J, who stated:

> As a general rule, in order to found a suit in England for a wrong alleged to have been committed abroad, two conditions must be fulfilled. First, the wrong must be of such a character that it would have been actionable if committed in England ... Secondly, the act must not have been justifiable by the law of the place where it was done.

This double actionability rule implies that the wrong must be actionable in England and the act must not have been justifiable under the law of the place where it was committed. In practice, the rule was very disadvantageous for the claimant, as he had to prove that he had a claim under both the law of the forum and the law of the place where the wrong occurred.

The double actionability rule was modified in *Boys v Chaplin* (1971). In this case, both parties were British servicemen domiciled in England but temporarily stationed in Malta. They had a car accident in Malta. The plaintiff, through the admitted negligence of the defendant, was seriously injured. Both parties were off duty at the time of the accident. By Maltese law, the plaintiff could only recover £53 in special damages for expenses and loss of earnings. However, under English law, he was entitled to recover £2,500 as general damages for pain and suffering.

Under the rule of double actionability, the plaintiff could only recover £53 as a lowest common denominator of both English and Maltese law. The House of Lords held unanimously that the plaintiff should recover the greater amount under English law. However, it is almost impossible to extract the *ratio decidendi* from this case. Indeed, English law was applied by their Lordships for different reasons. The right to claim damages for pain and suffering was justified as follows:

- Lords Guest and Donovan decided that it was a procedural matter and, as such, the *lex fori* applied – English law;
- according to Lord Hodson and others, it was a substantive issue. He stated that the rule in *Phillips v Eyre* should be applied with flexibility, taking into account public policy considerations as expressed in the American Restatement;
- Lord Pearson agreed that some flexibility should be allowed in the operation of the rule in *Phillips v Eyre*, but not in the present case;
- Lord Wilberforce considered the issue to be a substantive one and recommended flexibility in interpretation of the rule in *Phillips v Eyre*, especially in the context of important policy considerations. He emphasised that, in this case, Maltese public policy was not interested in denying the application of English law where both parties were so closely connected with England.

Furthermore, three judges rejected the approach of *Machado v Fontes* (1897) concerning the second limb of the rule in *Phillips v Eyre,* which required non-justifiability of a wrongful act under the law of the place where it was done rather than actionability under the *lex loci delicti.* In *Machado,* the second limb of the rule in *Phillips v Eyre* led the judges to the conclusion that the requirements of the rule were satisfied where the defendant's conduct attracted criminal, but not civil, liability under the *lex loci delicti.* Thus, actionability under the *lex loci delicti,* not wrongfulness, is required.

The decision in *Boys v Chaplin* has left English conflict of laws in foreign tort in a state of great uncertainty. It seems that the judgment of Lord Wilberforce is considered to be authoritative by academics and judges. It is safe to say that the rule of double actionability still applies but is subject to a more flexible interpretation. Thus, the law of the forum can be applied by way of exception. This rule has been applied in some cases. In *Johnson v Coventry Churchill International Ltd* (1992), an English employee working in Germany for an English company was allowed to sue his employer when the latter failed to provide a safe means of access to the place of work. He would have had no claim against his employer under German law. Furthermore, as the plaintiff and the defendant were English, they could not have benefited from the German 'no fault' insurance scheme which provides a remedy in such circumstances.

In that case, the rule in *Phillips v Eyre* was applied with flexibility – the plaintiff could sue even though his claim was not actionable under German law (the *lex loci delicti*). However, until *Red Sea Insurance Co Ltd v Bouygues SA* (1994), it was considered that the exception could only apply to a particular issue, not to the entire cause of action. *Red Sea* was decided by the Privy Council in July 1994. In this case, 23 plaintiffs brought an action in Hong Kong against Red Sea, an insurance company incorporated in Hong Kong, whose headquarters were in Saudi Arabia. The plaintiff claimed to be indemnified under an insurance policy issued by the defendant for loss and expenses incurred in relation to correction and repairs to structural damage which had occurred in Saudi Arabia. Red Sea argued that the loss claimed by the plaintiff was not covered by the policy and counterclaimed against Consortium PCG which, according to them, was in breach of its duty of care to the plaintiffs by supplying them with faulty pre-cast concrete building units which were unfit for their purpose.

Consequently, if Red Sea was liable under the policy, they were entitled to recover the loss from PCG by subrogating to the other plaintiffs' rights. PCG applied to strike out the counterclaim. In response, Red Sea applied for leave to amend the counterclaim. Red Sea claimed that they were entitled under Saudi Arabian law to sue PCG directly, in negligence, for the damage caused to the other plaintiffs. The Court of Appeal of Hong Kong struck out this part of the counterclaim on the ground that the direct action against PCG was not available because it was not part of Hong Kong law. The decision was reversed on appeal. The Privy Council endorsed the rule of double actionability and concentrated on the exception. It held that the exception was not limited to the application of the *lex fori*, as in *Boys v Chaplin*, but could also lead to the application of the *lex loci delicti* in cases where that law was more closely connected to the case as a whole or to a particular issue of the case, even though, under the *lex fori*, the liability did not exist as it was not recognised. Since the case was more closely connected with the law of Saudi Arabia, the Privy Council decided that the exception to the double actionability rule should apply. Consequently, the defendant was allowed to rely exclusively on the *lex loci delicti*.

In the light of these developments in conflict of laws, especially the decision of the Privy Council in *Red Sea*, it seems that Anthony's situation will be greatly improved. Previously, under the strict application of the double actionability rule, Anthony's action against James would be dismissed, as the claim was not actionable under the law of Malandia (though it would be actionable under the *lex fori*). Now, Anthony may rely on the exception in *Boys v Chaplin* (if it is actually an exception – not a new rule) and commence proceedings against James.

Until the decision in *Red Sea*, James could recover damages under the *lex loci delicti* but not under the *lex fori*. However, it was decided in *Red Sea* that the exception was not limited to the application of the *lex fori*. Thus, the departure from the strict rule in *The Halley* (1868) was, according to the Privy Council, justified;

otherwise, it would contradict the flexibility allowed by the exception as stated by Lord Wilberforce in *Boys v Chaplin*. Furthermore, the exception is not only limited to a specific issue but can be applied to the whole case. As a result, if all significant factors point in the direction of the *lex loci delicti*, the latter applies to the whole case.

Question 35

Explain why it was necessary to reform English conflict of laws rules in tort, taking into consideration the situation of a claimant who commences proceedings in England in relation to a tort committed abroad.

Answer plan

The main disadvantages to the claimant who brings proceedings in England in relation to a tort committed abroad must be examined. Particular attention must be paid to the following: the double actionability rule and its impact on the position of the plaintiff; the principle of the lowest common denominator in respect of recovery of damages; non-application of foreign law *ex officio* if the *lex loci delict* is a foreign law; and defences available to the defendant which will allow him to escape liability.

Answer

Prior to the enactment of Pt III of the Private International Law (Miscellaneous Provisions) Act 1995, the position of a claimant in a dispute involving a wrongful act committed abroad but tried and determined in England was particularly difficult.

Under the rule of double actionability (which was formulated in *Phillips v Eyre* (1971)), he had to prove that the wrong was actionable under the laws of both the forum and the place where the wrong occurred. This solution imposed a heavy burden on the claimant.

The need for actionability under the *lex fori* exaggerated the importance of the forum. This attitude, which is peculiar to English law, was nationalistic and parochial, since it afforded to English domestic law a special importance in matters which, as they concerned torts committed abroad, were primarily connected with foreign countries. The *lex fori* claimed its application regardless of the circumstances of a particular case and the situation of the parties. Furthermore, this approach produced astonishing results. It denied a remedy when an action was not recognised by the *lex fori*. Thus, if a claim was actionable under the *lex loci delicti* but not the *lex fori*, it would have been dismissed by an English court. In *Def Lepp Music v Stuart-Brown* (1986), the plaintiff brought an action for an infringement of UK copyright which he alleged took place abroad. It was held that such acts were not actionable as a tort under the Copyright Act 1956 (now repealed by the Copyright, Designs and Patents Act 1988) or at common law. As a result, his claim was dismissed. The same decision was reached in *Tyburn Productions Ltd v Conan Doyle* (1991).

A second difficult issue was that the *lex fori* set up a maximum amount of damages recoverable by the claimant. As a result, when the *lex loci delicti* was more generous to the claimant, the *lex fori* ignored it. Conversely, if the *lex fori* was more generous, the *lex loci delicti* intervened. As a result, the claimant could recover only the strict minimum under both laws. *M'Elroy v M'Allister* (1949) illustrates this point well. The widow of a man killed in an accident in England brought proceedings in England. At the time of the accident, her husband was a passenger in a lorry owned by his employer. All the parties – the man killed in the accident, his widow, the lorry driver and the defendant – were resident in Scotland. If the accident had occurred in Scotland, then, under Scottish law, the widow would have been entitled to substantial damages for *solatium*. If the accident had occurred in England and the parties had been resident in England, she would have been entitled to both substantial damages under the Fatal Accidents Act 1976 and loss of the deceased's expectation of life under the Law Reform (Miscellaneous Provisions) Act 1934. The Court of Session applied the double actionability rule and held that the widow was entitled to recover £40 in respect of funeral expenses, as it was the only point at which both laws agreed. The application of a lowest common denominator in respect of damages resulted in gross injustice to the plaintiff.

Thirdly, the defendant could easily escape liability, as any defence which was valid under English law was available to him. Similarly, he could plead any defence provided by the *lex loci delicti* unless it was a procedural defence. It was particularly unjust to the claimant if the defendant could defeat an action on the basis of a defence available under the *lex fori*. Indeed, the connection between a tort committed abroad and a defence provided by the *lex fori* but not *lex loci delicti* aggravated the disadvantageous position of the claimant. The defences available to the defendant included defences at common law. Additionally, under the Foreign Limitation Periods Act 1984, the defendant could defeat the action if the limitation period had expired under either the *lex fori* or the *lex loci delicti*, whichever was shorter. In this respect, in *Matall und Rohstoff AG v Donaldson Lufkin and Jenrette Inc* (1990), the distinction between substantive and procedural defences under the *lex loci delicti* in relation to the limitation period was abolished. As to contributory negligence, it constituted a valid defence; this meant that, if a tort was committed in a country which considered it to be a complete defence, the claimant's claim would fail.

Another disadvantage resulting from conflict of laws rules in tort still exists under the 1995 Act. It concerns the status attaching to proof of foreign law, which is treated as a question of fact and consequently must be pleaded and proved as any other fact. Judges are presumed to be technically ignorant of unproven foreign law. Even though the foreign law is 'a question of fact of a peculiar kind' (*Parkasho v Singh* (1968); *Dalmaria Dairy Industries Ltd v National Bank of Pakistan* (1978)), it is still a question of fact and consequently a matter which has to be proved, although a special status of foreign law is recognised by s 69(5) of the English Supreme Court Act 1981. It provides that:

> ... [when] it is necessary to ascertain the law of any other country which is applicable to the facts of the case, any question as to the effect of the evidence given with respect to that law shall, instead of being submitted to the jury, be decided by the judge alone.

Thus, not only is the cost of proving and pleading foreign law important to the claimant but also the fact that judges assess the competence of the experts and are entitled to their own opinion as to the meaning of submitted evidence. A judge's perception of foreign law may come as a total surprise to all the parties concerned (*Dubai Bank Ltd v Galadari* (1990)).

Because this area of English private international law was fraught with uncertainty, it was necessary to change conflict of laws in tort. In this respect, the rule in *Phillips v Eyre* was modified by subsequent case law, but it is difficult to assess the extent to which this was done. The House of Lords in *Boys v Chaplin* delivered five different and often contradictory judgments. After the judgment of the Privy Council in *Red Sea*, it was impossible to predict the outcome of a particular dispute.

It is submitted that English conflict of laws rules in multi-State torts have been rightly criticised. The claimant was disadvantaged for a number of reasons. He had to prove that both requirements of the double actionability rule, as formulated 129 years ago, were satisfied; thus, the alleged wrong must have been actionable if it had been a tort committed in England. It had to be actionable in the *lex loci delicti* regardless of the circumstances of the case and the parties. Furthermore, the plaintiff got the worst of both laws (that is, the *lex fori* and the *lex loci delicti*). He could only recover damages which were recoverable under both laws, which meant that the principle of the lowest common denominator was applied. Also, the defendant could easily escape liability as he was entitled to any defence available under the *lex fori* and the *lex loci delicti*. As a result, gross injustice was done to the claimant in situations where his claim was not recognised under the *lex fori* (and would thus be dismissed) but defences unknown to the forum would be available to the defendant (*Lieff v Palmer* (1937)) which would enable him to escape liability.

In general, English private international law exaggerates the importance of the *lex fori* to the detriment of foreign law. In multi-State torts, this tendency is even more obvious. Finally, the uncertainty as to the choice of laws solutions before entry into force of the 1995 Act did not improve the position of the claimant.

Question 36

Critically assess the solutions in conflict of laws in tort introduced by the Private International Law (Miscellaneous Provisions) Act 1995.

Answer plan

The most important features of Pt II of the Private International Law (Miscellaneous Provisions) Act 1995 should be examined. The main characteristic of the 1995 Act is that it abolishes the double actionability rule and the distinction between torts committed in England and foreign torts. The general rule under the 1995 Act provides that the law of the country in which the events constituting the tort or delict occur applies, that is, the *lex loci delicti commissi* governs multi-State torts. However, the exception in favour of the application of the proper law of tort provides the basis for the critical assessment of the 1995 Act. In conclusion, the following points should appear:

- whether the 1995 Act strikes the right balance between certainty and flexibility;
- whether it treats the claimant and the defendant equally;
- whether it leads to fair and just solutions;
- whether the 1995 Act should be preferred to the old common law rules on conflict of laws in tort.

Answer

The current rules on conflict of laws in tort have been strongly but rightly criticised. The Law Commission and Scottish Law Commission have recommended new solutions in order to provide rules of conflict of laws in tort appropriate to the requirements of modern society and in line with solutions in other countries. A Working Paper was published in 1984[1] which, after consultation, led the Law Commission to prepare recommendations which were accompanied by a Draft Bill in 1990.[2] Part III of the Private International Law (Miscellaneous Provisions) Act 1995 (ss 9–15) implements the Law Commission's

Draft Bill. The 1995 Act applies to England, Wales, Scotland and Northern Ireland. Its structure is very simple: it establishes a general rule regarding the determination of the applicable law to torts and then states the exceptions to that rule. The Act has no retrospective effect.

However, the tort of defamation, torts committed on the high seas and the question of contractual defences in a tort action are outside its scope of application. As a result, the common law rules will apply to the torts of defamation; therefore, uncertainty remains as to the possibility of contractual defences in a tort action (*Sayers v International Drilling Co* (1971)). As to torts committed on the high seas, these are still governed by the principles of maritime law.

The main innovation introduced by the 1995 Act is that the double actionability rule, as modified in *Boys v Chaplin*, is replaced by the *lex loci delicti commissi*: the law of the country in which the events constituting the tort occured. In order to identify the *lex loci commissi* when significant elements of those events take place in different countries, according to s 11(2):

> ... the applicable law under the general rules is to be taken as being:
>
> (a) for a cause of action in respect of personal injury, caused to an individual or death resulting from personal injury, the law of the country where the individual was when he sustained the injury;
>
> (b) for a cause of action in respect of damage to property, the law of the country where the property was when it was damaged; and
>
> (c) in any other case, the law of the country in which the most significant element or elements of those events occurred.

The application of the *lex loci delicti* is in line with solutions in most countries. The rule discourages 'forum shopping', as the substantive law in most cases will be the same, regardless of the country in which the court is situated. Also, in most cases, it constitutes the best solution, as the place in which the tort occurred is usually one country. Thus, the new rule responds to the reasonable expectations of the parties. Furthermore, s 9(1) of the Act provides that the characterisation of issues relating to a tort or delict is to be determined by the forum. This provision precludes English courts from deciding actions for torts unknown to English law, such as privacy, unfair competition and criminal compensation.

The general rule may be displaced and a law of another country applied if a more significant connection is established between that country and the tort. In order to ascertain the law which is substantially more appropriate than the one selected by the general rule, a comparison must be made between the significance, in all the circumstances, of factors which connect a tort with the law of the country which is *prima facie* applicable and the significance of any real and substantial factor connecting the tort with the law of another country. If, as a result of this comparison, it appears that the law of another country is more substantially appropriate than the *prima facie* applicable law, the law of that country should be applied.

In the search for the law with which the tort has the closest and most real connection for the purposes of applying the rule of displacement, certain factors may be taken into consideration. Although s 12 of the 1995 Act does not provide an exhaustive list, it specifies that such factors include those relating to the parties, any of the events which constitute the tort and any of the circumstances or consequences of those events. The proper law exception ensures the flexibility which is so necessary in deciding multi-State torts. It will apply in cases where it is difficult to determine the place of wrong, not only where the act and the damage may be dissociated geographically but also where the essential parts of those two elements of tort may be scattered over the territories of many States and the parties themselves may have no significant connection with the place of occurrence of the events leading to the tort.

The exception will apply in situations where it would be substantially more appropriate to apply a law other than the *lex loci delicti commissi* because all the significant factors point in the direction of one law, as occurred in *Boys v Chaplin* (where the applicable law was clearly the English law) and *Red Sea* (where the law of Saudi Arabia had the most real and substantial connection with the parties involved and the circumstances of the dispute). The exception causes some interpretational problems but is necessary in order to ensure flexibility.

Part III of the Private International Law (Miscellaneous Provisions) Act 1995 stipulates that the application of a foreign law which is determined by virtue of the above rules will be disregarded if it is contrary to the principles of English public policy, is penal in character or concerns foreign revenue or other public law. The 1995 Act also gives priority to mandatory provisions of the forum and makes it clear that any questions of procedure in proceedings before an English court are to be determined in accordance with the *lex fori*. The *renvoi* is expressly rejected by s 9(3). Thus, when an English court determines, according to the rules contained in the 1995 Act, that the applicable law is a foreign law, the substantive provisions of that law will be applied.

It is submitted that the Private International Law (Miscellaneous Provisions) Act 1995 is a step in the right direction in relation to multi-State torts. It is not perfect, as, in this area of law, it is impossible to find an ideal solution, but it strikes a good balance between certainty and flexibility. Indeed, the general rule is clear and poses no major interpretational problems. The exception, like any exception, is formulated in broad and imprecise terms. The Law Commission has indicated that it is against the application of different laws to different issues and favours the application of the exception to the whole of a tort or delict. It recommends that, in cases where there are three or more parties to the same proceedings, the applicable law should be determined separately for each pair of opponents. In general, the exception is not easy to apply and, thus, the nature of the issue in each case will dictate whether the general rule should be displaced. Furthermore, the exception should be applied restrictively so as not to undermine the general rule. It is submitted that, whatever problems may arise under the 1995 Act, its solutions should certainly be preferred to the old common law rules. Even if the 1995 Act does not achieve greater certainty, it eliminates unfair and unjust solutions which were inherent in the old rules. The claimant and defendant are treated equally. The disadvantages to the claimant which resulted in advantages to the defendant have been swept away.

Notes

1 Law Commission, *Private International Law: Choice of Law in Tort and Delict*, Working Paper No 87, 1984.
2 Law Commission, *Private International Law: Choice of Law in Tort and Delict*, Working Paper No 193, 1990.

Question 37

Examine the jurisdiction of English courts under Art 5(3) of the Brussels Convention in the tort of defamation and assess English conflict of law rules in this area.

Answer plan

For English courts, the question of jurisdiction has always been more important than the determination of the applicable law in tortious matters. In relation to Art 5(3) of the Brussels Convention, the ECJ decision in *Cheval v Press Alliance SA* (1992) is particularly important.

Part III of the Private International law (Miscellaneous Provisions) Act 1995 expressly excludes claims for defamation. For that reason, it is necessary to examine this question according to traditional conflict of law rules in tort. In this respect, once the place of tort is determined (which often has to be done in the context of jurisdiction), the rule of double actionability, as modified in *Boys v Chaplin* and interpreted by the Privy Council in *Red Sea*, applies.

Answer

Article 5(3) of the Brussels Convention covers many different kinds of tort. In cases of, *inter alia*, product liability, unfair competition, transnational pollution and defamation, the determination of the place where the harmful event occurred from a jurisdictional standpoint can be extremely difficult. In particular, defamation cases give rise to confusion and uncertainty because damage to reputation is of a non-physical nature and can only be located *in abstractio*.

In spite of the obvious attraction of granting a wider choice of jurisdiction to the claimant, the decision of the ECJ in *Bier v Mines de Potasse* (1976) gives rise to practical difficulties in the context of defamation which has been communicated through the media of radio, television and newspapers. It is difficult to separate the event giving rise to the damage from the damage itself. It may be argued that the place where the allegedly libellous article is written or where the defamatory remarks are uttered on radio or television is also the place where the damage first occured. It is also possible to claim that the distribution of newspapers or a broadcast on radio or television containing alleged defamatory statements constitutes the last event giving rise to the damage and thus completes the tort of libel.

For the victim of alleged defamation, the fact that both he and his family, friends, employers, etc, hears broadcast remarks is of the utmost importance. Neither the place of publication nor the place of distribution is important. The fact that a newspaper containing a defamatory statement can be bought at a local newsstand is critical for the claimant, no matter how many copies are available. Thus, it may be argued that, in cases involving defamation via the media, the domicile of the victim is the most important connecting factor, both in the choice of law context and from a jurisdictional point of view.

It may be suggested that all connecting factors as to the determination of jurisdiction for the purposes of Art 5(3) of the Convention should be ignored in favour of the solution which common sense dictates, namely that the place where the claimant's reputation is injured should be considered as the place where the harmful event occurred.

Nevertheless, the fact that complex and sophisticated techniques of modern mass media make it possible for a defamatory remark which is broadcast from Ireland to be heard in New Zealand, and the fact that almost any newspaper in any language may be bought in any civilised place on Earth, exposes the complexity of that question.

At this stage, it is useful to examine a few decisions made in Contracting States in the context of Art 5(3) with respect to transnational defamation.

In *Radio Monte Carlo v Syndicat National de l'Edition Phonographique* (1991), an action was brought against the owner of a radio station in Monaco for the unlawful broadcast of copyright material which was heard in France. The French court held that it had jurisdiction on the basis of Art 5(3), since the place where injury was caused was France.

In *The Unauthorised Publication of Approved Photographs* (1991), the claimant, a German domiciliary, sued the Dutch publisher, a Dutch domiciliary, in Germany for unauthorised publication of his photograph in the defendant's pornographic magazine. The German court declared that, since the Dutch pornographic magazine was not distributed regularly or even in small numbers in Germany, the mere fact that it was possible to buy copies in Germany did not justify the assumption of jurisdiction by the German court.

Even if we accept that the minimum requirement for the assumption of jurisdiction by a court is the circulation of the publication to a significant extent or a regular distribution, even if only in small numbers of copies, another problem arises. In *Shevill v Presse Alliance SA* (1992), the claimant (an English domiciliary) brought an action for libel against a French newspaper, *France Soir*, in respect of the publication of an article alleging that the claimant's workplace had laundered drug money. The defendant newspaper had a daily circulation of 200,000 copies in France and 15,000 outside France, including 230 copies in England and Wales. It was held that the English court was entitled to exercise jurisdiction, on the grounds that the libel had been published in England and constituted a harmful event in the light of Art 5(3). However, the claimant had limited her claim to the publication of the article in England and Wales. Thus, any harm she had suffered was minimal.

The Court of Appeal suggested that, had the claimant not limited her claim to the publication in England, the court might have declined jurisdiction. From this case, the question arose as to whether she might sue in France where, by reason of the larger circulation, she might expect to get higher damages. In order to clarify the meaning of 'the place where the harmful event occurred' under Art 5(3), the House of Lords referred *Shevill* to the ECJ for a preliminary ruling and asked seven questions.

The Court held that, in the case of defamation by a newspaper circulated in more than one Contracting State, the expression 'place where the harmful event occurred' under Art 5(3) must be interpreted as meaning that the claimant may sue either in the place where the publisher of the defamatory publication is established or in the place where the newspaper is distributed and where the victim claims to have suffered injury to his reputation. However, the court of the place where the publisher is established has jurisdiction to hear the action for damages for all harm caused to the claimant. The courts of each Contracting State in which the defamatory newspaper was distributed had jurisdiction solely in respect of the harm caused in that State.

Therefore, in international press defamation cases, the place of the event giving rise to the damage is the place where the publisher of the defamatory publication is established, since the damage originates from that place. The place where the damage occurred is the place where the event giving rise to the damage produces an effect upon the victim. Thus, it is the place where the defamatory publication is distributed and where the victim has a reputation.

Furthermore, the ECJ stated that the criteria for assessing whether the event is harmful and the evidence necessary to establish the existence and extent of the alleged harm are outside the scope of the Convention. It is up to the *lex causae* selected by the conflict of law rules of the forum to determine this question.

In the light of decisions of the ECJ regarding the application of Art 5(3) of the Convention in general and the cases of transnational defamation in particular, a few conclusions may be drawn.

Article 5(3) of the Convention should be interpreted restrictively as being an exception to a principle. As a consequence, the domicile of the claimant as a sole connecting jurisdictional factor is excluded. Therefore, in defamation cases, the jurisdiction of *forum actoris* should be rejected; this means that if, for instance, a defamatory letter or article was written in State A, published in State B and the reputation of the claimant was injured in State C, States A and C have no jurisdiction over the claim, even though the claimant is domiciled in State C.

Different approaches should be applied as to the determination of the place where the harmful event occurred for choice of law objectives and for jurisdictional purposes. It may be submitted that, in the context of choice of law rules, the place where the claimant's reputation is injured constitutes the most important connecting factor. This solution is, of course, easy to state but difficult to apply in practice. Nevertheless, in the majority of disputes, it would lead to the application of the *lex domicili*. On the other hand, for the purposes of Art 5(3) of the Convention, a distinction must be drawn between the place where the event which originally started the sequence of events resulting in the damage (and without which the damage could not have occurred) and the place where damage occurred at an earlier point in time. In the context of transnational defamation, the place where the first event in a series of events giving rise to the damage occurred (the event at the 'origin' of the damage) is the place where the defamatory statement is published and put into circulation. As to the allocation of jurisdiction to the courts of the place where the damage first occurred, an important practical difficulty arises, since the damage may occur in many Contracting States at the same time.

It has been clear since *Bier* and has been confirmed in *Shevill* that a court may exercise jurisdiction if any one element of the tort, the event which was at the origin of the damage, or the damage itself, first occurred in the territory of the court. As a result, the claimant is allowed, at his option, to bring the action in the courts of either country. However, only the court located in the place where the event which originally started the sequence of events and which eventually resulted in the damage occurred has the general competence to entertain all actions in respect of tortious liability and can award damages wherever the event happened to take place. This general competence is justified, since it is necessary to have a clear solution in cases of complex conflicts. The exceptional allocation of jurisdiction to the courts of the place where the damage first occurred must not obscure the fact that it is the court of the place where the wrongful event took place that possesses the general jurisdiction over the claim in its entirety. Furthermore, it is also important to realise that this is the only solution which can achieve a minimum of coherence in foreign tort matters under the Convention.

As to the court of the place where the damage was first suffered, it has only functional competence, since that court can only assess damage which occurred within the jurisdiction.

In the context of choice of law rules, Pt III of the Private International Law (Miscellaneous Provisions) Act 1995 excludes defamation from its scope of application. As a result, common law conflict of laws rules apply. Under those rules, the determination of the place where the wrongful event occurred has been examined principally from a jurisdictional point of view. In every decision concerning the purpose of Ord 11, it was held that the place where the defamation is committed is the place where the defamatory statement is published. Thus, in *Bata v Bata* (1948),[1] the Court of Appeal decided that leave to serve the defendant out of jurisdiction should be granted when a defamatory letter written in Switzerland was received in London, since publication completed the tort of libel and, therefore, the cause of action had arisen in England. In *Church of Scientology v Metropolitan Police Comr* (1976), the Court of Appeal held that, where an alleged defamatory report had been written in England and sent to a German Police Authority, the tort had been committed in Germany.

The same approach was applied in a case of defamation by radio broadcast from a New York studio which was heard in Ontario. The Ontario High Court stated that the tort was committed in Ontario and, therefore, local courts had jurisdiction over the claim (*Jenner v Sun Oil Co* (1952)).

At this stage, it is useful to remember that the assessment of damage is a matter for the *lex fori* (*Kohnke v Karger* (1951)). Thus, when an action is brought before an English court, as far as the recovery of damages is concerned, the principle of the lowest common denominator applies, which means that the claimant can only recover such damages as are recoverable under both the *lex loci delicti commissi* and the *lex fori*.

Notes

1 However, see *Kroch v Rossell et Cie* (1937), a case involving libel in the printed media, where a person having no connection with England claimed to be defamed in two

French and Belgian newspapers, of which only a few copies were sold in England. The Court of Appeal refused service out of the jurisdiction, but Slesser J said *obiter* that, on the facts of the case, he would have been prepared to assume that the alleged tort had been committed in England. See, also, *Pillai v Sarkar* (1994).

* by Alina Kaczorowska

CHAPTER 7

PROPERTY AND SUCCESSION

Introduction

This chapter examines the rules of private international law in relation to transfers of property, individual or universal. The former relates to transfers founded on a contractual agreement, whilst the latter is usually by will or other similar disposition.

Students should know the distinction between movable and immovable property. Conflict of laws is concerned not so much with the distinction between personal and real property as with the distinction between immovable and movable property. One of the fundamental problems in this connection is the classification of movables and immovables. English private international law provides that the classification of the property in question as movable or immovable is left to the *lex situs*.

The general rule vis à vis immovable property is found in Art 16(1) of the Brussels Convention, as incorporated into English law by the Civil Jurisdiction and Judgments Act 1982. This Article, which encapsulates the common law position, states that the courts of the *lex situs* have exclusive jurisdiction in proceedings which have as their object rights *in rem* in, or tenancies of, immovable property (see, also, *British South Africa Co v Compania de Mocambique* (1893)). The exceptions to this rule should be observed:

- where the court has jurisdiction *in personam* over the defendant, it also has jurisdiction to entertain an action against him in respect of contract or an equity affecting foreign land (RSC Ord 11 r 1(1)): *Arglasse Muschamp* (1682) and *Penn v Baltimore* (1750));
- where the court has jurisdiction to administer a trust or the estate of a deceased person and some of the property in question includes foreign land, there is no reason why the court cannot exercise jurisdiction over the claim (*Nelson v Bridport* (1845));

- a third exception is found in the law of admiralty. In *The Tolken* (1946), in the exercise of jurisdiction *in rem* by an English Admiralty court, that court also had jurisdiction over foreign immovables connected with the claim.

The transfer is subject to the *lex situs* in respect of its formal validity, essential validity and, to a lesser extent, the capacity of the transferor (*Bank of Africa v Cohen* (1909)).

In respect of movable property, the student should bear in mind the distinction between tangible and intangible movables. Some highly relevant issues in this area include:

- the general rule that proprietary rights in the movable property are to be determined by the *lex situs* operative at the time when the property was transferred;
- reservation of title clauses written into the foreign contract of sale as an exception to the general rule;
- the problems caused by goods in transit;
- the application of mandatory public policy considerations;
- the application of Art 12 of the Rome Convention to assignment of intangible movables.

In the area of succession, the distinction between intestacy and testacy is crucial; the rule for the former is that any distribution of movable property is to be carried out in accordance with the law of the deceased's place of domicile. With testacy, the distribution of movables must be made according to the terms of the will; the essential validity of the will and the capacity of the parties are to be determined by the law of the testator's domicile. The issue of formal validity is less strict, as long as the will complies with the provisions of s 1 of the Wills Act 1963.

In respect of immovables, the law is that their distribution *should* be in accordance with the *lex situs*.

Checklist

Areas which should be given particular attention include:

- the distinction between immovables and movables;
- the *lex situs* and immovable property;
- choice of law and validity of transfer of the property;

- the issue of capacity to transfer and to receive;
- the *lex situs* of tangible movables;
- reservation of title, goods in transit and public policy concerns as exceptions to the general rule;
- the proper law of assignment set out in Art 12 of the Rome Convention;
- assignment of debts, validity and capacity considerations;
- seizure of property by foreign governments.

Question 38

Sonny sells rare books and manuscripts. In January 2000, while he was on holiday in Wazland, he bought a book from Jaz. He has now returned to England and intends to sell the book to Jo, a very rich lady.

The book has, in fact, been taken out of Clubland by Jaz and smuggled into Wazland in breach of Clubbish law. Clubbish law prohibits the sale and export of rare manuscripts and books. The Government of Clubland has now issued a decree calling for the seizure of the book stolen by Jaz.

In another transaction made by Sonny while in Wazland, he agreed to franchise his business interest to Tony. The agreement stipulates that the law of Clubland shall be the proper law. The agreement further stipulates that Tony is not allowed to assign his rights to any third party or to subcontract out the franchise. This restriction is valid under English law but not under Clubbish law.

Tony has now entered into a contract with Ully, purporting to grant Ully the franchise to sell rare books in northern Clubland. This agreement is formally valid under English law but not under Clubbish law. Ully is domiciled in England.

Discuss how the rules of English private international law deal with these events.

Answer plan

The first distinct issue here is whether the Clubbish Government could retrieve the book by resorting to the English courts. The rule that an English court is slow to enforce a rule of public law, as pointed out by Lord Denning in *AG of New Zealand v Ortiz* (1984), is essential to the answer. Some discussion of the conditions set out in *Lecouturier v Rey* (1910) and *Luther v Sagor* (1921) should make good inroads into the problem.

The second issue turns on the question of assignment and the assignability of intangible movables, namely the franchise. Here, the student should identify the relevant articles in the Rome Convention – Arts 3, 9 and 12. The primary principles involved are: recognition of the parties' autonomy in choosing the applicable law; the use of the applicable law to determine the assignability of the franchise; and the operation of Art 9 on formal validity.

Answer

It is well settled law that the *lex situs* governs the validity and effect of the transfer of tangible movables. In the present case, the validity of the transfer of the book in Wazland is in issue. At English law, where the *situs* is constant, the position is that, if the proper law of the transaction vests the proprietary interest in the transferee, that interest in the transferee will be recognised. Where the *situs* is not a constant, as is the case here, assistance may be derived from *Cammell v Sewell* (1860).

In *Cammell v Sewell*, the English owner's goods were sold by a shipmaster in Norway after his ship was wrecked off the coast of Norway. His proprietary interest could not prevail over the right of the *bona fide* purchaser, who subsequently brought the goods into England. It was held that, although the sale in Norway was unlawful under English law, the purchaser's rights prevailed over those of the the original owner because, under Norwegian law (the *lex situs*), that transfer was valid.

It is unclear whether Wazzian law makes the transfer of the title in the book to Sonny bad, even though it does prohibit the sale and purchase of smuggled goods. The question of passage of title is separate to the issue of the unlawfulness of the sale; this distinction must be assessed at Wazzian law. If it does confer good title, regardless of the prohibition, the Clubbish Government will be unable to recover the book in the English courts.

On the assumption that the *lex situs* confers good title on Sonny through the sale, the fact that both Clubbish and Wazzian laws make the act an offence is irrelevant, to the extent that English law does not enforce foreign penal laws. It is envisaged that the Clubbish Government is likely to claim that the book is the property of State (by legislation or like manner) and should, therefore, be returned. This argument finds support in the general rule of English private international law that the English judge has no jurisdiction to entertain an action which affects a foreign sovereign's proprietary interest, subject only to the operation of the State Immunity Act 1978. This general rule must, however, be seen in the context of *Luther v Sagor* (1921) and *Lecouturier v Rey* (1910).

The position is that foreign governmental laws or decrees purporting to recover or seize private property will be recognised only if the property was within the territory of the foreign State at the time that the decree or the legislation concerned was made. In dealing with the present case, it would be imperative to determine whether the legislation or decree was in place when the book was in Clubland. Tangible things such as books are 'situated' where they are physically situated (*Standard Chartered Bank Ltd v IRC* (1978)). Secondly, the legislation must refer specifically to the property in question, and finally, the court must enquire whether the decree forms a part of the law of that place which is acceptable by English law.

According to the court in *Luther v Sagor*, before the seizure or purported seizure is to be given recognition at English law, the court must be satisfied that the decree has legal standing at the place where it was legislated. For example, a forcible seizure by an unlawful government will not be recognised. This does not arise in Sonny's case.

Although the information given does not go far enough to permit the determination of the validity and currency of the decree, the rule is that, if the decree was issued only after the book had been taken out of Clubland, then the extraterritorial effect of the decree will not be enforced by the English court.

On the third condition, it was held in *Banco de Vizcaya v Don Alfonso de Borbon y Austria* (1935) that decrees which confiscate property are to be treated as penal in nature and, as such, are not to be enforced. In *AG of New Zealand v Ortiz* (1982), the New Zealand authorities claimed that they were entitled to a Maori door which had been taken unlawfully from New Zealand to England to be auctioned. Lord Denning, in the Court of Appeal, held that the New Zealand statute which provided for the forfeiture of historic articles was a provision of public law and could not, therefore, be enforced by the English court. Moreover, on further examination, the statute provided that New Zealand authorises such a right only when the goods have been seized by the New Zealand Government. The House of Lords upheld this finding but, unfortunately, did not venture to address the issue of whether such a statute constitutes public law unenforceable at English law.

On the franchise contract, the relevant provision of law comes from the Contracts (Applicable Law) Act 1990, which incorporates the Rome Convention 1980. Voluntary assignments are governed generally by Art 12 of that Convention. Hence, since a franchise contract is an intangible movable, Art 12(1) should apply. It provides that the mutual rights and obligations of the parties are determined by the law which, under the Convention, applies to the contract. This law will effectively govern the issue as to formal and essential validity.

Assuming that either party is possessed of formal and essential capacity, it is important to consider whether the restriction on the assignment may be enforced in the English courts. It is ascertainable from the facts that the restriction is valid under English law but not under Clubbish law. In order to resolve this issue, it is important to establish whether the law applicable to the question of assignability is English or Clubbish law. Article 12(2) of the Convention states that the law governing the right to which the assignment relates shall also determine its assignability. What, then, is the 'law governing the assignment'?

In the current situation, the agreement between Sonny and Tony clearly prohibits the assignment of rights derived under the franchise. The contract, however, expressly prescribes that Clubbish law is to govern the contract. Under Art 3(1) of the same Convention, the law which is chosen by the parties will be the applicable law of the contract. Consequently, the assignment executed by Tony is not unlawful, since Clubland law allows such an assignment.

Upon the supposition that the franchise may be assigned or subcontracted to a third party under Clubbish law, the next issue is whether the lack of formal validity at Clubbish law would be fatal to Tony. Under Art 9(2), a contract concluded between persons who are in different countries is formally valid if it satisfies the formal requirements of either the law which governs it under the Convention or the law of one of those countries. Consequently, as the contract is formally valid where Ully is situated, this Article ensures that the contract is enforceable in England, even though it does not meet Clubbish formal requirements.

In this connection it would be useful to determine what it means by 'form'. The Giuliano-Lagarde Report defines it as 'includ[ing] every external manifestation required on the part of a person expressing a will to be legally bound, and in the absence of which such expression of will would not be regarded as fully effective'. Presumably, if the Clubbish formal requirements are set out to ensure that this 'purported intention' is evinced, then they could be properly regarded as 'formal'.

Question 39

In March 1995, Isaac bought a tractor from Harry in Erewhomes, subject to the condition that, 'until the legally required transfer fee of heavy vehicles has been paid, the title to the tractor remains with Harry and Harry shall have the right to claim possession of the vehicle'. Before settling the full transfer fee, Isaac drove the tractor into Erewhon and sold it to Jason. The law of Erewhon prohibits the removal of vehicles outside its territory until all transfer and registration charges have been settled.

Jason paid Isaac partly in cash and partly by assigning to him a percentage of his royalties on his new album in Erewhomes. In Erewhomes, the assignment of future royalties is not permitted.

Under the law of Erewhomes, the sale of the vehicle gives Jason good title, provided that he was an innocent purchaser and had no notice of the defect in title. Under the private international law of Erewhomes, however, this is not possible.

Jason has now brought the tractor into England. Harry wishes to recover the tractor and Isaac wishes to sue Jason in England for the outstanding royalties which he claims Jason has failed to settle.

Discuss with reference to English private international law.

Answer plan

This question examines the scope of the transfer of tangible movables under English rules of private international law. The main part of this question revolves around the validity and enforceability of the reservation of title clause. This matter is one of considerable doubt and uncertainty. It would be prudent to examine two well known, non-English cases in this regard – *Goetschius v Brightman* (1927) and *Century Credit Corp v Richard* (1962). There is an express invitation to discuss what the proper law of the transaction is when the *situs* changes. In this connection, the rule in *Cammell v Sewell* (1860) should be discussed.

The second limb to this question, albeit the lesser of the two, requires a careful explanation of the ambit of Art 12 of the Rome Convention and, consequently, the determination of the applicable law under Arts 3 and 4.

Answer

There are two distinct situations that warrant discussion here. One relates to the reservation of title condition placed on the sale and purchase agreement between Isaac and Harry, and its validity and subsequent enforceability at English law. The second turns on whether the assignment of future royalties could be enforced by Isaac.

Where the transfer of the vehicle is valid according to its *lex situs* at the time of the transfer, that transfer will be recognised in England. In *Winkworth v Christie Manson & Woods Ltd* (1980), for example, the transfer of stolen art works was recognised because, under Italian law (the *lex situs*), such a transfer was valid. The fact that Isaac has unlawfully (under Erewhomes law) removed the vehicle from the jurisdiction and sold it in Erewhon is irrelevant, to the extent that the *lex situs* (Erewhomes) recognises the transfer. This was confirmed by Staughton LJ in *Macmillan Inc v Bishopsgate Investment Trust plc (No 3)* (1996) in the following terms:

> A purchaser ought to satisfy himself that he obtains good title by the law prevailing where the chattel is ... but should not be required to do more than that, And an owner, if he does not wish to be deprived of his property by some eccentric rule of foreign law, can at least do his best to ensure that it does not leave the safety of his own country.

On the reservation of title clause in the contract between Isaac and Harry, the rule is that the act of reserving or retaining title is not a contractual matter but a proprietary one. This proposition finds support in *Simpson v Fogo* (1863). It was held there that the law of the place where the reservation took place should prevail, provided that the goods were in that country when the title was reserved.

In *Century Credit Corp v Richard* (1962), a Canadian case, a car had been sold under a conditional sale agreement in Quebec. In breach of the agreement, the person in possession took the car into Ontario and sold it to a third party, who resold it to the defendant. Under the law of Quebec, the reservation of title clause was valid but, under Ontarian law, reservation of title was only valid if such clauses were registered and, further, a purchaser in good faith and for value was entitled to a good title under certain circumstances. There was thus a conflict between the two legal systems.

The court first identified the *lex situs* of the transaction in question (that is, the sale to the defendant). That took place in Ontario. It was then decided by the court that, while any attempt by Ontarian law to equip itself with extraterritorial effect over, for example, the laws of Quebec, was unenforceable, the situation where the transaction in question takes place wholly within Ontario should naturally be governed by Ontarian law.

If the English courts were to follow this line of approach, it would appear, then, that the recognition of the transaction between Isaac and Jason in Erewhomes should be enforceable because, first, it is the *lex situs* and, secondly, there is no extraterritorial effect intended or caused.

Further guidance may perhaps be adduced from an American case. In *Goetschius v Brightman* (1927), the law of New York provided that all reservations of title were void against subsequent purchasers in good faith unless the contract had been registered in New York. The seller sought to enforce such a clause against the buyer, a Californian resident, who had taken the car in breach of the contract into New York and sold it to a third party without the seller's consent or knowledge. Under Californian law, the original owner's title prevailed over all other derived titles. On the issue of the statutorily required registration, the New York court held that, although the contract was not initially registered, the original owner could satisfy this requirement by registering as soon as he became aware of it. This was because the statutory registration requirement could not be extended beyond domestic transactions generally.

The two cases may be reconciled on the basis that, in the latter case, New York law had not stated unequivocally that valid title had passed to the third party. In the Canadian case, the position was that the registration issue was of less importance because, under Ontarian law, there had been good passing of property to the third party purchaser.

The impact of these cases on the present situation is this: whether Harry lost his title when his tractor was taken into Erewhomes and sold to Jason depends on the reason why Erewhomes law would deny him his title. Two possible reasons might be offered in this regard:

- Erewhomes, as the country where the subsequent transaction took place, may say that an event which has occurred in its territory has the effect of overriding prior titles; or
- it may not recognise the transaction whereby the original owner acquired or reserved his title in the first country (in the present case, Erewhon).

If the former were the case, the law of Erewhomes governs as the *lex situs* and Harry's title is lost, because that law makes an innocent purchaser without notice of the defect in title capable of receiving a good title, even though the transferor has no title. If it were the latter, the law of Erewhon would govern as the *lex situs* and Harry should thus retain his title. The law of Erewhomes would be irrelevant to the transaction.

These propositions take the discussion back to *Cammell v Sewell* (1860), where English law recognised a title to goods acquired in the first State until a new title overrode the original title. Two key points are to be noted: the inclination of the English courts to avoid giving effect to extraterritoriality of foreign laws; and the *lex situs* always takes precedence generally. The issue is frequently one of determining the *situs* of the transaction. Where it is proved that Jason obtains a good title to the tractor under the *lex situs* (Erewhomes), then that title will be similarly recognised by English law.

On the issue of the royalties, it should be pointed out that royalties are a form of intangible movables. As such, the assignment of royalties is to be seen in the light of Art 12 of the Rome Convention, which has been incorporated into English law by the Contracts (Applicable Law) Act 1990. Article 12 provides that the mutual obligations of assignor and assignee under a voluntary assignment shall be determined by the law which, under the Convention, is applicable to the contract in question.

Hence, the first task in relation to the royalties is to ascertain the law applicable to the contract made between Jason and Isaac. The general rule under the Convention is that, where the parties have expressly elected the applicable law for the contract, that election shall apply. Where there is an absence of an express choice of law, Art 4(1) states that the law of the country most closely connected with the contract will be the applicable law. In determining the law of the country most closely connected with the contract, Art 4(2) presumes that that country is the one where the party who is to effect the performance characteristic of the contract had his habitual residence at the time of the conclusion of the contract.

If the delivery of the tractor to Jason is to be treated as the obligation performance of which is characteristic of the contract, then Erewhon would appear to be the country with which the contract is most closely connected, because that is presumably the place where Isaac (the party who is to effect that performance) has his place of habitual residence. This proposition would be in line with the Giuliano-Lagarde Report, where performance characteristic of the contract was linked with that for which consideration in payment of money is due.

Article 4(2), however, is not irrebuttable. Under Art 4(5), the presumption is not to be used if it appears from the circumstances that, on the whole, the contract is more closely connected with another country. The law of that country will be the applicable law. It may be argued that, as the contract was actually made and performed in Erewhomes, the provisions of Art 4(2) are displaced.

Accordingly, if the law of Erewhon governs the substance of contract, the prohibition on future royalties under Erewhomes law would be ineffective and could not be applied by the English courts.

Question 40

> Any inability of the court to enforce the decree *in rem* is no reason for refusing the plaintiff such right and means of enforcement as equity can afford him [*Richard West & Partners (Inverness) Ltd v Dick* (1969), *per* Megarry J].

Critically examine the operation of equity on private international law in this context.

Answer plan

It is important to know the context of the quote. The 'inability of the court to enforce the decree *in rem*' refers to the rule both at common law and under the Brussels Convention against the interference with another country's jurisdiction over its land or immovable property. Taking that as the starting point, it would be useful to explain the operation of the general position with reference to case law (see *British South Africa Co v Compania de Mocambique* (1893)).

Next, discuss how equity intervenes to offer some form of redress for the claimant whose rights are rights *in personam* but tied with immovables in a foreign State. Examine the difficulties involved and comment on the lack of consistency evident in the case law.

Answer

The general rule at common law and under the Brussels Convention (Art 16(1)(a)) is that English courts have no jurisdiction when the subject matter in a dispute is the title to or right to possession of foreign immovable property. At the end of the 19th century, the House of Lords decided in *British South Africa Co v Compania de Mocambique* (1893) that the Judicature Act 1873 and the subsequently drafted Rules of Court prevented any English court from exercising jurisdiction over an action to determine the title to or right to possession of any immovable property situated outside England and Wales. The quote taken from Megarry J's judgment is, however, a reflection of the more flexible approach and practice of the Court of Equity to grant relief even though the action may involve such a title claim or right to possession.

This essay will examine the rationale of equitable relief principles vis à vis the so called *Mocambique* rule (and/or Art 16 of the Brussels Convention) and consider the extent to which these principles have been applied.

The rationale behind the English law rule of restraint is that to exercise jurisdiction over immovable property situated in another country is an unwarranted interference with that State's territorial sovereignty. On the other hand, where the matter concerns personal rights, there is no conflict with the principle of territorial sovereignty where an English court exercises jurisdiction over a person who has submitted to jurisdiction or is within the jurisdiction. In the latter case, the rights involved are generally rights *in personam*, and jurisdiction over these rights is not interventionist in nature as far as international comity between States is concerned. The problem arises, however, when these personal rights connote or implicate rights over immovable property in a foreign country.

The basic rule, as espoused in *Re Smith* (1916), is that the enforcement of such personal rights may be lawful, provided that the *lex situs* over the immovable property is not affected. In that case, the court ordered specific performance of the undertaking in order to create an effective mortgage over immovable property in the West Indies. This was permissible because the specific performance ordered was based on the personal relationship between the parties and was not founded on rights *in rem*.

There is, however, inconsistency in judicial approach and practice in this regard. In *Bank of Africa v Cohen* (1909), the *lex situs* (the Transvaal) prohibited the transfer of land as security without the surety first renouncing certain protectionary legislation. The surety, an English domiciled married woman, had not done so, and the court found that the surety agreement could not, therefore, be enforced in England. Although the legislation dealt with her personal rights, the court appears to have taken a rather strict approach.

This inconsistency, which is unfortunately all too often a side effect of the application of equity, has motivated some of the later decisions to prescribe certain conditions before applying or refusing to apply equity in this manner.

The first rule is that jurisdiction *in personam* must be established. This may be achieved by showing that the defendant is in England when the claim is served or that he submits (expressly or by implication) to the jurisdiction; or secondly, where leave to serve notice of the claim out of jurisdiction under RSC Ord 11 r 1(1) has been obtained.

Respect for the *lex situs* is of fundamental importance, hence the second condition. According to *Re Courtney ex p Pollard* (1840), before jurisdiction may be exercised, 'the law of the country where the land is situated should not permit or enable the defendant to do what the court might otherwise think it right to decree' (*per* Lord Cottenham). It would be useless and unjust to direct him to do so. In that case, the mortgagor deposited title deeds to land in Scotland with the mortgagee and undertook to take steps to ensure that the security was good. Under English law, the deposit of title deeds was tantamount to an equitable mortgage, but this was not the position at Scots law. The mortgagee subsequently attempted to enforce the mortgage. He succeeded on the basis that there was nothing to prevent a valid mortgage being created over Scottish land, the mortgage being a right *in personam*, and there was also a personal duty on the mortgagor to create such a mortgage.

The emphasis on rights *in personam* was taken further in *Re Hawthorne* (1883), where the court held that there 'must be some personal element, something more than a mere naked question of title to foreign land'. In that case, the title to property in Germany was in dispute. One of the parties sold the property and received part of the purchase price. On whether the other person could compel him to account for the money, the court declined jurisdiction. Jurisdiction cannot be exercised unless there is some 'personal equity running from the plaintiff to the defendant'.[1] These rights *in personam* must be recognisable at equity.

In *Norris v Chambres* (1861), for example, the court had to decline jurisdiction because the person against whom equitable relief was sought was not privy to the equity. There, the seller agreed to sell land in a foreign country but had instead later transferred it to a third party. Although the third party had notice of the agreement between the seller and the original buyer, the court could not wield any jurisdictional control over him. This is not an easy issue for the courts, thus limiting further the scope of equity in this realm. The position in *Norris v Chambres* was not followed in *Mercantile Investment Co v River Plate Ltd* (1892), where the third party's notice of a charge on the land in question was subject to equity. Jurisdiction was exercised accordingly.

Yet another difficulty in relying on equity is the fact (or rule of practice) that an English court will not issue any equitable relief unless it can effectively supervise the execution and enforcement of the decree. In *Grey v Manitoba Railway Co* (1897), the court was invited by the mortgagee to order relief against the mortgagor who had land in a foreign country. The court refused to order the sale of the land in question because there was little likelihood of effective supervision of the execution of such an order.

Where fraud or other unconscionable conduct is alleged, the courts are prepared to order equitable relief where doing so will not be repugnant to the control of the *lex situs* over the property. In *Webb v Webb* (1991), for example, even though the property involved was immovable property situated in a foreign country, the court did not hesitate in ordering a trustee of a constructive trust situation to perform his obligations.

In conclusion, it may be opined that, while equity does in fact equip the common law courts to grant relief to a person whose rights are dependent or connected with immovable property in a foreign State, there are four major difficulties: the cardinal priority of avoiding encroachment on the foreign country's territorial sovereignty; the problem of defining the connection with the immovable property; the problem of identifying the existence of an equitable element; and the practical matter of supervision of the equitable remedy granted. Further, all the conventional equitable norms or maxims shall apply, since the remedy sought in founded on equity.

Note

1 McLean, *Morris – The Conflict of Laws*, 4th edn, 1993, p 307.

Question 41

Siti, who was domiciled in Highland, married Abdul, a domiciliary of Lowland. She moved to Lowland to be with Abdul. By an ante-nuptial agreement, Siti, who was then under the age of majority under the law of Highland, covenanted to settle her property on her husband. According to the law of Lowland, the settlement is valid, but, under the law of Highland, a woman cannot settle her property on marriage.

The law of Highland provides that a married woman's property is to be divided equally between her husband and children.

Assuming that Siti and Abdul were subsequently domiciled in England until Siti died in 1999, advise Abdul regarding the settlement.

Answer plan

The emphasis of this question is on the operation of a marriage settlement contract and on questions of validity, formal and essential. The student should be versed in the general rule that matrimonial property rights created by an ante-nuptial agreement are governed by the terms of that agreement (*Duke of Marlborough v AG* (1945)). The exclusion of the Rome Convention should be pointed out in this regard.

There is also the added issue of the distinction between rights accruing to immovable property as against movables.

The proposition that capacity is to be determined by the law of the matrimonial domicile rather than the proper law of the settlement should be examined critically. The three cases usually cited in support, *Re Cooke's Trusts* (1887), *Cooper v Cooper* (1888) and *Viditz v O'Hagan* (1900), should be discussed in the light of academic opinion.

Answer

Generally, the effect of marriage on the property of a wife or husband will depend on whether there exists between them a marriage settlement or ante-nuptial agreement. According to Dicey and Morris, where there is no marriage settlement and no subsequent change of domicile of the parties to the marriage, the governing law so far as movables are concerned is the law of the matrimonial domicile, which is normally the husband's domicile at the time of the marriage. Where there has been a change of domicile, the rights of the spouses vis à vis movables will be governed by the law of the new domicile, except in so far as vested rights have been acquired under the law of the former domicile. With immovable property, the implication in *Welch v Tennant* (1891) is that the *lex situs* shall apply.

In our situation, there is a marriage settlement between Siti and Abdul. The terms of the contract will govern the substantive rights of the parties to all property within its terms, regardless of whether the property was then owned or subsequently acquired. This is notwithstanding any change in domicile. The determination of whether the property in question is within the governance of the contract is a question of construction based on its proper law.

The proper law of the ante-nuptial contract between Siti and Abdul is the law of the matrimonial domicile at the time the agreement was made. Consistent with the rule in *Duke of Marlborough v AG* (1945), the matrimonial domicile is the husband's domicile. This is to say that the proper law is that of Lowland; accordingly, the ante-nuptial contract is valid.

At this juncture, it might be added that the Rome Convention, as incorporated in the Contracts (Applicable Law) Act 1990, has no application, even though an ante-nuptial contract is a contract properly enforceable at law. By virtue of Art 1(2)(b) of that Convention, contracts relating to 'rights arising out of a matrimonial relationship' are expressly excluded from its operation.

Before a claimant is entitled to enforce the ante-nuptial agreement in England, he must show not only that the agreement is valid under the rules of private international law, but also that the parties had the necessary capacity to enter into the agreement. The question is one of determining the relevant law that is to govern the issue of capacity. It has been suggested on the authority of *Re Cooke's Trusts* (1887) and *Cooper v Cooper* (1888) that the question of capacity should be settled by reference to the *lex domicilii*, that is, the law of the domicile of the party alleged to be incapable. In the present case, the law of Highland should apply. This would make the ante-nuptial contract null and void, as, under Highland law, Siti was not of the age of majority when she entered into the agreement.

The contrary view is to be found in Professor Morris' argument.[1] The argument (as modified) is that there is no reason why capacity should not be governed by the law of the settlement, an analogy to be drawn from the Rome Convention rules and commercial contracts.

An assessment of the two cases is necessary. In *Re Cooke's Trusts*, the question of capacity to enter into a notarial contract in French form was not to be determined by the proper law of the contract but by the *lex domicilii* of the maker. Professor Morris argued that this case as an authority is not particularly cogent because it was based on an erroneous assumption that, under English law, marriage settlements made by infants are not void but are merely voidable.

In *Cooper v Cooper*, while Lords Halsbury and Macnaghten allowed a widow to repudiate an ante-nuptial contract on the basis that she was a minor when she made it, they were inconsistent in their finding of validity of the infant's marriage settlement at Irish law. Whilst Lord Macnaghten found that such contracts were void *ab initio*, Lord Halsbury thought that they were simply voidable.[2] As observed by Lord Lindley in *Viditz v O'Hagan* (1900), the position in *Cooper v Cooper* was that the claimant succeeded in repudiating the settlement after the lapse of much more than a reasonable time, if the fact of her change of domicile between the execution of the settlement and the repudiation is shut out. In *Viditz v O'Hagan*, the Court of Appeal had to consider an ante-nuptial agreement entered into by an Irish domiciled girl under the age of 21. She married an Austrian domiciled man. The settlement was expressed in English form. The parties then moved to Austria and became domiciled there. About 30 years later, they applied to revoke the settlement by a notarial act in Austria. The court held that the revocation in Austrian form was valid because the wife had never possessed the capacity to make an irrevocable settlement, either before or after her marriage. Under Austrian law, she could never confirm or ratify the settlement; she could only repudiate it, which she did.

The clear inference, according to Professor McLean, is that the House of Lords in *Cooper* did not shut out consideration of the proper law of the settlement.[3] Hence, it is no authority for saying that the capacity to make a marriage settlement is governed by the law of domicile of the party alleged to be incapable. He therefore submitted that such capacity is to be governed by the proper law of the contract, which is the system of law most closely connected with the contract, not the law intended by the parties.

If the court finds that the ante-nuptial contract is null and void, the rule relating to movable matrimonial property ought to apply in the absence of a marriage settlement. This means that, once the domicile is changed, the law of the new domicile will be used to determine Abdul's rights. Thus, under the circumstances, his rights will be governed by English law.

In terms of immovable property, the rights of the parties would appear to be governed by the law of the matrimonial domicile. There is no direct authority on this issue. Some assistance may perhaps be gained by referring to *Chiwell v Carlyon* (1897). The court held that land bought by the husband in Cornwall was subject to South African (the original domicile) community of property where there was no marriage settlement on the disposition, even though the parties were then domiciled in England. If this case is followed, the *denouement*, it would seem, is that the law of Lowland will govern any property rights accruing to Abdul vis à vis immovable property.

One last issue is perhaps that of formal validity. The law, as set out in *Guépratte v Young* (1851) and *Van Grutten v Digby* (1862), is that, where the settlement conforms with the law of the place where it is executed or the proper law, it meets the requirement of formal validity.

Notes

1 See (1938) 54 LQR 78.

2 It should be pointed out that, in *Edwards v Carter* (1893), the House of Lords held that, at English law, a minor's marriage settlement agreement is neither void nor voidable whenever the minor wishes to repudiate it, but voidable only within a reasonable time after the minor has attained the age of majority.

3 McLean, *Morris – The Conflict of Laws*, 4th edn, 1993, p 375.

Question 42

In January 1998, Matt committed suicide in Popia. He had been suffering from acute depression for more than 10 months. A week before he killed himself, he visited his mistress, May. Matt was domiciled in Manna, while May is domiciled in England.

He made a videotape containing the following instructions in her presence:

> Please make sure that my freehold cottage, Rose Cottage, in Luton, England, is left to my dear daughter, Mo. I should also want my younger girl, Marie, to have my collection of rare books on Mannan history now kept on loan by the Mannan National Archive. And you, May, shall have the residue of my movable property.

May then signed the videotape label, stating that she witnessed the making of the 'will'. Under Popian law, such a recording constitutes a formally valid will.

On 4 January 2000, the Mannan ruler decreed that all rare books shall vest in the State upon the death of the owner. The decree was to have effect as of 1 January 1995, Manna's Independence Day.

There is also a Mannan statute to the effect that no Mannan testator may leave his property to a mistress. Furthermore, it is illegal for Mannan nationals to own freehold property overseas.

Mo, a Mannan national, is domiciled in Manna, and her sister, Marie, is domiciled in Ireland.

Discuss the legal implications of the above events under English rules of private international law.

Answer plan

In matters of testacy, the distribution of the property of a deceased will generally be executed according to the terms of his will. The question is: when there is an international element to the will, how should the validity of the terms (essential validity) and the formal validity of the will themselves be determined?

The rule is that capacity to make a will relating to movables must be determined by the law of the testator's domicile, whilst capacity to make a will of immovables is arguably governed by the *lex situs*.

On essential or material validity, the position is very much the same. The problem, however, emerges when the court has to characterise the issue as one relating to capacity or form.

Answer

The first issue is whether Matt's will satisfies the formal validity requirements for a will made overseas. Section 1 of the Wills Act 1963 provides that a will shall be treated as properly executed if its execution conformed to the internal law in force in the territory where it was executed. In this context, under s 6, 'internal law' refers to the law that would apply in a case where no question of conflict of laws arose. Since it is pellucid that the will was made on video in Popia, whose law provides that such a will is valid, the will satisfies the element of formal validity.

Before moving on to the issue of essential validity, the question of which law is to determine the personal capacity of the testator should be resolved. It is conceivable that this might be in issue, since Matt was under severe depression when the will was made. The rule at common law is that the law of the testator's domicile determines whether he has personal capacity to make a will of movables (*In bonis Maraver* (1828); *In bonis Gutteriez* (1869); *Re Fuld's Estate (No 3)* (1968)). Following this rule, the law of Manna is to be applied in order to determine whether Matt had the legal capacity to make dispositions by will. On the law that governs capacity in making a will relating to immovables, it may be suggested that, in line with *dicta* in *Bank of Africa v Cohen* (1909), the *lex situs* should govern. This would mean the law of the place where the freehold cottage is situated should govern the issue of Matt's legal capacity to dispose of the cottage to Mo. The *lex situs* is, therefore, English law. Under English law, unless it can be proved that Matt was labouring under bodily or mental illness so as to deprive him of the soundness of mind to make a will, mere depression should not be enough.

On the issue of material or essential validity, a similar distinction between a will for movables and a will for immovables should be made. In *Whicker v Hume* (1858), the issue was determined by the law of the testator's domicile at the time of his death vis à vis gifts of movables. Thus, the material validity of the disposition of the rare books and the residue of the movable property is to be adjudged under Mannan law, the law of Matt's domicile when he died. The fact that he died in Popia is immaterial.

The gift of immovables is to be governed by the *lex situs* (*Nelson v Bridport* (1846)). Thus, the gift of the freehold to his daughter, being a disposition of immovables, is to be determined by English law. Under English law, the gift would have been materially valid. The seeming difficulty is whether Mo, being a Mannan national who, by Mannan law, is prohibited from owning land abroad, could still acquire title to Rose Cottage. It may be argued that this is a question of capacity and, therefore, falls to be governed by the relevant *lex domicilii*. It is, however, submitted that the issue cannot be severed from the original disposition of immovables and must, therefore, be governed by the *lex situs*. If this is accepted by the court, then Mo will have the essential capacity to take the gift. It was held in *Re Miller* (1914) that the incidents of the estates owned by the testator should be determined by the *lex situs*. Similarly, an analogy could be extracted from *Duncan v Lawson* (1889), where the question of whether the testator could make a gift to charities was held to be governed by the *lex situs*. The essence of the question is how severable the disposition is from the issue of capacity.

On the gifts of the movables, Mannan law will apply. The gift to May may be caught by the Mannan statute prohibiting the leaving of property by will to mistresses. But it could be argued in favour of May that the Mannan law simply turns on the issue of the mistress's capacity to inherit property under a will, and is, therefore, not a question relating to the essential validity of the will. This being the case, the law of the beneficiary's domicile should govern the issue of her capacity (*Re Hellman* (1866)).

The gift of the collection of rare books falls to be considered by Mannan law. Under this law (the *lex causae*), the gift would have been permissible but for the retrospective decree. According to Lord Penzance in *Lynch v Provisional Government of Paraguay* (1871), a change in the *lex causae* having retrospective effect is not relevant, as English law adopts the law of the domicile 'as it stands at the time of the death'. This rather wide characterisation of the position of English private international law may be criticised on the basis that it does not give effect to the transitional law of the *lex causae*. Also, to exclude such law regardless of its content is untenable.[1]

Subsequent to *Lynch*, the court in *Re Aganoor's Trust* (1895) adopted very much the same judicial attitude. In that case, the testatrix's legacy was valid under Austrian law, which was the law in force in Padua at the time of her death. However, when the retrospectively effective Italian Civil Code came to replace the Austrian code, the trust substitutions she had purported to make by will became unlawful. The court disregarded the new legal position on the basis that, after the death of the testatrix, the change in the *lex causae* was irrelevant.

An interesting contrast may be made with a case on succession to immovables. In *Nelson v Bridport* (1846), Lord Langdale MR held unequivocally that he had to apply the law of

Sicily as it existed from time to time and not as it was at the time of the original grant of the entail in issue and/or at the time of the death of the party concerned.[2] Taken in this context, Marie has a right to the collection of rare books held by the Mannan Archive. There is, however, the practical issue of whether the Mannan Government will relinquish its possession of the collection in recognition and enforcement of the probate granted in England.

Notes

1 For a criticism of the rule, see Mann (1954) 31 BYIL 217 and Grodecki (1959) 35 BYIL 58.

2 According to Professor McLean, if it is true that, in succession to movables, no account is to be taken of subsequent changes in the *lex causae* made after the death of the testator, that proposition is subject to an important qualification so far as the formal validity of wills is concerned (*Morris – The Conflict of Laws*, 4th edn, 1993). This is because s 6(3) of the Wills Act 1963 states that regard shall be had to retrospective alterations in the *lex causae* which enable the will to be treated as properly executed. The same regard shall be had to retrospective amendments in the *lex causae* which invalidate the will.

Question 43*

> In modern law, it is a quite unnecessary complication to have different conflict rules for intestate succession to movables and immovables [Dicey and Morris, *Conflict of Laws*, 12th edn, 1993].

Comment.

Answer plan

It is necessary to explain the principle of scission and the complications it creates:

- it requires the classification of the item of property as either a movable or an immovable: *Re Berchtold* (1923);
- it requires an application of different laws to the same estate;
- it may lead to unfair results: *Re Collens* (1986); contrast with *Re Thom* (1987).

Finally, the solutions of the Hague Convention on the Law Applicable to Succession to the Estates of Deceased Persons of 1989 should be examined.

Answer

English conflict of laws rules relating to intestate succession recognise the principle of scission, according to which intestate succession to immovables is determined by the law of the country where the immovables are situated (*lex situs*) and intestate succession to movables is governed by the law of domicile of a deceased person at the time of his death. In contrast, under the principle of unitary succession, a single system of law is applied for movables and immovables and testate and intestate succession. Only common law countries (that is, France, Belgium and Austria) adhere to the principle of scission. The Hague Conference on private international law favours the principle of unitary succession, which was adopted by the Convention on the Law Applicable to Succession to the Estates of Deceased Persons of 1989.[1]

The principle of scission creates many unnecessary complications. First, it involves a classification of an item of property as a movable or an immovable. This distinction is not always easy to make. In *Re Berchtold* (1923), the *propositus* died intestate, domiciled in Hungary. He left a freehold interest in English land which was subject to a trust for sale. As he died before the conversion took place, it was necessary to determine whether the freehold interest was to be considered as an interest in an immovable (and thus governed by the *lex situs*) or on the basis of the doctrine of conversion (according to which, the land directed to be sold and turned into money is to be regarded as that species of property into which it is directed: *Fletcher v Ashburner* (1779)) as a movable (money). It was therefore governed by the law of domicile of the deceased person at the time of his death. Although it was argued that the unsold land was already considered to be money in the eyes of equity, the court held that there was no connection between the doctrine of conversion and the classification of the subject matter of ownership and that the unsold land was an immovable property irrespective of the binding direction for its conversion into money. Although the classification was governed by the law of the *situs*, by deciding that the freehold interest in land was an interest in immovable property, the English court avoided consulting Hungarian law, which may have led to a different solution. Furthermore, legislation sometimes decides *a priori* whether a subject matter of ownership is to be considered as immovable or movable (*Re Cutcliffe's Will Trusts* (1940)).

Secondly, the principle of scission divides a single unit, that is, a whole estate comprising movables and immovables, into as many separate legal entities as the number of different laws applicable. Each legal entity is autonomous and does not take into consideration what happens to other items of the estate. For example, if the estate of a deceased person is composed of immovable property scattered around the world and, in order to decide the question of intestate succession to movables, the court applies the doctrine of *renvoi*, many legal systems will be involved. In addition, the same individual may accept succession to movables in one country and refuse the succession to immovables in another country.

Finally, in respect of intestate succession to immovables, the order of descent or distribution provided by the law of the *situs* is applied regardless of the domicile of a deceased person. This may lead to unfair and surprising results. In *Re Collens* (1986), the *propositus* died intestate domiciled in Trinidad and Tobago, leaving assets in Trinidad, Tobago, England and Barbados. According to the law of Trinidad and Tobago, his widow was entitled to one-third of the estate, and the children from his first marriage to two-thirds of the estate. The widow accepted $1 million as her share of the assets in Trinidad and Tobago under a deed of compromise. In connection to immovables in England, the question arose as to whether she was entitled to claim the statutory legacy due to her under s 46 of the Administration of Estates Act 1925 (as amended) (at that time, £5,000) in addition to her share of assets agreed under the law of domicile of the deceased. Although Sir Nicolas Browne-Wilkinson VC regretted that he could not exclude her from the statutory legacy, the meaning of the English statute was clear and left no room for doubt: she was entitled to £5,000 in addition to the sums already received under the deed of compromise. However, in the Canadian case of *Re Thom* (1987), it was decided that a widow could claim only one of the two statutory legacies.

It is submitted that the principle of scission should be abandoned in favour of the principle of unitary succession governed by the law of the habitual residence of the deceased person at the time of his death. The solution adopted by the Hague Convention on the Law Applicable to Succession to the Estates of Deceased Persons is modern, fair and appropriate to solve today's problems posed by intestate succession. As such, it should be part of English law. The traditional common law rules in this area were suitable before 1926, when English domestic law of succession distinguished succession to land and succession to personalty, notwithstanding the fact that, even before 1926, this solution had produced unfair results (*Re Rea* (1902)).

Note

1 The Convention on the Law Applicable to Succession to the Estates of Deceased Persons is not in force. It was opened for signatures on 1 August 1989. Form, capacity and matrimonial property are excluded from its scope of application. The Convention recognises the principle of unitary succession for movables and immovables. The law of the habitual residence of the deceased person at least five years before his death or, in default, his nationality, is applicable to succession. The *propositus* may select the law of his habitual residence or his nationality as applicable to the succession of his estate at the time of drafting his final will and testament.

* by Alina Kaczorowska

CHAPTER 8

FAMILY LAW*

Introduction

Conflict of laws rules relating to family matters are constantly challenged. The reason is obvious: it is the area of private international law which concerns the essential and fundamental structure of any society – the family. It reflects the political, sociological and religious peculiarity of each State. National legislation in family law is increasingly affected by the internationalisation of everyday life, resulting in the growth of international conflicts in this area. Furthermore, conflict of laws in family matters is of potential interest to everybody. Nowadays, we travel abroad, marry abroad, and we live in multi-national, multi-faith and multi-racial societies. Even the notion of marriage is subject to different definitions. In *Hyde v Hyde* (1866), private international law refused to recognise the existence of polygamous marriages. Today, it struggles with new issues such as homosexual marriage and the capacity of transsexuals to marry. Even the self-evident notions of father and mother pose difficult problems. The old problem of proving paternity, which, in the eyes of conflict of laws rules, is a matter of procedure and, as such, is governed by the *lex fori*, has been resolved beyond reasonable doubt through DNA profiling; but, in cases of new artificial reproductive technology, such as donor insemination, egg and embryo transfer and surrogacy, it is not always evident who the mother or father of a child is.

On the other hand, transnational divorces are more common. In England, one in three marriages ends in divorce. This rate is similar in many countries. The recognition of overseas divorces, both judicial and extra-judicial, constitutes an important consideration of English private international law.

Children from broken multi-national families are at risk of being abducted by one of their parents. Once again, private international law, by way of international conventions, helps to restore the status quo and brings children back home as promptly as possible.

Finally, as the number of children available for adoption in England steadily declines, inter-State adoptions are almost the only option for British couples. Once again, the rules of private international law are vitally important in the recognition of overseas adoption. The clash between old and new is constantly present in conflict of laws in family matters.

Checklist

An understanding of the following is particularly important:

- marriage: its meaning and formal and essential validity;
- matrimonial causes: polygamous marriages, recognition of overseas divorces, annulment of marriage;
- legitimacy and legitimation and the rights to succession;
- international abduction of children;
- new challenges in family law: homosexual marriage, a transsexual's capacity to marry, new reproduction technology, succession rights of children born as a result of artificial insemination.

Question 44

Janusz, an officer in the Polish Army, married Isabelle, a French national, in Rome in 1946. At that time, Janusz was serving in Italy with the British Army. They were married by a Polish Roman Catholic priest according to Catholic rites. Isabelle has recently commenced proceedings in England to declare her marriage invalid. She claims that:

- the marriage is invalid under Italian law, since it has not been registered in Italy;
- it is invalid under Polish law, since Janusz did not obtain the authorisation of the Commander of Polish Forces in Italy to marry Isabelle;
- it is invalid under French law, since Isabelle was only 14 years old at the time of marriage.

Janusz argues that Isabelle lied about her age at the time of their marriage. She told him that she was 20 years old, although to him she looked at least 25.

Advise Isabelle.

Answer plan

The question concerns both formal and essential validity of marriage. First, it is necessary to determine the formal validity of the marriage. Formal validity concerns issues such as the form of ceremony (which may be civil or religious), registration of marriage, witnesses, the time and place of celebration, the presence of a priest, prior medical examination and parental consent.

The fundamental principle in this area is that the *lex loci celebrationis* applies. Thus, if a marriage is valid under the law of the country where it was celebrated, it will be valid in England, provided that statutory and common law exceptions do not apply. As to the essential validity of marriage, it relates to such matters as consanguinity, affinity, bigamy, lack of age and lack of consent. In English private international law, controversy lingers over whether capacity to marry is to be determined according to the ante-nuptial law of domicile of each party (the dual domicile theory) or the law of the intended matrimonial home (the matrimonial home doctrine). Case law is inconclusive, but it seems that the doctrine of the dual domicile prevails. The following points should be examined:

- the *lex loci celebrationis* and exceptions to its application;
- marriage of military forces in belligerent occupation: *Taczanowska v Taczanowski* (1957);
- parental consent in relation to the authorisation to marry given by the Commander of Polish Forces in Italy: *Simonin v Malloc* (1860); *Ogden v Ogden* (1908);
- minority as an incapacity: s 2 of the Marriage Act 1949; *Pugh v Pugh* (1951); *Mohamed v Knott* (1969).

Answer

The formal validity of marriage is governed by the *lex loci celebrationis*. This is a fundamental rule of English private international law (*Brook v Brook* (1861); *Berthiaume v Dastous* (1930)). Thus, if a marriage is valid under the law of the place where it was celebrated, it would be valid in England. In *Herbert (Lady) v Herbert (Lord)* (1819), it was held that 'every marriage must be tried according to the law of the country in which it took place'. More recently, the rule has been applied in *McCabe v McCabe* (1994). In that case, an Irishman domiciled in England, who was living in London with an Akan woman domiciled in Ghana, consented to a marriage ceremony in Ghana according to the tribal custom of Akan (a Ghanan tribe) at the suggestion of her uncle, who was visiting them. The uncle asked the Irishman to give him a bottle of gin and some money (as 'aseda') and took it to Ghana, where the ceremony was performed. The parties were neither present at the ceremony nor represented by proxy. The Court of Appeal, based on expert witnesses' testimonies on the ceremony of marriage of Akans, decided that they were validly married. The only requirement for contracting a valid marriage under Akans custom was the consent of the parties and their families (however, consent is not a formal requirement!). According to the expert witnesses, neither the ceremony nor the 'aseda' were essential.

In respect of Isabelle's first claim, it seems that, since their marriage was not valid under Italian law, it would not be valid in England. However, it was decided in *Starkowski v AG* (1954) that a marriage which is void at the time of celebration may be validated by subsequent changes in the law of the place of celebration, that is, if legislation subsequent to the ceremony validates the marriage retrospectively. In *Starkowski*, two Polish nationals who were domiciled in Poland went through a religious marriage ceremony in Austria in 1945. Their marriage was void according to Austrian law, since only civil marriages were regarded as valid. However, subsequent Austrian legislation validated such religious marriages if they were registered in a public register. On the facts, one of the parties had registered the marriage; thus, its validity was upheld. If the parties in our case have neglected to satisfy the requirement of registration, the marriage will be void in England (*Pilinski v Pilinski* (1955)). At first glance, it seems that Isabelle is right to question the formal validity of her marriage to Janusz. The marriage was neither valid nor subsequently validated by Italian law.

However, the rule *lex loci celebrationis* is subject to exceptions. Some are statutory, others are derived from the common law. The common law exceptions are relevant to our case. In this respect, it is recognised that, in some exceptional circumstances, a marriage celebrated in breach of the formal requirements of the law of the place where it is solemnised would be valid if it satisfied the form accepted by the common law. The first exception applies when there is extreme difficulty in conforming to local custom. The parties must show not only that there was difficulty but that it was virtually impossible to celebrate their marriage in conformity with the local law. In our case, this exception is not applicable, since the parties could comply with the requirements of Italian law.

The second exception, on the other hand, is relevant to our question, since it concerns the marriage of a member of the military forces in belligerent occupation. In this respect, the leading case is *Taczanowska v Taczanowski* (1957), where two Polish nationals domiciled in Poland went through a marriage ceremony in Italy in 1946. The husband was serving in the Polish 2nd Corps in belligerent occupation of Italy. The religious ceremony was celebrated by a Polish Army chaplain, who was a Catholic priest. The marriage was formally invalid according to Italian law. The Court of Appeal decided that, since the parties were in Italy not of their own free will but because the husband was a member of the military forces in occupation of Italy, they were not presumed to submit to the local law. Accordingly, English common law was applied and their marriage's validity was upheld.

The theory of submission produces uncertainty as to the validity of marriage and, for that reason, it has to be construed very narrowly. In *Merker v Merker* (1963), Sir Jocelyn Simon P stated that the principle in *Taczanowska v Taczanowski* should be applied to cases of:

> ... marriage within the lines of the foreign army of occupation (which constitute, so to speak, an enclave, within which it is

> reasonable to hold that the local law has no application), or of persons in a strictly analogous situation to the members of such an army, such as members of an organised body of escaped prisoners of war.

As a result, the marriage in *Lazarewicz v Lazarewicz* (1962) was declared void because the wife was a national of a conquered country. In that case, a Polish corporal, serving with the Polish forces in Italy, married an Italian woman. They were married in a Polish refugee camp by a Catholic priest. The case was distinguished from other cases on the basis that the parties submitted to Italian law.

In our case, Isabelle is a French national, not an Italian. It is submitted that the principle in *Taczanowska v Taczanowski* will apply and, consequently, their marriage, although invalid under Italian law, will be held as a valid marriage under English common law.

The next question to examine is whether the lack of authorisation by the Commander of Polish Forces in Italy invalidates the marriage. In this respect, it is necessary to determine whether authorisation relates to formal or essential validity. It is submitted that an authorisation from a superior officer is analogous to parental consent. Under English law, parental consent is considered to be a formal requirement, and is thus governed by the *lex loci celebrationis*. Historically, the English courts made no distinction between form and capacity to marry, and thus parental consent became only a matter of form. In the 17th century, many English couples went to Scotland to get married because, under Scottish law, no parental consent was necessary. Once the distinction was made, English courts had to find a justification for validating those marriages and, as a result, parental consent has been classified as a formal requirement. Furthermore, English private international law rejects the doctrine of evasion of law; that is, if the marriage is contracted abroad in order to escape mandatory provisions of national law, it will be considered to be valid in England. In *Simonin v Malloc* (1860), the marriage was solemnised in England without the parental consent required by Art 154 of the French Civil Code. It was held valid in England although it was void in France (see, also, *Ogden v Ogden* (1908)). It is submitted that the lack of authorisation constitutes a formal requirement and, as such, is determined by the *lex loci celebrationis*. Italian law does not contain this requirement, and thus has no effect on the validity of marriage. In any case, the marriage would be invalid under Italian law.

Finally, Isabelle claims that she was only 14 at the time of marriage. Age is considered to be an essential requirement. In England, s 2 of the Marriage Act 1949 (re-enacting the Age of Marriage Act 1929) stipulates that a marriage between persons, one of whom is under the age of 16, is void. However, different countries have different perceptions of the minimum age for contracting a valid marriage. As to lack of age, two principles are established: first, a marriage solemnised in England will be void if one (or both) of the parties is under the age of 16, regardless of their domicile; and, secondly, if one party is under the age of 16, neither party is domiciled at the relevant time in England, their marriage was celebrated abroad and is regarded as valid under local law, then it will be valid in England. In this respect, the marriage celebrated in *Mohamed v Knott* (1969) in Nigeria between parties domiciled there was held to be valid, even though the wife was only 13 at that time.

As to English domiciliaries, it seems that case law in this area is rather limited. The best case is *Pugh v Pugh* (1951). A British officer, domiciled in England but stationed in Austria, and a Hungarian girl of 15, domiciled in Hungary, got married in Austria. Their marriage was valid under Hungarian and Austrian laws. However, since the husband was domiciled in England, the Age of Marriage Act 1929 applied, and so it was held void in England.

It is submitted that, no matter what law will be applied to determine Isabelle's capacity to marry (that is, whether it be the law that was applicable before the marriage ceremony (French law) or the law of common domicile (which may be English or Polish law)), the result will be the same: her marriage will be held invalid by reason of her age. Whatever Janusz believed or thought about her age at the time of marriage is irrelevant.

The marriage between Janusz and Isabelle is void on the ground that, at the relevant time, Isabelle lacked the capacity to marry, as she was only 14. As regards the formal requirements, the *lex loci celebrationis* is displaced in favour of the common law of England.

Question 45

Anna, domiciled in England, is an anthropologist. She went to Zimu-Zimu, an island in the Pacific, to conduct research on the customs and traditions of the Kumu-Kumu, a rare tribe that inhabits the island. The Kumu-Kumu practise polyandry. During her stay, she met Atu, a member of the tribe, and, in 1990, she married him in a ceremony performed according to rites of the Kumu-Kumu. Two years later, she was attracted to Batu and decided to marry him. Once again, she went through the traditional marriage ceremony of the Kumu-Kumu. They all lived happily until Anna had to go back to England for a few months. She is worried that her marriages will not be recognised in England and wants to know more about the way English private international law deals with polygamy in general and polyandry in particular.

Advise Anna.

Answer plan

First, polygamy should be discussed, particularly how the English private international law has changed since *Hyde v Hyde* was decided in 1866. Also, the recognition of polygamous marriages and its limitations are relevant in answering the question. The second part of the answer should focus on Anna's problem. In this respect, the most important question is whether, as an English domiciliary, she has capacity to contract a polygamous marriage. Two cases are important in this area – *Radwan v Radwan* (1973) and *Hussein v Hussein* (1983) – since they give indications as to the meaning of s 11(d) of the Matrimonial Causes Act 1973. Furthermore, s 5(1) of the Private International Law (Miscellaneous Provisions) Act 1995, which embodies the recommendation of the Law Commission and abolishes the notion of potentially polygamous marriages (*de facto* monogamous), should be discussed. It should be noted that, although most parts of the Act have not yet come into force, s 5(1) has been in effect since 8 January 1996.

Answer

A polygamous marriage may take two forms: polygyny – a man may have more that one wife during the length of his first marriage; and polyandry – a woman is entitled to have more than one husband during the subsistence of her first marriage.

It used to be of great importance to determine the nature of a marriage, as parties to polygamous marriages could not commence proceedings for matrimonial relief. The hostility to polygamy was expressed by Lord Penzance in *Hyde v Hyde* (1866): '... the matrimonial law of this country is adopted to the Christian marriage and is wholly inapplicable to polygamy.' As a result, it was not proper for an English court to be 'creating conjugal duties, not enforcing them, and furnishing remedies when there was no offence'. By this, he meant that, under English law, the religious nature of a marriage is unimportant. The relationship between man and woman is essential. Thus, a marriage must have two main characteristics: it must be a voluntary union of indefinite duration and it must be contracted between man and woman to the exclusion of all others. Also, a very important distinction was made in *Hyde v Hyde*: a marriage is considered under English law to be polygamous if either party is entitled to have another spouse, although it may in fact be a monogamous marriage. Thus, a *de facto* monogamous marriage which is polygamous by nature is still polygamous for the purposes of law even though the husband has never exercised the right to take a second wife or has never intended to do so (*Hyde v Hyde; Sowa v Sowa* (1961)). In cases of concubinage, it was decided in *Lee v Lau* (1967) that a marriage (under customary Chinese law) which allowed a husband to take '*tsipsis*' (concubines or secondary wives) during the marriage but not to remarry was polygamous.

Since *Hyde v Hyde*, English law has changed greatly in respect of polygamy, and many, but not all, obstacles have been removed in order to give parties to polygamous marriages similar rights to those enjoyed by monogamous spouses. A valid polygamous marriage is recognised in England (*Mohamed v Knott* (1969)) for many purposes. Children from *de facto* (*Baindail v Baindail* (1946)) and actually polygamous marriages (*Hashmi v Hashmi* (1971)) are regarded as legitimate. Furthermore, s 1 of the Matrimonial Proceedings (Polygamous Marriages) Act 1972 provides that parties to polygamous marriages are entitled to matrimonial relief such as a decree for divorce, judicial separation and declaration under Pt III of the Family Law Act 1986, which may involve the determination of the validity of a marriage. Section 47(1) of the Act states that the matrimonial law of England applies to polygamous marriages; thus, the approach in *Hyde v Hyde* is abolished. The Social Security Contributions and Benefit Act 1992 provides in s 121(1)(b) that a polygamous marriage shall be treated as a monogamous marriage for any day, but only for any day throughout which it is *de facto* monogamous. A husband to a polygamous marriage who maintains his wife or wives is entitled to a deduction of tax under s 257(1) of the Income and Corporation Taxes Act 1988. The Matrimonial Homes Act 1983, as well as s 17 of the Married Women's Property Act 1882, applies to a polygamously married wife (*Nabi v Heaton* (1981)). The Law Commission and many academics agree that the Fatal Accidents Act 1976 should be applied to a wife or wives of a polygamous marriage.

In Anna's case, it is necessary, first, to determine whether as an English domiciliary she has capacity to enter a polygamous marriage. In this respect, s 11(d) of the Matrimonial Causes Act 1973 states that such marriages celebrated after 31 July 1971 shall be void if, at the time of marriage, either party was domiciled in England or Wales. However, the construction of this statutory provision, which seems clear and straightforward, produced unexpected results in *Radwan v Radwan* (1973). In that case, a polygamous marriage was celebrated in the Egyptian Consulate in Paris between a woman domiciled in England and a man domiciled in Egypt. The parties set up a home in Egypt. Cumming-Bruce J considered that s 11(d) of the Matrimonial Causes Act 1973 applies only if either party is domiciled in

England and the parties intend to have their matrimonial home in England. He justified his conclusion on the basis of s 14, which applies the substantive law of another country if English conflict of laws rules determine its application. Thus, according to *Radwan v Radwan*, capacity to contract a polygamous marriage is governed by the law of the intended matrimonial home.

On the basis of *Radwan v Radwan*, Anna would have capacity to contract a polygamous marriage. However, the question of whether she has acquired a domicile of choice in Zimu-Zimu remains, and the answer to this is uncertain. The Court of Appeal's decision in and the implications of *Hussein v Hussein* (1983) are also relevant to Anna's case. In that case, it was decided, *inter alia*, that capacity to enter into an actually polygamous marriage is governed by the law of the ante-nuptial domicile of each party. This means that Anna could not contract a polygamous marriage.

The conflicting decisions in *Radwan v Radwan* and *Hussein v Hussein* prompted the Law Commission to suggest amendments to s 11(d) of the Matrimonial Causes Act 1973. The Private International Law (Miscellaneous Provisions) Act 1995 has been enacted to incorporate its recommendations. This Act provides in s 5(1) that an English domiciliary should have capacity to enter a marriage outside the UK which, though polygamous in form, is *de facto* monogamous. Section 5(1) came into force as of 8 January 1996.

This rule applies to all marriages, wherever celebrated, provided that the marriage has not been declared void by a nullity decree and that a party to a polygamous marriage has not entered into a later marriage which would be rendered invalid by the retrospective validation of the earlier one. What the Act abolishes is the old division between a polygamous and potentially polygamous marriage. As a result, s 11(d) will apply to polygamous marriages, as in Anna's case. However, even under new legislation, she will lack capacity to contract a truly polygamous marriage; that is, she will not be entitled to have two husbands and, if she does, she may be guilty of the crime of bigamy, as defined in s 57 of the Offences Against the Person Act 1861.

Question 46

Anita was born into a Sikh family in England in December 1981. Both her parents are very religious and deeply attached to traditional values of Sikh culture. Anita has always admired and loved her older sister, Meera. In 1998, Meera met James and fell in love. James proposed but Anita's parents opposed the marriage because James was not a Sikh. Meera left the family home and went to live with James. In January 1999, Anita decided to leave her parents and establish herself with Meera. Both Meera and James were delighted and welcomed Anita. In February 1999, Anita's father sought police assistance and brought Anita home. Shortly afterwards, Anita was taken by her parents to a village in northern India, the home town of Anita's parents. Anita managed to send a desperate letter to Meera, describing her circumstances in terms of imprisonment and begging Meera to help her to escape as soon as possible, as their parents were about to arrange a marriage between Anita and a 60 year old Sikh.

Meera obtained advice from Reunion, a charity, and issued an originating summons in England to make Anita a ward of court. During wardship proceedings, orders were made and, with the assistance of the Foreign and Commonwealth Office, the British High Commission in New Delhi, the Indian police and Interpol, Anita returned to England, unfortunately apparently married to the Sikh.

Anita wishes to clarify her legal status: she wants to know whether she is married and, if so, whether she can seek annulment of her marriage or a divorce. Also, she wants to start proceedings against her parents for abduction.

Advise Anita.

Answer plan

The main points that should be examined are as follows:

- the differences between a void and a voidable marriage;
- the grounds for annulment of void and voidable marriages: ss 11 and 12 of the Matrimonial Causes Act 1973;
- the jurisdiction of English courts in nullity proceedings: s 5(3) of the Domicile and Matrimonial Proceedings Act 1973;

- the controversial issues regarding grounds for annulment in conflict of laws for lack of consent (*Apt v Apt* (1948); *Szechter v Szechter* (1971)).

In relation to Anita's abduction, the relevant case is *Re KR (A Minor)* (1999).

Answer

Unfortunately, Anita is married. However, it is not necessary for Anita to petition for a divorce. She can start proceedings for annulment of her marriage on the ground of lack of consent. In this respect, it is necessary to make a distinction between void and voidable marriages. There are three main differences between them.

The first and most important is that a void marriage is null *ab initio*. In other words, in the eyes of the law, a void marriage has never existed and 'spouses' are cohabitees. As to a voidable marriage, in *De Reneville v De Reneville* (1948), it was described as 'one that will be regarded by every court as a valid subsisting marriage until a decree annulling it has been pronounced by a court of competent jurisdiction'.

The second difference is that a void marriage can be challenged by anyone, and no proceedings are necessary in order to nullify a void marriage. In contrast, a voidable marriage can only be challenged by the parties themselves, through nullity proceedings or otherwise.

Finally, the voidness of a void marriage has retrospective effect, while the voiding of a voidable marriage is retrospective only at common law. A decree of annulment granted after 31 July 1971 nullifies a voidable marriage prospectively from the date of the decree absolute.

The grounds for annulment of a void marriage celebrated after 31 July 1971 are listed in s 11 of the Matrimonial Causes Act 1973. The list is exhaustive and contains the following:

- the parties are within the prohibited degrees of relationship (consanguity and affinity);
- either party was under the age of 16 at the time of marriage;

- the parties have intermarried in breach of certain requirements as to the formation of marriage;
- either party was already lawfully married at the time of the marriage (bigamy);
- the parties are not respectively male and female;
- either party was, at the time of the marriage, domiciled in England or Wales and the marriage to be voided was one contracted as a polygamous marriage outside England and Wales.

Section 12 of the Matrimonial Causes Act 1973 stipulates that a marriage celebrated after 31 July 1971 will be voidable only on the following grounds:

- the marriage has not been consummated, due to the incapacity of either party to consummate it or a wilful refusal of the respondent to consummate it;
- either party did not validly consent to it, whether in consequence of duress, mistake, unsoundness of mind or otherwise;
- either party, although capable of giving a valid consent, was suffering (whether continuously or intermittently) from mental disorder within the meaning of the Mental Health Act 1959 of such a kind or to such an extent as to be unfit for marriage;
- the respondent was suffering from a venereal disease in a communicable form;
- the respondent was pregnant, by a person other than the petitioner, at the time of the marriage.

However, the last two grounds can only be invoked if the petitioner was not aware of the respondent's venereal disease or pregnancy at the time of marriage.

Anita's marriage is voidable on the ground of lack of consent.

The jurisdiction of English courts in annulment proceedings is governed by s 5(3) of the Domicile and Matrimonial Proceedings Act 1973. Thus, in relation to nullity petitions, the courts in England have jurisdiction if:

- either party was domiciled in England on the date of commencement of proceedings; or

- either party was habitually resident in England throughout a period of one year ending with the date when the proceedings were commenced; or
- either party has died before proceedings are commenced but was, at death, domiciled in England or habitually resident in England throughout the period of one year ending with the date of death.

Under s 5(5), an English court has an additional ground of jurisdiction, notwithstanding that the requirements of s 5(3) are not satisfied, if proceedings are pending for the same divorce, judicial separation or nullity of marriage. This sub-section concerns a supplemental or cross-petition. Thus, if neither party is domiciled or has habitual residence in England but an English court has entertained the original proceedings and the petition is still pending, the court has jurisdiction over the supplemental or cross-petition.

Under s 5(3) of the Domicile and Matrimonial Proceedings Act 1973, the English court will have jurisdiction on the ground that Anita was domiciled in England on the date of commencement of proceedings.

Once an English court has jurisdiction to entertain proceedings, it must classify the defect which is allegedly affecting the marriage and decide whether it regards formal or essential validity. As a matter of procedure, this classification is governed by the *lex fori*. This stage is sometimes crucial for the outcome of the case, since different laws classify the same defect differently. For example, in *Solomon v Walters* (1956), a marriage celebrated in Nevada which did not satisfy the requirement of parental consent of the *lex loci celebrationis* was declared void, even though parental consent was not required by the ante-nuptial law of domicile of the party (the law of British Columbia). The court held that parental consent was a question of form. As a result, the marriage was nullified and the law of Nevada was applied.

The conflict of laws rules in nullity, apart from a few exceptions, are simple. If the defect concerns the formal validity of marriage, the *lex loci celebrationis* applies. If the essential validity is challenged, the ante-nuptial law of domicile of the concerned party governs the matter. The most controversial question in this area is whether the lack of consent should be considered as a formal or as an essential requirement. In this respect, it seems that the English courts have primarily applied the *lex fori*, ignoring the distinction between jurisdictional and conflict of laws rules. Thus, cases on nullity where a foreign law was applied are scarce and controversial.

In *Apt v Apt* (1948), the question of validity of proxy marriage was at issue and the Court of Appeal made a distinction between consent itself and the method of giving consent. The latter was considered to be a formal requirement. The marriage was held valid and the *lex loci celebrationis* was applied. In *Way v Way* (1950), an English domiciliary married a Russian national in a ceremony which took place in Russia, under the mistaken belief that, under Russian law, spouses had a duty to live together. He thought that he would be allowed to stay in Russia or that his wife would be allowed to join him to live in England. It was held that: 'Questions of consent are to be dealt with by reference to the personal law of the parties rather than by reference to the law of the place where the contract was made.' However, in that case, the marriage was held valid by both Russian law (the ante-nuptial law of domicile of the wife and the *lex loci celebrationis*) and English law (the ante-nuptial law of domicile of the husband).

Similarly, in *Szechter v Szechter* (1971), a Polish professor domiciled in Poland divorced his wife and married his secretary (also a Polish domiciliary) in order to rescue her from prison and help her to emigrate. She was serving a prison sentence for 'anti-State activities' and was suffering from ill health. In England, the secretary petitioned for nullity, in the hope that the original marriage of her rescuer would be resumed. The second marriage was invalid for duress under both Polish law (the ante-nuptial law of both parties and the *lex loci celebrationis)* and English law. Although Polish law was applied, the same result would be reached by applying English law.

Another interesting case is *Vervaeke v Smith* (1983), in which the test of the most 'real and substantial connection' was applied to determine the 'quintessential validity' of marriage. According to Lord Simon, the law of the territory with which the marriage had the most real and substantial connection was the law of the intended matrimonial home. He believed that his solution would clarify the law applicable to consent.

It is submitted that marriage, although a special kind of contract, is still a contract. For that reason, the *lex loci celebrationis* is inappropriate, since the place of contracting has nothing to do with the consent of parties. Consent should be determined by the law of the ante-nuptial domicile of the party who alleges that he did not consent.

It is submitted that English law will determine the question of Anita's consent. Under English law, the meaning of duress has been extended. No longer does it require a threat to 'life, limb or liberty'; 'an overbearing of the will' will be sufficient. As a result, Anita's marriage should be annulled (see *Hirani v Hirani* (1982)).

In respect of the proceedings that Anita wishes to bring against her parents, it was decided in *Re KR (A Minor)* that child abduction was still child abduction even where the parents were the abductors and the child was nearly an adult. Therefore, Anita can bring proceedings against her parents.

Question 47

> Those who can afford to travel abroad may have their foreign divorces recognised, whereas those who cannot afford to make the journey are left with limping marriages.

Discuss the above observation in the context of divorce proceedings conducted under religious laws commenced in England and concluded abroad.

Answer plan

The concept of the 'limping marriage' should be explained, especially in relation to the 1970 Hague Convention on the Recognition of Divorces and Legal Separations. The different form of religious divorce should be examined, in particular the Muslim *talaq* and the Jewish *ghet*. The distinction between overseas divorces obtained by means of judicial or other proceedings and the situation where no proceedings are involved should be discussed. The application of the Family Law Act 1986 to overseas divorces, including religious divorces, is important. Finally, the following decisions are particularly relevant:

- *R v Secretary of State for the Home Department ex p Fatima* (1985);
- *Berkovits v Grinberg* (1995).

Answer

Lord Diplock stated in *Quazi v Quazi* (1980) that a 'limping marriage' is one which is recognised as dissolved in one jurisdiction and considered as subsisting in another. Indeed, a limping marriage is a result of discrepancy and divergence in rules of conflict of laws, both jurisdictional and choice of laws, which refuse to recognise a divorce or an annulment of marriage obtained in another country. This situation creates many legal problems which have an impact, not only on the parties themselves (since they do not know whether they are still married or divorced or bigamists or, depending on the country, whether their marital status has changed), but also on their partners in new relationships. More importantly, the legal status of their children from previous and subsequent unions is unclear. In order to alleviate the 'acute misery and frustrations' that 'limping marriages' create, the Hague Conference on Private International Law adopted the Convention on the Recognition of Divorces and Legal Separations in 1970, which was implemented in the UK by the Recognition of Divorces and Legal Separations Act 1971.

In relation to religious divorces, different religions offer differing approaches to the question of termination of marital relationships during the lifetimes of spouses. This question has been of considerable importance since England became a multi-faith society, a fact which was recognised by the Archbishop of Canterbury, Dr George Carey, in relation to the revision of the coronation oath. It is impossible to examine all the different forms of religious divorce, but the most important should be discussed. The Roman Catholic Church has not changed its view on divorce for centuries. Marriage is a sacrament and, as such, its sanctity cannot be challenged under any circumstances. Thus, no earthly authority can terminate a valid marriage, as man does not have the right to separate what God united.

The Church of England, however, makes concession for human weakness, though, since the promulgation of the Matrimonial Causes Act in 1857, secular jurisdiction has replaced the ecclesiastical courts. Other Reform Churches on the continent also permit divorce. The Eastern Catholic Church is very generous in this respect. Marriages in the Eastern Church could almost be said to be dissolved at will. A marriage may be terminated if the original commitments in the sacrament are no longer in existence and where the marriage is morally dead, psychologically hateful and there is no love between the spouses.

In Islamic law, divorce is permissible. Although Islamic law (the *Sharia*) is basically the same in all Muslim countries, there are marked differences between *Sunnis* and *Shias*. The fundamental form of divorce for both sects is the unilateral repudiation of a wife by the husband, known as the '*talaq*' (literally, 'I divorce you'). Under the classic Muslim *Sunni*, no formalities are required. Thus, the *talaq* may be explicit: by words (involving the pronouncement of the word *talaq* three times) or in writing (the *telegnama*); or it may be conveyed by a gesture where the husband is incapable of expressing his wish by words or in writing. The most common form of repudiation for *Sunnis* is the revocable *talaq*. A certain time must elapse before *talaq* is effective: usually, as Sura Bagara II v 228 specifies, 'Repudiated women shall wait ... for three monthly periods'.

For *Shias*, *talaq* is irrevocable and immediately effective. Consequently, it requires a specific form. The husband must expressly tell his wife that she is repudiated *(talaq)* and point in her direction. Two male witnesses are necessary and the *talaq* can be pronounced only while the wife is in a period of menstrual purity during which no sexual intercourse occurs. Although Islamic law recognises other forms of divorce, for example, the termination of a marriage by mutual consent of the spouses at the request of the wife (*khula*) or its judicial form (*tafriq*), the husband in many countries retains his right of unilateral repudiation. On the other end of the scale are Muslim countries which have abandoned the *Sharia* and secularised their family law on the European pattern (for example, Turkey and Tunisia).

Finally, Jewish law allows for divorce, called the '*ghet*'. The fundamental requirement of the Jewish law is the mutual agreement of both spouses. The Jewish procedure for divorce is complicated, time consuming and involves considerable hardship for both spouses. A special document (also called the '*ghet*') must be drafted and mutual consent must be proved, and then the husband must appear in person before the Rabbinical Court (*Beth Din*), which is composed of three judges specialising in family law. At this stage, the *ghet* document is scrutinised and, if there is a mistake, the entire procedure must be repeated. The *ghet* document terminates the matrimonial bond once it is officially delivered by the husband or his proxy to his wife in the presence of witnesses, usually judges of the Rabbinical court, in order to ensure that the wife accepts the document of her own free will. Since Jewish law is personal law for Jews, regardless of their place of residence, they must apply to the Rabbinical Court and follow the *ghet* procedure.

The question of whether such religious divorces are recognised in England is governed by the Family Law Act 1986. According to s 44(1), no divorce obtained in the British Isles shall be effective unless it takes the form of a judicial decree. As a result, an extra-judicial divorce pronounced in a foreign embassy in London is considered as having been obtained in the UK and, consequently, is not recognised. In *Radwan v Radwan* (1973), an Egyptian national married to an English woman repudiated her by *talaq* in the Egyptian Embassy in London. Their divorce was not recognised under s 44(1) of the Family Law Act 1986.

As regards overseas divorces, a distinction is made between overseas divorces obtained by means of judicial or other proceedings and divorces which do not involve proceedings. When a divorce is obtained by judicial or other proceedings, the jurisdictional basis for recognition is much wider than where there are no proceedings. For the recognition of overseas divorces in the first category, the following requirements must be satisfied: they must be effective under the law of the country where they were obtained; and, at the date of the commencement of the proceedings, either spouse must have been habitually resident, domiciled in or a national of that country. The crucial question is what constitutes proceedings under the 1986 Act. In this respect, there is no definition in the 1986 Act itself, but it seems that some formalities external to the parties, such as registration or conciliation proceedings, are necessary.

In *Chaudhary v Chaudhary* (1985), Oliver LJ said that proceedings 'must impart a degree of formality and at least the involvement of some agency, whether lay or religious, or recognised by the State as having a function that is more than simply probative', which is not the case when both spouses, or one of them, make a private declaration of divorce, even if the act is solemnised by the party and witnesses are present. Consequently, a 'bare' *talaq*, that is when the husband unilaterally repudiates the wife by pronouncing three times the word *talaq* and which is immediately effective does not amount to 'proceedings' within the meaning of the 1986 Act (*Chaudray v Chaudray* (1976)).

Where there have been no proceedings, that is, where a divorce takes all similar forms to the bare *talaq*, s 46(2) of the Family Law Act 1986 may be referred to on the issue of recognition. Thus, it will be recognised if it is effective under the law of the country in which it was obtained and both parties were domiciled in that country at the date the divorce was obtained, or, if only one party to the marriage was domiciled in that country, the divorce must be recognised as valid under the law of domicile of the other party. Furthermore, it will be recognised if neither party was habitually resident in the UK throughout the period of one year immediately preceding that date.

However, our question concerns the situation where one of the parties is present in the UK while the other spouse is abroad and the religious divorce has been obtained by way of proceedings which are commenced in the UK and concluded abroad. In *R v Secretary of State for the Home Department ex p Fatima* (1985), the appellant was a Pakistani national, resident in the UK, who pronounced *talaq* in England against his wife (who was in Pakistan) and made a statutory declaration in this respect before a solicitor in Bolton, England. Copies of the document were sent to Pakistan to the wife and the chairman of a local union council. In Pakistan, under the 1961 Muslim Family Laws Ordinance, a husband who pronounces the *talaq* must notify the chairman of the relevant local union council of his decision in writing and as soon as possible. The wife must be informed of her husband's decision. The chairman of the local union must then, within 30 days of receiving the notice, set up an Arbitration Council in order to commence reconciliation proceedings. If they fail, then, 90 days after the notice of the *talaq* is delivered to the chairman, the *talaq* is effective.

In *Fatima,* the appellant obtained a divorce in Pakistan. Once his marriage was dissolved, he wanted to marry Ghulam Fatima. However, she was refused leave to enter the UK and the immigration officers declared that the appellant was still validly married. The appellant argued that his marriage to Fatima could take place within a reasonable time, since, as it was 'obtained' in Pakistan, the *talaq* was effective, even though it was pronounced in England. The House of Lords held that the pronouncement of the *talaq* amounted to the institution of the proceedings. However, the proceedings, in order to be effective, 'must be a single set of proceedings which have to be instituted in the same country as that in which the relevant divorce was ultimately obtained'. As a result, the divorce was not obtained overseas: the so called 'divorce by post' attempted by Pakistani nationals residing in the UK is not recognised.

The entry into force of Pt II of the Family Law Act 1986 has not changed the position of English law in this respect. However, it was uncertain whether the divorce obtained by way of a Jewish *ghet* in similar circumstances would also be refused recognition in the UK. In *Berkovits v Grinberg* (1995), it was held that a marriage is considered to be dissolved when the *ghet* is handed to the wife and the writing of the *ghet* is a step in proceedings. It was also held that all proceedings must be conducted in a country outside the UK in order to be recognised as an overseas divorce under s 6(1) of the Family Law Act 1986. Consequently, when the proceedings are commenced in England but the *ghet* is delivered in another country, the principle in *Fatima* applies.

It is submitted that, when the divorce proceedings conducted under religious laws were commenced in England and concluded in another country, the divorce, although valid under religious laws, would not be recognised in England. Section 46(1) of the Family Law Act 1986 applies only to divorces obtained by means of a single set of proceedings conducted outside the British Isles. Consequently, the statement that 'those who can afford to travel abroad may have their divorces recognised ... whereas those who cannot afford to make the journey are left with limping marriages' is true in the context of divorce proceedings conducted under religious laws which were commenced in England and concluded abroad. For that reason, in *Berkovits v Grinberg*, Wall J said that there were strong policy arguments against the conclusion which the construction of the Family Act 1986 required.

Question 48

Jane, a devout Catholic, domiciled and resident in Belgium, has always dreamt of getting married in Lourdes. When she met John, an English domiciliary and also a Catholic, they decided to marry at a Catholic ceremony in Lourdes. Their marriage took place in 1975 and was performed by a Catholic priest according to Catholic rites.

Jane and John decided to set up a home in Belgium. In 1976, their daughter, Faith, was born. Soon after that, their marriage began to deteriorate. In 1977, John decided to get a divorce and consulted a solicitor on the matter. He was told that his marriage was void since, under French law, only civil marriages are valid. John left Jane and Faith and moved back to England. In 1988, he married April in a Registry Office in London. They had a son, Malcolm, in 1989. In 1995, John died intestate.

Discuss the succession to movable property of John's children, Faith and Malcolm.

Answer plan

In order to answer the question, it is necessary to deal separately with legitimacy and succession to movable property. Legitimacy concerns the determination of John's children's status. Succession is a question of construction of words such as 'children' and 'issues' under the relevant Act of Parliament (because John died intestate) in order to determine whether Faith and Malcolm can inherit their father's movable property. The position of illegitimate children under English law has been gradually improved, although the Family Law Reform Act 1987 has not abolished the distinction between legitimacy and illegitimacy. For the purposes of succession, it is not conclusive if a child is considered to be legitimate under a foreign law. For example, only a child born in lawful wedlock can succeed as heir to English real estate. Conversely, statutory rules may disregard the distinction between legitimate and illegitimate children and allow children to succeed, regardless of their status. The following points should be examined:

- the distinction between legitimacy and legitimation;
- s 1(1) and (2) of the Legitimacy Act 1976;
- ss 1 and 18(1)(4) of the Family Law Reform Act 1987;

Answer

At the time of birth, a child acquires the status of a legitimate child if he is born in lawful wedlock. Legitimation occurs where a child who is born illegitimate becomes legitimate as a result of subsequent events, such as the marriage of his parents after his birth (the only event under English domestic law which renders a child legitimate) and parental recognition.

The first question concerns the status of John's children. The traditional manner of determining the question of legitimacy is to examine whether the marriage of a child's parents is valid. Until the passing of the Legitimacy Act 1959, the English rule of domestic law was that, when a child was born of parents whose marriage was valid at the time of his birth, he was considered to be a legitimate child. In this context, Faith is not a legitimate child, since the marriage of her parents was void for lack of form. Jane and John celebrated their marriage in France in breach of French law, according to which only civil marriages are valid. Since the matter is governed by the *lex loci celebrationis* (French law), their marriage is void. However, the traditional test has been displaced by statutory provision and developments in common law. As to the statutory provision, the concept of putative marriage has been introduced by s 1(1) of the Legitimacy Act 1976. This states:

> The child of a void marriage, whenever born,[1] shall ... be treated as the legitimate child of his parents if, at the time of the insemination resulting in the birth or, where there was no such insemination, the child's conception (or at the time of the celebration of the marriage if later), both or either of the parties reasonably believed that the marriage was valid.

Section 28 of the Family Law Reform Act 1987 further develops this section by setting up a rebuttable presumption in favour of children of void marriages: if one of the party to a void marriage reasonable believes that, at the relevant time, the marriage was valid, the child is regarded as legitimate. This presumption is not retrospective, as it applies only to children born after 4 April 1988, the date of the coming into force of that section. It is thus irrelevant to our case. However, under s 1(1) of the Legitimacy Act 1976, Faith may be considered to be a legitimate child, since both her parents believed that their marriage was valid at the time of her birth. The bad news is that s 1(1) of the Legitimacy Act 1976 is subject to s 1(2), which provides that the Act applies only to the child whose father was domiciled in England at the time of the birth or, where the father died before the birth, whose last domicile was England. At the time of Faith's birth, both her parents were domiciled in Belgium. As a result, she cannot rely on s 1(1) of the Legitimacy Act 1976. This yields strange results. The legislation legitimates children whose fathers were domiciled in England at the relevant time but denies the benefit of the status of legitimacy to a person who would have been born in England but whose father was, at the time of birth, domiciled abroad.

According to Dicey and Morris,[2] it would not be appropriate to draw any inference from s 1(2) of the Legitimacy Act 1976 as to the choice of law issue, as the rule only establishes the territorial scope of English domestic law and constitutes solely an assumption of law in an Act of Parliament which is not necessarily correct or binding on the courts. In this context, it is submitted that, if the law of the parents' domicile at the relevant time recognises the concept of a putative marriage and thus confers the status of a legitimate child to a child born of a void marriage, it is difficult to accept that an English court would not follow that law's solution.

Secondly, we may accept North's theory that, in order to determine his status, a child's domicile should be governed by the law of his domicile of origin and the validity of his parents' marriage should be irrelevant. In this respect, where parents have the same domicile at the time of their child's birth, no problem arises. However, if they have different domiciles, we enter a vicious circle since, if a child is legitimate, he acquires the domicile of origin of his father, but, if he is illegitimate, he aquires the domicile of his mother. In those circumstances, it is impossible to ascertain the domicile of a child without answering the question of his legitimacy. According to North, in order to break the vicious circle, the domicile of the natural father should prevail. In favour of this solution, it can be said that it is admitted in cases of legitimation (*Goodman's Trust* (1881)). In *Re Bischoffsheim* (1948), a testator gave a share of residue to the children of his granddaughter, Nesta, who was domiciled in England. Nesta had married her deceased husband's brother, also an English domiciliary, in New York in 1917. Their marriage was void under English law but valid under the law of New York. It was held that, at the time of marriage, they still had English domicile but had acquired a domicile of choice in New York by 1920, when their son, Richard, was born. In order to determine whether Richard was entitled to succeed under the will of the testator, who died domiciled in England, the relevant question was whether he was the legitimate child of his mother. The court held that the validity of Nesta's marriage to her second husband was irrelevant to the question of succession and that the legitimacy of Richard should be established by reference to his domicile of origin (the domicile of his parents at the time of his birth). Thus, there is no reason to treat legitimacy and legitimation differently. Indeed, this was confirmed in *Motala v AG* (1990) (which was reversed by the House of Lords on a different point). In addition, the introduction of the concept of the putative marriage further enhances this approach (see, also, the decision in *Royal Trust Co v Jones, Re Jones* (1961)).

As to our case, ascertaining Faith's domicile of origin is not difficult, as her parents were domiciled in Belgium at the time of her birth. Thus, Belgian law will be used in deciding whether she is legitimate or illegitimate. If Belgian law makes no distinction between legitimate and illegitimate children, as is the case in the New Zealand (Status of Children) Act 1969, she should be considered as legitimate in England. In this context, it is interesting to mention the decision of the Supreme Court of Canada in *Re MacDonald* (1962), in which it was held that a child considered as illegitimate in Mexico (a child of an unmarried couple) should have the status of a legitimate child in Canada.

In relation to Faith's rights to the intestate succession to movables (only), her position is not affected by her status. If she is recognised as a legitimate child, she should succeed to property under English deeds, wills or intestacy as if she were legitimate by English domestic law (*Re Bozzelli's Settlement* (1902)). However, if she is still considered as an illegitimate child, ss 1 and 18(1)(4) of the Family Law Reform Act 1987 provide that, on intestacy occurring on or after the entry into force of that Act (4 April 1988), references in the intestacy rules (in Pt IV of the Administration of Estates Act 1925) to any relationship between two persons are to be interpreted without regard to whether either of the persons, or any person through whom the relationship is inferred, were at any time married to each other.

As to Malcolm, the marriage of his parents is valid and he is the legitimate son of his father.

The intestate succession to movables will be distributed according to the law of the deceased's domicile at the time of his death, and, since John's last domicile was in England, English law applies.

It is submitted that, for the purposes of intestate succession to John's movable property, Faith and Malcolm enjoy exactly the same rights.

Note

1 However, the child must be born after the marriage was entered into (*Re Spence* (1990)).
2 *Conflict of Laws*, 12th edn, 1993.

Question 49

Anna, a British national, married Isaak, an Israeli national, in 1984. They set up a home in England. Their children, Paula and Jane, were born in 1990 and 1991. Both children have dual (British and Israeli) nationality.

In 1994, when the marriage broke down, Isaak returned to Israel to live with his parents. Their divorce became final (*nisi*) in 1997. Both Paula and Jane have remained in the custody of their mother. In March 2000, Isaak came to England to visit his children. At that time, Paula was sick and stayed with Anna, but Jane went away with Isaak for a weekend. She never returned. Isaak took her to Israel and she is still living there.

Isaak refuses to bring her back to England. He claims that Jane is perfectly happy living with him and his parents in Israel,and her return, taking into account the fact that Anna is mentally unstable, would represent a risk to Jane's health and welfare.

Anna wants to know what she can do in order to get Jane back. Advise her, taking into account the fact that Israel is a Contracting State to the Hague Convention on the Civil Aspects of International Child Abduction 1980.

Answer plan

The Hague Convention on the Civil Aspects of International Child Abduction 1980, which is in force in the UK, applies. The main features of the Hague Convention should be examined. Article 13(b) is especially relevant, as it concerns a refusal of the abductor to return the child if he alleges that there is a grave risk that the return would expose the child to physical or psychological harm or otherwise place him in a intolerable situation. The interpretation of Art 13(b) by courts in Contracting States is very important:

- *B v K* (1992);
- *Macmillan v Macmillan* (1989).

Answer

Many factors contribute to aggravate the problem of international child abduction: marriages between parties of different nationalities; the growing number of broken marriages (in the UK, more than one in three marriages ends in divorce); and the facility to travel and set up a home abroad. In the UK, around 350 children are abducted each year.

The question of abduction of children in the UK is regulated by various laws which may be relevant to our case. The UK has ratified two conventions in this area:

- the Hague Convention on the Civil Aspects of International Child Abduction, signed at the Hague on 15 October 1980; and
- the European Convention on Recognition and Enforcement of Decisions concerning Custody of Children and on Restoration of Custody of Children, signed at Luxembourg on 20 May 1980.

Both Conventions are implemented in the UK in the Child Abduction Act 1984. This Act considers abduction to be a criminal offence in England and Wales. Further, the Children Act 1982, in force since 14 October 1991, provides that the fundamental principle in proceedings concerning children in England and Wales is the welfare of the child; thus, the courts should always take into account the child's best interests.

First, the question of Jane's return will be examined. Jane has already been taken abroad by her father. Fortunately for Anna, Israel is a Contracting State to the Hague Convention. The main objectives of this Convention are to facilitate the speedy return of an abducted child and the recognition of custody rights in Contracting States. According to Art 1 of the Convention, the Contracting States should take all appropriate measures to secure implementation of the Convention and shall use the most expeditious procedures available. The Hague Convention has been very successful in returning children. In 1998, the Child Abduction Unit received applications from, and made applications to, a total of 29 countries. In respect of applications made to England and Wales, three countries stand out: the US – 44 applications; Ireland – 20 applications; and Australia – 19 applications. In relation to outgoing cases, 42 applications were made to the US; 40 to Ireland; and 21 to France. In respect of these cases, 48 resulted in a judicial return; 11 resulted in voluntary return; and 32 cases were withdrawn. Only 10 cases were subject to a judicial refusal to return. Among the incoming cases, 61 resulted in voluntary return; 36 resulted in cases being withdrawn; 36 cases ended in judicial return; and seven cases resulted in a refusal to allow the child to be returned.

The Hague Convention applies if the following requirements are satisfied: a child must be under 16 and habitually resident in a Contracting State prior to the abduction; the applicant, in our case Anna, must exercise her right to custody in relation to the child; and finally, the Convention must be in force in both Contracting States. All requirements are fulfilled in respect of Jane.

The Hague Convention comes into operation when the removal or retention of a child is wrongful. Article 3 of the Convention states that that happens when: (a) it is in breach of rights of custody attributed to a person, an institution or any other body, either jointly or alone, under the law of the State in which the child was habitually resident immediately before the removal or retention; and (b) at the time of the removal or retention, those rights were actually exercised, either jointly or alone, or would have been so exercised but for the removal or retention. The House of Lords held in *Re H; Re S* (1991) that removal is wrongful when a child is removed without the other parent's consent and is wrongful at the point of removal.

It is very important for Anna that she exercises the custody rights over Jane. Indeed, the Hague Convention draws the distinction between rights of custody and rights of access. Only rights of custody include the right to determine the child's place of residence. Furthermore, the expression 'right of custody' has been widely interpreted by the courts where there is no order or any other official custodial status (*Re B (A Minor)* (1994)). Finally, fortunately for Anna, the prompt return of a child who has been wrongfully taken away is the primary concern of the Hague Convention, not the welfare of the child. Thus, Art 12 of the Convention requires the mandatory return of a child within 12 months of abduction. Once the mandatory period expires, the return may be refused if it is demonstrated that the child has settled into his new environment.

Jane was abducted in March 2000, thus, the mandatory period has not yet expired. As a result, apart from exceptions contained in Art 13 of the Convention, the court of a Contracting State in which the child has his habitual residence has exclusive jurisdiction to make decisions on the merits of the case and the requested State must solely order the return of the child. The rule on jurisdiction is absolute and the Israeli court cannot exercise any discretion but must order the return of Jane.

Sometimes, this rule produces an interesting result. In *H v H* (1994), it was held that, although England was the appropriate forum for the determination of the child's future, under the Hague Convention, the child had to be returned to France, the place of his habitual residence, and French courts had jurisdiction to investigate the merits of the case. Under the Hague Convention, the doctrine of *forum non conveniens* does not apply.

However, Art 13 may change Anna's situation. It provides that a judicial or administrative authority of a requested State may refuse the return of the child if the person opposing the return establishes: (a) that the other party was not actually exercising the rights of custody or consented to or subsequently acquiesced in the removal or retention; or (b) that there is a grave risk that the return of the child would expose him to physical or psychological harm or otherwise place the child in an intolerable situation. In our case, Isaak bases his claims on Art 13(b). Furthermore, in the context of Art 13(b), the child's views may be taken into account by a requested State (Israel) if the child is of sufficient age and maturity. The court must decide those issues, since no age is mentioned by the Convention. However, the objectives and spirit of the Convention require the prompt return of wrongfully removed children and the investigation on the merits should be conducted by the court of the child's habitual residence. As Jane is only nine years old, the chances of her opinion being taken into account by the court are slim. However, in *Re R (A Minor)* (1991), when a 14 year old girl threatened to commit suicide if sent back, the court did allow her to stay.

In the light of Art 13(b), the question arises as to Isaak's chances of retaining Jane in Israel. For many reasons, it seems that it will be extremely difficult for Isaak to prove that her return to England constitutes a grave risk to her mental health. In England, there has been only one case where the party was able to prove that the return would place the child in an intolerable situation (*B v K* (1992)). In this case, the court decided that the child should return without his older sister, who succeeded in convincing the court that to let her stay would constitute a grave risk within the meaning of Art 13(b) (see, also, the unreported case of *Re C* (1990)).

No adjournment would be allowed in order to gather information, thus encouraging the delaying tactics of the abductor (*Re E (A Minor)* (1989)). Case law indicates that the defence under Art 13(b) has been strictly interpreted by the courts in Contracting States.[1] Only where the applicant has a history of mental illness or alcohol abuse is it possible for the abductor to succeed (*Macmillan v Macmillan* (1989)). Nothing in our case indicates that Anna has any mental problems. Secondly, as already discussed, an objective of the Convention is the return of the child and not his welfare (*Re S (A Minor)* (1991)). Furthermore, Isaak can bring proceedings in England and seek to obtain the custody rights once Jane is back home. Article 19 of the Convention provides that any decision regarding the child under the Convention should not be taken into account in any subsequent custody hearings. Finally, even if Isaak succeeds in proving that Anna is mentally unstable, the Israeli court exercises a discretion in deciding the return of a child under the Convention.

On the practical side, under the Convention, Contracting States shall establish a central authority to discharge the duties imposed by the Convention. In England and Wales, the Child Abduction Unit of the Lord Chancellor's Department is the central authority for processing the application. Thus, Anna should contact the Unit, which will help her to prepare a formal application for the return of Jane and will send it to the central authority of Israel. It is important to emphasise that, under the Convention, no payment for legal proceedings is required, although expenses relating to the return of the child are not covered. Anna should indicate in her application that an order for travel costs should be made against Isaak.

It is submitted that Anna should expect a prompt return of Jane. The Hague Convention, although criticised for not taking into account the best interests of a child, constitutes a very efficient mechanism for returning unlawfully removed or retained children.[2] So far, it has been ratified by 50 countries. Its effectiveness will certainly encourage more countries to become Contracting States. In this context, Art 11(2) of the UN Convention on the Rights of the Child 1989 recommends the ratification of the Hague Convention, while its Art 11(1) urges all States to take appropriate measures to prevent child abduction.

Notes

1 See the Second Special Commission Report on the Application and Effectiveness of the Hague Convention, as summarised in (1994) 33 ILM 225, p 241.

2 See the Reports of the two Special Commissions on the Application and Effectiveness of the Hague Convention, as summarised in (1990) 29 ILM 219, p 224 and (1994) 33 ILM 225; Lowe, N and Perry, A, 'International Child Abduction: The English Experience', 1998, a report on research sponsored by the Nuffield Foundation.

Question 50

James, domiciled in England, married Anna, a French national, in 1991. They set up a family home in England. They wanted to have a child but both had medical problems. Anna could get pregnant but could not give birth. James and Anna decided to use artificial reproduction techniques. Anna asked her friend, Maria, domiciled in California, to be a surrogate mother. An embryo, created with the gametes of Anna and Hans, a friend of James, was implanted in Maria's womb. Maria gave birth to Mark in 1993 and handed him over to James and Anna. In 1994, James noticed that Anna often wore his clothes and aftershave. He was worried, but Anna assured him that she was doing it just for fun. However, in 1995, Anna declared that she was really a man and would shortly have gender reassignment surgery in Switzerland. She left James and Mark and returned to France. After a successful operation, Anna has become Steve. In the meantime, Maria died intestate in California, without next of kin, leaving movable property in France and her house in Los Angeles.

James is very confused. He wants to know:

- whether he is still married to Anna/Steve and, if so, how he can legally terminate the marriage;
- whether he is legally the father of Mark;
- whether Mark can succeed to the immovable and movable property of Maria.

Advise James.

Answer plan

Each issue should be answered separately. The answer will be rather speculative, as there are no authorities on many of the issues. However, the following points should be examined:

- transsexuals: *Corbett v Corbett* (1970); *Rees v UK* (1986); *Cossey v UK* (1990); *X, Y, Z v UK* (1997); *Sheffield and Horsham v UK* (1998);
- the validity of marriage: s 11(c) of the Matrimonial Causes Act 1973;

- the determination of the legal status of Mark: the Human Fertilisation and Embryology Act 1990;
- succession: *Johnson v Calvert* (1993).

Answer

The traditional perceptions of marriage, parentage and family, which are at the centre of conflict of laws rules in family law matters, risk being challenged. On the one hand, new artificial reproductive technology, such as donor insemination, egg and embryo transfer and surrogacy, result in uncertainty as to who are the legal parents of a child. In international adoption and succession matters, those questions are of great importance. The notion of 'mother', which used to be self-evident, is no longer easy to determine. On the other hand, the acceptance of relationships between two individuals of the same sex will have to be legally recognised sooner or later. In some countries, homosexual 'marriages' are accepted (in Denmark and Norway, for example, a form of registration which produces legal consequences similar to marriage is available to homosexual couples). This is not so in England.

Another interesting question arises in relation to transsexuals. Do they have capacity to marry a person who is of the opposite sex but was originally of the same sex? What happens if a person who is already married changes her or his gender during the marriage?

The first problem concerns the effect of a sex operation on the validity or even existence of the marriage. Anna had the operation, which resulted in giving her the outward appearance of being a man. Legally, she changed her name to Steve. Can she/he be still married to James? There is no authority on this matter. However, Lord Penzance's definition of marriage in *Hyde v Hyde* (1866) as 'the voluntary union for life of one man and one woman to the exclusion of all others' still applies. The question is whether Anna/Steve is still woman. This question, like any question concerning personal status, will be answered by reference to the law of domicile. Anna/Steve is now domiciled in France. If, under French law, she/he is considered to be a man, then James is married to a man. The Matrimonial Causes Act 1973 provides that a marriage in England is void if the parties are not respectively male and female (s 11(c)). In *Corbett v Corbett* (1970), it was decided that, for the purposes of marriage, a sex change operation could not be of legal effect. In England, the original gender survives the sex change operation. In other words, a transsexual has no capacity to marry.

In *Rees v UK* (1986), the European Commission of Human Rights unanimously stated that 'the right to marry, guaranteed by Art 12, refers to the traditional marriage between persons of opposing biological sex'; thus, a Contracting State is not in breach of Art 12 if it precludes a transsexual from marrying. The Commission was divided on the question of whether the issue was formal or substantial. If it is formal, then a Contracting State should allow a person to legally change their status after a sex change operation. Otherwise, a State would be in breach of Art 8 of the Convention. Thus, with their new status, there would be no reason why a transsexual should be prevented from marrying a person of the opposite sex. However, if it is a substantive question, then the essence of marriage is at stake, including the 'physical capacity to procreate'. As a result, on this ground, the right to marry should be denied to transsexuals.

However in *Cossey v UK* (1990), the Commission changed its opinion. A majority decided that there was a violation of Art 12 (10 votes to six) and rejected the distinction between capacity to marry and capacity to found a family. The European Court of Human Rights disagreed, re-affirmed the decision in *Rees v UK* and decided that the denial of transsexuals' right to marry did not violate Art 12.

Slowly, the perception of marriage has changed, even in Strasbourg. In *Sheffield and Horsham v UK*, the European Court of Human Rights re-affirmed that the traditional concept of marriage underpinning Art 12 of the Convention provided sufficient reason for the continued adoption by the UK of biological criteria for determining a person's sex for the purposes of marriage, although as many as nine judges disagreed (compared to three in *Rees* and eight in *Cossey*, while the Commission was in favour of recognising transsexuals' right to marry by 15 votes to one). The Court refused to take into consideration new medical evidence, although it recognised the increased social acceptance of transsexualism. The UK is one of the four remaining Contracting States to the European Convention on Human Rights refusing to update the birth certificates of post-operative transsexuals. In this respect, it is interesting to note that the Conservative Government introduced the Gender Identity (Registration and Civil Status) Bill 1996, which recognises the possibility of amending the register of births for post-operative transsexuals.

It appears that James is married to another man. It seems difficult to imagine that an English court today would decide that there is no marriage and deny matrimonial relief, as happened in *Hyde v Hyde*. His marriage will probably be annulled under s 11(c) of the Matrimonial Causes Act 1973.

As to Mark, his biological father is Hans. However, James was the husband of the mother (if Anna is considered to be the mother) at the time of his birth. The Human Fertilisation and Embryology Act 1990 provides definitions of 'mother' and 'father', which apply for all legal purposes. A mother is 'the woman who is carrying or has carried a child as a result of the placing in her of an embryo or of sperm and eggs, and no other woman is to be treated as the mother of the child'. Thus, in England, a surrogate mother has parental rights over the child. Therefore, Maria is the legal mother of Mark. As to the father, the 1990 Act specifies that, in cases of artificial donor insemination and egg or embryo transfer, the husband or the consenting partner of the woman who becomes pregnant is considered to be the father. Thus, neither James nor Hans is legally the father of Mark. James has to adopt Mark.

Finally, the question of succession falls to be examined. The principle is that intestate succession to immovables is determined by the law of the country where the immovables are situated (the *lex situs*) and the intestate succession to the movables is governed by the law of domicile of the deceased person at the time of his death. Maria is domiciled in California and the immovable property is situated in California. The law of the State of California will determine whether Mark is entitled to succeed. In this respect, in *Johnson v Calvert* (1993), where a surrogate mother refused to give up her child after the birth, the Supreme Court of California held that the surrogate mother had no parental rights and the biological parents were considered to be the parents for all legal purposes. Therefore, Mark is not considered to be Maria's son under the law of the State of California.

It is submitted that, in the future, many interesting cases will have to be decided concerning the two issues discussed above. Traditional rules of conflict of laws are not appropriate to solve such complicated issues. Although national legislation has been introduced in many areas, the divergencies and disrepancies among them may produce unjust results. In our example, Mark legally has no father. Under English law, his mother is Maria, but, under the law of California, Anna is his mother. As a result, depending on jurisdiction, he may end up with three fathers: James, Hans and Steve; and two mothers: Maria and Anna; or he may be an orphan. It is necessary to harmonise national legislation – the best solution is to unify law at an international level by way of international conventions.

* by Alina Kaczorowska

INDEX